Greener
Marketing

Greener Marketing

John Grant

This edition first published 2020
© 2020 John Grant.

Edition History
John Wiley & Sons Ltd (1e, 2007)

Registered office
John Wiley & Sons Ltd, The Atrium, Southern Gate, Chichester, West Sussex, PO19 8SQ, United Kingdom

For details of our global editorial offices, for customer services and for information about how to apply for permission to reuse the copyright material in this book please see our website at www.wiley.com.

Wiley publishes in a variety of print and electronic formats and by print-on-demand. Some material included with standard print versions of this book may not be included in e-books or in print-on-demand. If this book refers to media such as a CD or DVD that is not included in the version you purchased, you may download this material at http://booksupport.wiley.com. For more information about Wiley products, visit www.wiley.com.

Designations used by companies to distinguish their products are often claimed as trademarks. All brand names and product names used in this book are trade names, service marks, trademarks or registered trademarks of their respective owners. The publisher is not associated with any product or vendor mentioned in this book.

Limit of Liability/Disclaimer of Warranty: While the publisher and author have used their best efforts in preparing this book, they make no representations or warranties with respect to the accuracy or completeness of the contents of this book and specifically disclaim any implied warranties of merchantability or fitness for a particular purpose. It is sold on the understanding that the publisher is not engaged in rendering professional services and neither the publisher nor the author shall be liable for damages arising herefrom. If professional advice or other expert assistance is required, the services of a competent professional should be sought.

Library of Congress Cataloging-in-Publication Data

Names: Grant, John, 1964- author.
Title: Greener marketing / John T Grant.
Other titles: Green marketing manifesto.
Description: First Edition. | Hoboken : Wiley, 2020. | Revised edition of
   the author's The green marketing manifesto, c2007. | Includes
   bibliographical references and index.
Identifiers: LCCN 2020008311 (print) | LCCN 2020008312 (ebook) | ISBN
   9781119689119 (hardback) | ISBN 9781119689102 (adobe pdf) | ISBN
   9781119689133 (epub)
Subjects: LCSH: Green marketing.
Classification: LCC HF5413 .G722 2020 (print) | LCC HF5413 (ebook) | DDC
   658.8/02—dc23
LC record available at https://lccn.loc.gov/2020008311
LC ebook record available at https://lccn.loc.gov/2020008312

10 9 8 7 6 5 4 3 2 1

Cover Design: Pentagram Design

Set in 11/15pts Goudy Std by SPi Global, Chennai, India

Printed and bound by CPI Group (UK) Ltd, Croydon, CR0 4YY

Contents

Foreword for 'Greener Marketing' By John Grant

Come the day when historians can reflect properly on this particular, post-1980s era of capitalism, I have no doubt that marketing (and advertising in particular) will be seen, in the round, as an egregiously irresponsible and damaging industry – driving decades of wasteful consumption, converting 'wants into needs', exploiting the worst aspects of human nature – whilst frittering away the creative talents of countless young people indentured into the dark and demeaning arts of 'flogging more stuff'.

In that regard, I find myself closely aligned with Pavan Sukhdev, banker turned sustainability guru, who has described advertising as 'the drug we need to quit'.

So you may wonder why the author of this splendidly insightful and stimulating book should have entrusted me with the task of contributing a Foreword? It may be that he has some sympathy with my overall position (he himself sourced that quote from Pavan Sukhdev, for instance!), evidenced by the fact that John Grant has worked as hard as any marketing person I know to encourage his colleagues to think more deeply about their industry – to change their mindsets, to stop treating everything as if it was a bit of a game. Or it may be that he and I are united in our belief that time genuinely is running out to 'reset capitalism' (as John puts it) – which in turn means fundamentally resetting marketing.

Today's converging crises (accelerating climate change, collapsing ecosystems and worsening inequality) pose a radically different challenge to today's prevailing economic paradigm – not least because there's no possibility of trying to grow our way out of them. Any more of today's growth-at-all-costs will put our chances of enjoying in the future a stable climate (let alone a fair and thriving economy for the whole of humankind) permanently out of reach.

That's a pretty tough call for companies wrestling with these dilemmas – even for those that have built up an impressive track record over the last decade or so. The achievements of a lot of those 'sustainability leaders' are generously celebrated here, as well as those of many less well-known innovators and champions – and John has plenty of wise and timely words for those just waking up to the reality of today's 'galvanic tipping-point'.

John wears his own impressive expertise in sustainability lightly – but it's not possible either to critique today's marketing industry, or to propose fundamental improvements in the way it operates in future, without that kind of expertise. There are many, many years of front-line experience reflected in these pages.

Jonathon Porritt

Greener
Marketing

Introduction

Marketing rightly has a mixed reputation.

If you write a list of what is wrong with the world, marketing is implicated in overconsumption, inequality, fake news, populism, obesity, ocean plastic, climate change, and so much more.

But if you want to change the world fast – as we have to – then marketing can be pretty useful.

This book is a handbook for creative marketers who are up for that challenge.

It is full of inspiring examples and strategic angles, as well as things to avoid (like greenwash).

Let's start with why we need to change the world.

We are in a climate and ecological emergency. Don't just take my word for it – 11 000 scientists signed a declaration in November 2019 saying as follows:

> Scientists have a moral obligation to clearly warn humanity of any catastrophic threat and to 'tell it like it is.' On the basis of this obligation and the graphical indicators presented below, we declare, with more than 11,000 scientist signatories from around the world, clearly and unequivocally that planet Earth is facing a climate emergency.
>
> An immense increase of scale in endeavours to conserve our biosphere is needed to avoid untold suffering due to the climate crisis (IPCC 2018).[1]

We have very little time left to radically transform our economies and societies.

If we don't succeed, we will see global temperatures rise far enough to do untold damage.

If we do succeed, we also stand a chance of building a fairer, more human and liveable society.

And whether we succeed or not, just the attempt could be a hugely worthwhile adventure.

Extinction Rebellion say the first step is each of us declaring an emergency. And committing to respond accordingly. This book covers what 'respond accordingly' might mean for marketers. It is based on the early efforts of a diverse global movement of marketing clients, creative agencies and entrepreneurs committed to doing good during their day jobs. Not just seeming good or being fashionably on trend – but actually doing good.

There are environmentalists who wish marketers would simply stop. Stop selling more stuff. Stop fuelling lifestyle aspirations. Stop lying. Stop getting people addicted to sugar, shoes, screen time. Stop putting a friendly face on industrially produced crap. Stop 'innovation' that is pointless and wasteful. Stop wrapping everything in plastic and graphics. Stop promoting things that destroy the world, like gas guzzling cars or cheap commodities that result in extensive deforestation.

Extinction Rebellion recently called on people to boycott fashion in 2020. To buy not one new item in the next 12 months. Because they see the buying of dresses and shoes at an accelerating rate in the midst of ecological collapse as obscene. They say we need to send a clear message to industries and governments that 'enough is enough'.[2]

One answer to our critics is a simple shift. We need to eradicate cynicism from marketing. And adopt sincerity. It's not what we do, or even the way that we do it, so much as *why* we do it. Sincerity means that we want to change – not just because the public are clamouring for it, but because it's the right thing to do, consistent with basic human values. We need to be sincere in intent. But we also need to stay playful, flexible, imaginative in execution. We can't afford to be stiff, boring, and politically correct. We need to apply every trick in the marketing book to bring people with us, to get them to wake up, enthuse, delight, share, and press for change.

Hence, we need to invert the marketing mindset.

The mindset used to be one of strategic insincerity – 'it's all just a game' – wrapped up in a serious pretence of aspiration, political correctness, or whatever fashionable attitude sells more and looks good. We used to conflate fripperies like laundry conditioner or countline bars with all the pretension of advertising, complete with Oscar style creative awards for 30 second films.

Now we need to have strategic sincerity – acting for the right reasons, with a core purpose – wrapped up in much bolder, more inventive, playful, humble, collaborative, and open campaigns. So that we bring people with us. And so that the destination is worth getting to.

We need to shift business thinking in many other ways covered later in this book. For instance, shift from short termism to longer termism. But none of these other shifts will work if marketers cannot be sincere. Without sincerity, every brand purpose campaign is just a pose.

If you do one thing, have a sincere conversation with colleagues. Talk about the climate emergency, about society, about your business, your products and services. Talk about what matters to each of you and how you could pursue that at work. Talk about whether you are proud of what you make and how you sell it. Talk about what is good for the world, for your friends and families. If you can get past 'it's all a game' to genuinely looking to do the right thing . . . everything else in this book will make sense. If you can't, think about changing job.

Cynicism leads to manipulation and to the overconsumption that got marketing a bad name. What is worse in recent decades is that those cynical approaches have been applied to eco and cause campaigns. The public are getting better at seeing through phony attempts. As Pepsi discovered with its Kylie Jenner video (attempting to co-opt the *Black Lives Matters* protests). Cynical fake purpose campaigns are starting to look like the old royal courts of Europe dressing up like shepherds. And rightly, when caught out, they face the guillotine. Marketing cynicism stems from company culture, from how politics work, what is and isn't up for discussion, who gets rewarded and for what, the example leaders set, and (often) the lack of voice for the rest.

Our track record is far from exemplary. But even Extinction Rebellion think marketers might – just maybe, if we get our act together – stand a chance of doing some good. How else to mobilise a system change, than with communicators, content creators, and entrepreneurs?

Once you are sincerely committed to marketing that makes a positive difference, there are plenty of helpful trends that will support your efforts.

First is the public appetite for change. Any change. A new generation has taken to the streets across the world to protest things ranging from climate to food prices. People feel the system is loaded against them. Public opinion is excitable and electrified by social media. One documentary about ocean plastic can change what is acceptable in waste, packaging, retail. People want change. That's the underlying force splintering politics – driving voters to both Trump and Ocasio-Cortez. Something has to give. The world seems broken and needs fixing.

Second, business leaders are becoming open to radical change too. Because of the climate crisis. But also, the growing public anger at the inequality of a system that only benefits a few and is putting intolerable pressure on everyone else. Even the *Financial Times* is calling for a 'reset' of capitalism and the reform of business to accommodate social purpose.

Third, the public will now pay for sustainable alternatives. Unilever showed that its Sustainable Living Brands – those supporting positive change for people and planet – grew 69% faster than the rest of its portfolio in 2018 and delivered 75% of Unilever's overall growth.[3] A comprehensive study of 71 000 products by NYU Stern's Center for Sustainable Business found that those marketed as sustainable grew 5.6 times faster than those that were not.[4]

Eco used to mean niche. With authentic brands sold at a premium. Allbirds is one recent example – selling 1 million pairs of shoes with uppers made from wool rather than plastic. But while VEJA, Allbirds, VivoBarefoot, and others cater to conscious consumers, Adidas sold 11 million pairs of their ocean plastic Parlay trainers. That's several billion dollars of sustainable shoe sales in only a few years. An example showing that mainstream brands can play too.

What's needed goes far beyond marketing. And there are hopeful signs. The EU, along with many nations, cities, and companies, declared a climate emergency. More and more institutions are signing up to Science-based Targets. And there is radical enough innovation happening from regenerative farming, to grid scale storage, to sustainability linked loans. There has been a real shift. But this all does need marketing and communication. Which is where we come in.

This book covers the new wave of environmental and social marketing, innovation, and business. It's a sequel to my *Green Marketing Manifesto*. In terms of scope it should really have been called *The Sustainable Marketing Manifesto* (but I didn't want to deter potential readers!) In 2007, when that book came out, we had seen what the *Financial Times* called 'a wave of eco marketing' (12 February 2007). Al Gore's movie *The Inconvenient Truth* had spiked climate concerns. Everyone from GE (Ecomagination) to Toyota (the Prius) to Ariel (Turn to 40) was jumping on the green marketing bandwagon. My book was an attempt to make sense of what was working and why. The book concluded that green marketing is about *making green things seem normal, not making normal things seem green*. Meaning that green-minded companies should avoid greenwash (presenting themselves as greener than they were) and instead focus on radical green innovations and behaviours, then use marketing to persuade people to adopt them.

In the intervening decade, green and climate concerns went away. Other news stole the headlines, like the global financial crisis and the Arab Spring. IPSOS MORI found that the population concerned about climate change in the UK fell from a peak of 82% in 2005 to only 60% in 2013. By 2019, this had risen again to 85%.[5] Public concern is back, riding on the awareness generated by the climate protests. And it has developed. For instance, a much higher proportion now perceive climate change as an issue affecting them personally. Global climate strikes and the Green New Deal are not the only focus. Single issues have pressed for attention; like the BBC's *Blue Planet 2* documentary series which sparked global concerns about plastic waste; or like the #metoo awakening to issues of equality, diversity, and fairness.

A lot has changed in 12 years. We have seen a shift in modal verb: from *should* to *must*. Those that don't respond now will likely be punished, whether by carbon taxes, share valuation, boycotts, or simply falling out of favour. You don't want to be one of the companies that still wraps everything in excessive plastic then stacks it in open fridges, nor one of those fashion brands that isn't committed to no fur. Any more than you want to be a company with no women on the board, nor sheltering abusive executives. Now is not the time.

That need to move with the times is the first imperative of *Greener Marketing* – covered in the first section of this book – which is to be Not Bad. This is an extension of all the sustainability work companies have done.

Reducing negative impacts on communities and ecosystems. And in the process reducing risk and improving reputation. Not Bad is a commitment to minimise negative impacts. With no skeletons in your closet. No child labour, no excessive carbon emissions, no carcinogenic ingredients. But it goes beyond harm reduction into innovation. Embracing new technologies, market segments. Hybrid cars were a typical Not Bad innovation.

Companies now need to be Not Bad. It is the base of the pyramid. Companies need to show, for instance, how they will reduce their own carbon emissions in line with the Paris Agreement. BP has been mandated (in a 99% majority vote) by their shareholders to do this. I'd say this is the new baseline. Your operations must be on track to halve carbon emissions by 2030 relative to 2010 levels (and to halve your environmental footprint – given the many other dire crises in water, biodiversity loss, deforestation . . .). And then reduce them to net zero by 2050.

The 2050 part isn't easy. Technologies to achieve this may not even yet exist. But you will only find them in time if you set the objective and start the search now. The private sector is great at this sort of thing. Setting a stretch goal then devising strategies to reach it. Companies can also be good at transparency and owning up when they don't achieve their targets.

Six hundred and eighty-two leading companies have signed up to Science-based Targets. Meaning they are setting goals that conform to the 1.5/2 °C targets of the Paris Agreement. This includes companies that you probably knew were progressive like Danone, Unilever, IKEA, British Telecom, Seventh Generation, HP, Natura – and ones that you perhaps didn't know were like Walmart, Nestlé, Burberry, Sony, Levi Strauss, and Zurich Insurance. Science-based Targets is rapidly becoming the way to show that you are serious. Although measurement is no substitute for action.

Given the pressure from governments and publics, companies can no longer afford to be just Not Bad and to report some reduction in the harm that they do. The new sustainability standard is being Net Good – which is covered in the second section of this book. Net Good means the world is a better place for your business existing. Everything has a cost, in energy, emissions, and entropy. But there can still be ways to bring enough 'good' in some parts of your business to cancel out or justify any inevitable 'bads' from the raw impact of your operations.

A key implication of Net Good for brands and businesses is the need for a social purpose. So that the aims of the business become two-fold: commercial success and social purpose success. Unilever in its 2010 Sustainable Living Plan defined its purpose through three key objectives:

> By 2020, help more than a billion people take action to improve their health and well-being.
> By 2030, halve the environmental footprint of our products as we grow our business.
> By 2020, enhance the livelihoods of millions of people as we grow our business.[6]

Purpose has increasingly become a factor in marketing as well as corporate objective setting. Unilever CEO Alan Jope told journalists at the Cannes adverting festival that:

> We will dispose of brands that we feel are not able to stand for something more important than just making your hair shiny, your skin soft, your clothes whiter or your food tastier.[7]

With a new wave of bandwagon jumping to espouse causes has come concern about social versions of greenwash or 'woke-washing' as Jope called it. He lamented the brands that devalue the currency by espousing causes without taking action:

> It's polluting purpose. It's putting in peril the very thing which offers us the opportunity to help tackle many of the world's issues. What's more, it threatens to further destroy trust in our industry, when it's already in short supply.[8]

Greener Marketing is defined in this book as integrating sustainability and social purpose – building brands and businesses that are both Not Bad and Net Good.

This is no longer a niche or an afterthought. The Green Economy may be as central to business strategy in the coming decades as the Digital Economy has been in the last decades.

Mark Carney (along with other central bank governors) warned that companies which don't have climate change mitigation baked into the balance sheet face a 'Minsky Moment' when their shares could be abruptly revalued. There are two levels of economic risk to factor in. The first level of risk is direct losses due to catastrophic storms, flood, heatwaves, epidemics. Hurricane Katrina cost $41 billion in damages to insured property alone. The second level is what Sarah Breedon from the Bank of England describes as Transition Risk; due to changes in regulation, technology, and market sentiment as we *necessarily* transition to a lower-carbon economy. Breedon estimated that the potential losses due to inaction could lead to a crash with asset values as high as $20 trillion – over a quarter of the world's wealth – being wiped out.[9]

The Green Economy also offers the promise of growth, innovation, and success for leading players – companies like TESLA prepared to lead the transition. There has already been a boom in Environmental, Social, and Governance (ESG) investment. Sustainable assets under management reached $30 trillion globally and this grew 34% between 2016 and 2018. Impact Investing in entities directly targeting social and environmental problems grew to $502 billion.[10]

Many large companies have clear commitments and programmes of action on ESG. But there are opposing pressures. The main one being generating short term returns. It's a critical choice for the planet. Businesses every day have to choose between feeding this quarter's results or investing now in greener alternatives. A 2016 report (by the Global Commission on the Economy and Climate) highlighted this issue. The *Guardian* reported their findings with the headline 'World needs $90tn infrastructure overhaul to avoid climate disaster, study finds'.[11] This is slightly misleading. What the study actually says is that the world is *already* likely to spend $90 trillion on infrastructure over the next 15 years. And that with *little additional net cost* these investments could also help us meet climate goals: 'the additional up-front costs can be fully offset by efficiency gains and fuel savings over the infrastructure lifecycle'.[12] All that is needed is some additional capital expenditure that will pay back later through efficiencies. Which leads us to the unlikely conclusion that bankers could save the world. Later in the book we will meet the Sustainability Linked Loan – tying interest rates on a line of credit with companies achieving sustainability targets. Companies from Phillips to Prada have taken SLLs, and this innovative green banking product grew from zero in 2016 to $40 billion in 2018.

Another unlikely hero in coming decades could be purposeful creative marketers.

I was at a creative industry meeting recently – hosted by the D&AD. It was heartening that so many people in the industry were passionately involved in the climate strikes. A representative from Extinction Rebellion suggested that 'no-one will give a shit about advertising and design in five years' time when the food starts to run out'. That's definitely a scenario to bear in mind. But I suspect our skills could still be helpful in the transition.

That doesn't mean it is open season for greenwashing again. A key theme of this book is that the correct response in this critical moment is more doing and less saying.

A company whose sustainability journey I have been involved in over several decades is IKEA. In 2001, the global CEO Anders Dahlvig called Naresh Ramchandani and I in to take a brief. I will let my previous *Green Marketing* book pick up the story:

> One of my first forays into big company CSR work was a project on how best to communicate IKEA's environmental and ethical commitments. They had spent twelve years putting their house in order. In many areas they were not only meeting but exceeding any standards in the world; from forestry and transport, to the way they worked with partner factories and influenced their operations.
>
> Yet our advice, as far as external communications went, was very simple: 'DON'T!'
>
> IKEA decided this was the right advice at the time, and instead we focused on an internal programme. IKEA hardly needed posters to tell people they were a company who could be trusted to do the right thing. Not only could NGOs and other interested parties view all of their information in detail if they wanted, but a number of the NGOs who had worked with IKEA to develop these programmes used it as a case study to show other businesses what could be done.
>
> Lo and behold, in Landor's survey of green brands, IKEA was rated the 7th greenest brand in the US, ahead of GE (at number 9), who spent $90 million on advertising proclaiming their newfound commitment to *Ecomagination*. And in a recent survey, IKEA was rated the trustworthiest institution in Sweden; 80% said they trusted IKEA, compared to 46% who said they trusted churches and 32% the leading political party.

The evidence we took to this meeting was the BP *Beyond Petroleum* advertising. A $200 million campaign that was seen as the epitome of greenwash and had earned a lot of criticism. Anders Dahlvig, the IKEA CEO, took one look at the BP ads and agreed. It sat better with the Swedish idea of *lagom* (moderation) to get on with things more modestly.

What happened next in the story?

IKEA kept innovating on sustainability. They shortened the global supply chain, so that these days most of the goods bought in Europe are now made in Europe. By 2017, IKEA UK was able to announce it sent zero waste to landfill – instead, for instance, using its own packaging waste to make new products in store.

But IKEA also recognised that sustainability did not go far enough. At a meeting in 2010 attended by around 200 internal and external stakeholders (including myself) IKEA set a 10-year sustainability goal: 'to be like a forest, putting more good into the ecosystem than bad'.

Of course, IKEA continued to attract criticism. At the 2009 Copenhagen Climate Summit, the first audience question for a panel including a spokesperson from IKEA came from a student activist (Jakob from Energy Crossroads) who asked: 'I hear what you say about sustainability Mr IKEA, but when are you going to stop selling so much shit?' In recent years, IKEA has started to respond on issues like this. In 2016, the IKEA sustainability head Steve Howard told the media that he thought we had reached 'peak stuff'. In 2019, IKEA announced the expansion of its circular economy scheme (piloted in Switzerland) whereby they refurbish and resell returned furniture.

IKEA also creates thought-provoking purpose content. IKEA Dubai's video 'Bully a Plant' supported initiatives in schools by showing the effects on two plants of being talked to nicely or denigrated for 30 days (the bullied plant withered, the other thrived). IKEA UK celebrated banning disposable plastic straws by exhibiting *The Last Straw* at London's Design Museum.

The whole IKEA story – from our early decision about avoiding greenwash, to engaging with criticisms, circular schemes, purpose, and plastics campaigning today – is an example of how the field has been shifting. The 'like a forest' idea pretty much nails one core theme of this book which is aiming higher than *Not Bad* and also going for *Net Good*.

This story is far from over. IKEA was founded with a lofty mission – 'to improve the everyday life of the majority of people'. In the consumer boom years of the 1950s, 1960s, 1970s, 1980s . . . the clear implication was to create well-designed affordable furnishings so everyone could afford a beautiful home. Today, IKEA's business model is blighted by deforestation, pollution, landfill, and the sheer waste of a category that relies on 'disposable furniture' (as opposed to the heirloom-grade furniture our grandparents bought or made and kept in use). It will take deep circular economy innovation for IKEA to continue to be Net Good and improve everyday life.

What IKEA can't do is continue to tear up the world to make kitchens for a rapidly expanding middle class in countries like China and India. There is still some profit and growth left in that direction. But its impact on resources, emissions, and habitats cannot be sustained. Sooner or later regulation – for instance a carbon tax – will make profiting from planet destruction uneconomic. Meanwhile for a purpose-led company like IKEA, it is easy to see habitat destruction, waste, and resource depletion already does not improve everyday human life.

As this IKEA case shows, the story of sustainability and marketing is a complex evolving dance. The two fields at times seem in direct conflict; yet at others to desperately need each other.

There are fresh debates to be had on how and whether to advertise your sustainability efforts. We advised IKEA against this 20 years ago. My own view – with notable exceptions – is that advertising your green credentials is generally best avoided. It's a different matter if you need to use your marketing to enlist the audience in achieving a social or environmental purpose. But otherwise don't tell people how green and virtuous you are, show this in your actions.

This book is far from the last word. But it seemed high time to respond to what is happening all around us. To capture the stories of pioneering case study brands and campaigns. To educate the marketing community on issues like transparency, the rebound effect, and the circular economy. And once again to sift through what is working, why, and how to apply it. To which end, the last section of the book covers specific tools, strategies, processes that are tried and tested in my own projects. And also offers a hasty summary of some recent creative marketing campaigns and initiatives that came out in response to the climate crisis in 2019.

Notes

1. William J. Ripple, Christopher Wolf, Thomas M. Newsome, Phoebe Barnard, William R. Moomaw (2020). World scientists' warning of a climate emergency. *BioScience*, biz088: https://doi.org/10.1093/biosci/biz088
2. https://rebellion.earth/event/fashion-costs-the-earth-xr52-boycott-new-clothing/

3. https://www.unilever.com/news/news-and-features/Feature-article/2019/brands-with-purpose-grow-and-here-is-the-proof.html
4. https://www.stern.nyu.edu/experience-stern/faculty-research/actually-consumers-do-buy-sustainable-products
5. https://www.ipsos.com/sites/default/files/ct/news/documents/2019-08/climate_change_charts.pdf
6. https://www.unilever.co.uk/sustainable-living/the-unilever-sustainable-living-plan/
7. https://www.thedrum.com/news/2019/06/19/unilever-chief-alan-jope-keith-weed-s-successor-working-with-networks-and-the-need
8. https://www.thedrum.com/news/2019/06/19/unilever-ceo-alan-jope-laments-the-woke-washing-ads-polluting-brand-purpose
9. https://www.bankofengland.co.uk/-/media/boe/files/speech/2019/avoiding-the-storm-climate-change-and-the-financial-system-speech-by-sarah-breeden.pdf
10. https://www.greenbiz.com/article/global-sustainable-investing-assets-surged-30-trillion-2018
11. https://www.theguardian.com/environment/2016/oct/06/climate-change-infrastructure-coal-plants-green-investment
12. https://newclimateeconomy.report/2016/

SECTION I

Not Bad

What is 'Not Bad'?

I met the 'Not Bad' idea while working with IKEA on its sustainability initiatives way back in 2001.

We were trying to come up with a simple way to communicate the programme internally. And it was flipping complex. Like only a Swedish multinational's supply chain could be. My colleague Naresh Ramchandani had the genius idea of simplifying all the reporting under three headings, depending on what they implied for taking further action:

Not Bad (things we don't need to improve this year).
Fix This (things we need to improve this year).
Urgent (things we should have improved last year).

It was a clever way to simplify and create a common framework for action. Like a traffic light.

Not Bad stuck with me. It's so Swedish and modest (after investing 12 years and millions on sustainability efforts . . .). Not Bad is the truth of corporate responsibility. Reducing the 'bads' that happen when making, transporting, selling things and whatever happens after.

Think of it as a verb. To Not Bad.

We need to Not Bad our climate emissions, keep them well within Science-based Targets.

We need to Not Bad our social impacts, from farms and forests, to consuming at home.

Obviously, it would be sad if Not Bad was the height of our ambition.

But it's a pretty good first step.

1.1 Waking up to an Environmental Crisis (again)

It all starts with farming.

I wasn't born in 1962 when Rachel Carson's *Silent Spring* was published. But I grew up in a world where my teachers and other hippy-leaning adult figures were part of a global movement with ecological concerns that crystallised around 1970 with the first ever Earth Day. They were often the same people who campaigned for peace and nuclear disarmament. My maths teacher Leon subscribed to all this and also wrote cookbooks while running the local Vegan Society.

Silent Spring was an eloquent whistleblowing book about the devastating damage done by the agrochemical industry. The establishment dismissed Rachel Carson as a hysterical crank and whispered that she must be a communist. The industry then as now argued that intensive use of fertilisers and pesticides was the only way to feed the world. And yet studies since the1960s (the original study being by Nobel Prize winning economist Amartya Sen) consistently show that the smaller the farm is, the more food is grown per hectare.[1] If small farms grow more food per hectare, why have big farms? The answer is economics. Big farms with mechanised equipment (replacing expensive labour) produce more profit per acre. That wouldn't be true if they were taxed for their impact on climate. Or if the marketing tactics of big agro were curbed. Or if trade deals stopped pushing developing nations to apply a 'green revolution' that is actually anything but green and often leads to fragile food resilience and sovereignty.

There was a fresh uprush of eco concern across the 1970s. And this is when the attention shifted from farming to energy. An Arab oil embargo in 1973 triggered a series of energy crises. By the late 1970s, Jimmy Carter had installed solar panels on the roof of the White House. When Ronald Reagan came into power these were removed – as were Carter's subsidies for renewable energy. Trump isn't the first American president to make a virtue of eco ignorance. Ronald Reagan once said: 'Trees cause more pollution than automobiles do.' His administration weakened pollution standards and cut the budgets of the Environmental Protection Agency.[2]

How was this possible? Part of the reason was that public concern fell asleep in the 1980s. There were exceptions – like James Lovelock's seminal book *Gaia: A New Look at Life on Earth*. And it was Margaret Thatcher (ironically) who, mixed up in a war on coal miners, warned about the dangers of climate change. But mostly the issue seemed to go quiet.

Some readers will remember 1989, the year the Berlin Wall came down and when an extraordinary series of natural disasters triggered a global groundswell of ecological concern and millennial angst. Earth Day 20 was marked by massive public participation. The demonstrations continued across the 1990s in places like Seattle. It was the era when the focus of activism shifted from farming and energy to the effects of globalisation and supply chains.

Later in the 1990s the public seemed to fall asleep again. We had the internet boom, Y2K Millennium Bug, and Asian Financial Crisis to keep us preoccupied.

Then, in 2006, Al Gore's *Inconvenient Truth* movie about climate change triggered a fresh uprush of concern resulting in what the *Financial Times* called 'a wave of eco marketing', with corporations from GE and Yahoo to M&S and Walmart, flanked by Prius-driving Hollywood celebrities, declaring their support.

In 2007, I published a book on the subject of Green Marketing and not greenwashing. And found myself speaking at an average of three events a week for the next two years. Everyone was convinced that this was a sea change. Lee Daley, chief executive of Saatchi & Saatchi UK, said:

> Brands will not be able to opt out of this. Companies which do not live by a green protocol will be financially damaged because consumers will punish them. In the longer term, I do not think they will survive.[3]

Then, a few years later, the global financial crisis seemed to divert corporate and public attention: 2008 was a good year for carbon emissions, but it cost us in the longer term. People forgot about their carbon footprint and went back to business as usual. They fell asleep again.

Now here we are in 2019 and we see a global movement of climate and environment protests. School children are on strike. Extinction Rebellion are gluing themselves to buildings and blocking bridges. And the public are awake again. And alarmed. One 2019 report from an Australian think tank suggested our species could face 'an existential threat' by 2050.[4] The oft quoted idea is we have '12 years left to act' (12 years from 2018, as this stems from a UN report that year saying that we must make sharp reductions by 2030 to stand any chance).

It's not exactly confidence inspiring that we have reached this point before and then seen public interest and business and government resolve ebb away. Perhaps this time at last we will really wake up enough to effect permanent system change?

That kind of deeper change requires a combination of urgency and sub-stance. We need to keep calm and worry on. We need to do more than wage a 'war on sugar' or plastic straws.

Let's start with the worry. How concerned are the general public today? And what do they worry about. Is it the same old range of concerns or does it have a different complexion?

First: climate change. IPSOS MORI have been asking the UK public the same question for several decades as part of their Political Monitor poll:[5]

'How concerned, if at all, are you about climate change, sometimes referred to as "global warming"?'

	Concerned	Not concerned
2005	82%	15%
2010	71%	27%
2011	63%	35%
2013	60%	34%
2014	67%	31%
2019	85%	14%

This data tells us what we already knew: there was huge public interest around 2006 and again in 2019, but climate concerns went away in-between.

The concerns expressed in April when UK climate protests were under-way seemed to 'spike'. YouGov regularly polls the UK public on what the most important issue facing the country is. 'Environment' usually hovers somewhere around 10th on the list. It leapt to 5th in February 2014 after widespread flooding dominated the news. In April 2019 it reached 4th ahead of Economy and behind only Europe (Brexit), Crime, and Health. Then there is the Greta factor. In October 2019, 28% of adults mentioned it as a top priority, but that figure rises to 45% among 18–24 year olds.[6] I met a FTSE 250 CEO recently who wanted to talk about radical options on climate, not least – as he explained – because 'I have two Gretas living at home'.

The message of the protestors seems to be filtering through. A poll by Opinium on behalf of Greenpeace found that 63% of UK adults agreed with the statement 'we are facing a climate emergency' and that 76% said they would vote differently to protect the planet.[7] This is evidence for what I said in the Introduction – most people do now agree it's an emergency.

Another poll by Comres tested the more extreme position that climate change 'threatens our extinction as a species' and found that 54% agreed. Two-thirds of adults, 67%, believe that human activity 'is the principal cause behind climate change'; 51%, would be willing to forego at least one overseas trip per year for the sake of the climate.[8]

It's not just the UK. In fact, we are only middling in our level of public concern. YouGov compared responses from 30 000 people in 28 countries.[9] They found less than 7% in any country did not believe the climate was changing at all. Only a few countries like the USA and Saudi are lagging on believing people are responsible. The key difference was over whether people thought that human activity was mainly responsible or only partly responsible.

Percentage who agree the climate is changing and human activity is:

	Mainly Responsible	Partly Responsible	Mainly or Partly
India	71%	23%	94%
Thailand	68%	27%	95%
Spain	69%	27%	96%
Indonesia	69%	24%	93%
Italy	66%	29%	95%
Vietnam	64%	32%	96%

(continued)

	Mainly Responsible	Partly Responsible	Mainly or Partly
Philippines	62%	31%	93%
Singapore	54%	39%	93%
Taiwan	53%	42%	95%
Qatar	52%	41%	93%
Kuwait	52%	34%	86%
UAE	52%	33%	85%
Great Britain	51%	37%	88%
Hong Kong	50%	45%	95%
Finland	49%	38%	97%
Germany	49%	36%	85%
France	48%	37%	85%
Malaysia	48%	43%	91%
Bahrain	46%	41%	87%
China	45%	48%	93%
Australia	44%	43%	87%
Oman	43%	47%	90%
Egypt	42%	38%	80%
Denmark	40%	48%	88%
USA	38%	37%	75%
Sweden	36%	48%	84%
Saudi Arabia	35%	36%	71%
Norway	35%	48%	83%

The next question is: how much impact do you believe that climate change will have on your life?

Here we can see a huge discrepancy as some regions are already on the frontline or are seeing a different scale and tone of media reporting. China and America have huge environmental stresses (fires and floods in America, water stress and pollution in China), for instance, but their media might not be giving the same level of attention to these as European media.

'How much of an impact, if any, do you believe that climate change will have on your life?'

% who say that it will have 'a great deal of impact'

Philippines	75%
Vietnam	71%
India	70%
Qatar	65%
Egypt	58%
UAE	56%
Kuwait	55%
Thailand	55%
Bahrain	53%
Malaysia	47%
Oman	46%
Indonesia	45%
Singapore	41%
Saudi Arabia	41%
Taiwan	38%
Spain	32%
Italy	29%
Australia	29%
China	26%
France	26%
Hong Kong	25%
USA	24%
Great Britain	17%
Germany	16%
Finland	14%
Norway	12%
Sweden	11%
Denmark	10%

These public perceptions of who will or won't be affected have some truth to them. Climate change will affect developing countries more than rich ones. Standard & Poor found that 'vulnerability to climate change is inversely proportional to prosperity'. Asian countries like India and the Philippines do have the highest climate risk, while Western Europe and the USA rank as the least vulnerable.[10] But we live in a vastly interconnected world. Food shortages originating in countries like the Philippines in 2011 contributed to global protests, including the Arab Spring. These food shortages were also due to a 200% increase in oil prices, increasing the cost of agrichemicals and the demand for biofuels. One study found that Maize (Corn) for ethanol fuel production rose from 15% of total US maize production in 2006 to 40% in 2012.[11]

1.2 Actually, Consumers Do Buy Sustainable Goods

Climate change concerns come and go.

Interest in sustainable goods has been growing more steadily in recent decades.

One reason for this is health. In the 1990s, there was a sea change from thinking of health as scientific (foods with unsaturated fats, added vitamins) to thinking of natural, unprocessed food, avoiding nasty chemicals. This trend is now global. China is on track to be the fourth biggest organic food market (as well as seeing a shift from meat to plant-based diets) with research showing this is mainly due 'due to health concerns that are linked to inorganic food'.[12]

Organic food does have a role to play in the climate crisis. One recent Swiss study (based on data going back as far as 1978) found that 'Long-term organically farmed soils emit 40 percent less greenhouse gases per hectare than conventionally farmed soils,'[13] Plus, chemical spraying of pesticides and fertilisers has a broader impact on natural ecosystems. But people are clearly buying organic and natural products for their health, rather than just for the environment. As a result, the US organic market totalled $52.5 billion in 2018. Across Europe sales reached $97 billion. Denmark has the highest organic share of food (13%).[14]

Alongside organic food, wellbeing has been a huge trend; from gluten free and avocado a few years ago to this year's CBD, adaptogens, and vinegar shrubs. But the biggest recent shift in both health and climate terms has been eating less meat.

Beyond Meat recently made a $200 million public share offering. Their competitor Impossible Foods raised over $700 million in investment from

Bill Gates, Google Ventures, and others. This is not some elite Silicon Valley trend (like Bulletproof Coffee). The Impossible Whopper is now on sale at Burger King, 'for a trial period'.[15] Reviews have picked up on the fact that the Impossible Whopper may be made entirely of plants, but is processed and packed with salt and saturated fats (not to mention worries about GMOs in human diets) and not much healthier than a regular burger. The Impossible Burger is a pure response to the climate emergency – designed to be an environmentally conscious replacement for beef.

Fast food might seem an unlikely starting point. But if you want system change then shifting mass markets can have more effect than purist green niches. (I'm not sure about the sustainability of their launch offer of a regular Whopper and an Impossible Whopper together for $7 so customers can try them side by side. But if this does convert meat eaters to plant-based food, I guess it's a win overall?) Max Burgers of Sweden have been on this same trajectory for decades. Back in 2008 they took advice from the *Natural Step* consultancy which was: 'your problem is that you make hamburgers'. Max won a Green Award for their next move which was to divide the menu into climate-friendly options and less climate-friendly options based on carbon ratings (and behind the scenes they had also added more non beef options like chicken, fish, and veggie burgers). Just by dividing the menu in this way they saw a 28% shift in purchasing towards the more climate-friendly options.

Max have kept innovating on many fronts, including packaging, sourcing, and food waste. And in 2018 they announced their Climate Positive Burger. How they achieve this is through monitoring and reducing emissions from farm to fork. They even look at consumer journeys to their restaurants. And then they plant sufficient trees to cover 110% of the remaining emissions. Max also committed to one in two products sold being non beef by 2020, extending their range of vegan burgers fourfold and launching a Climate Positive Products association to encourage others to follow suit. They also planted 1.5 million trees in Africa. Not Bad indeed.

Offsetting emissions does have a mixed reputation in green circles. (A funny activist spoof on offsets was provided by Cheat Neutral – an online trading platform where those faithful in sexual relationships could sell credits to others who had extramarital affairs.) But all power to Max. And if they have to plant trees to be climate positive, it's better than not trying.

Natural food can be expensive. Particularly in the USA where Whole-foods was nicknamed 'Whole Paycheck'. But people are increasingly willing to pay more for what Nielsen described as 'the intersection of healthy for me and healthy for we'. Nielsen found that fast moving consumer goods food and drink brands with a sustainability claim grew 7.2% in 2017 while others declined by 0.2%. Organic brands grew 12% in the same period. This despite an unbelievably high premium for organic products in the US: 87% for milk, 122% for eggs, and 43% for pasta sauce.

At the time I wrote my *Green Marketing* book, commentators often pointed to an attitude–behaviour gap: 30% of consumers reported that they were concerned about environmental issues, but research by the *Guardian* showed only 3–5% would act on these beliefs.

Commentators still moan about the gap today, but the figures for both thinking and doing tend to be much higher.

In one survey 65% said they want to buy purpose-driven brands that advocate sustainability, yet only 26% actually do so.[16]

Here we can see that the gap has narrowed: from 10:1 down to 3:1. You can build a huge brand based on 26% of people being willing to pay more.

And it's not just organic food. NYU Stern's Center for Sustainable Business found that 50% of all consumer-packaged goods growth in 2013–2018 came from sustainability-marketed products. The study covered 36 categories and 71 000 SKUs. Products marketed as sustainable accounted for $114 billion in sales and grew 5.6 times faster than those that were not. In 90% of categories, sustainability-marketed products grew faster than their conventional counterparts.[17]

What's really important here is captured by the HBR headline reporting this research:

Research: Actually, Consumers Do Buy Sustainable Products.

1.3 From Plastic Brands to the Circular Economy

Green brands are maturing to become mainstream and normal. This is common in the adoption of new technology. Gartner describes this transition to maturity as a later stage of their *hype curve*:

Technology Trigger: prototypes and demonstrations catch media interest.

Peak of Inflated Expectations: publicity, sales of early versions to early adopters.

Trough of Disillusionment: problems emerge, some attempts flop.

Slope of Enlightenment: new generations of product find a more mature form.

Plateau of Productivity: the tech becomes invisible, boring, the new normal.

Plastic bank cards were once remarkable. A UK TV advert once featured a comedian flashing a wallet full of credit cards while uttering the line 'more plastic than Michael Jackson's face'. It was aspirational and new. Cards went mainstream and started to differentiate themselves with offers like bundled insurance. Then they became universal and invisible – while paying with cash money started to look old. Next came contactless which was notable for a while. Now paying with your phone (or your face) is starting to make using plastic cards look out of date.

Speaking of plastic, one big shift recently has been attitudes to packaging. In 2018, UK research by Thoughtworks found that (thinking about purchasing over the next 10 years) 62% were concerned to reduce plastic packaging, compared to only 57% being concerned about price.[18]

Unpackaged goods are on the rise. Catherine Conway started Unpackaged in 2005 as a result of having a mouse at home and transferring her foods into glass jars. Conway started selling unpackaged dry goods in a market – rice, cereals, nuts, washing powder – that people would use their own containers for. Then opened a shop in Marylebone. And now helps larger chains like Planet Organic create nicely designed Unpackaged sections. In 2019, Conway helped Waitrose open its first packaging free zone in Oxford. After *Blue Planet* raised public concerns, sales through Unpackaged sections of supermarkets went up 40%.[19]

Another industry struggling to reduce its addiction to plastic is sports shoes. Allbirds became one of the coolest brands in America. Wired gave it a breathless roll call: 'The shoes quickly became popular with the Silicon Valley tech crowd, followed by entrepreneurs, celebrities and politicians. Former US President Barack Obama has been seen wearing them, Google co-founder Larry Page, celebrities Oprah Winfrey and Matthew McConaughey, venture capitalists Ben Horowitz and Mary Meeker. Actor Leonardo DiCaprio even became an investor.'[20]

Bit shallow I know. But it's the same following that propelled the Prius after an entrepreneurial Green Car to the Red Carpet service cornered the Oscars chauffeuring market and created a priceless (for Toyota) association in the public mind between hybrid cars and celebrity.

Allbirds founder Tim Brown is a former professional footballer from New Zealand. Brown came up with the idea of a wool-based shoe while studying at the London School of Economics in 2013. Brown started by offering 1000 shoes on the Kickstarter website and raised $120 000 in four days. A year later Brown teamed up with Joey Zwillinger, a product designer and expert in sustainable materials based in San Francisco. Allbirds then racked up $100 million in revenues while a fresh investment of $50 million brought a valuation of $1.4 billion.[21]

Pretty impressive. But it's only 1 million shoes in an industry that sells 20 billion shoes a year.

Compare this with the Adidas sustainable shoe. Adidas teamed up in 2015 with ocean conservation non-profit Parlay to make a trendy knitted shoe from ocean plastic. In 2019, Adidas sold 11 million pairs of these shoes. Each item in the range uses at least 75% marine trash recovered by Parlay and their partners from the Maldives. What's more, Adidas committed to the Parlay protocol called AIR (Avoid Intercept Redesign) across its entire product range; for instance, removing microbeads from their anti-perspirants.

The next Adidas hero sustainable product – due to launch in 2021 – will be the Futurecraft Loop. This will be a closed loop shoe designed to be disassembled and the components reused in future shoes (rather than recycled and the plastic used in a water bottle or tote jacket).

How is Adidas doing commercially from all these efforts? Eleven million pairs of Parlay shoes mean sales of over $1 billion. Clearly Adidas do not think that sustainability is a niche or that green should be left to eco disruptors like Allbirds (1 million pairs) and VEJA (500 000 pairs).

The circular economy isn't only about upcycling or design for reassembly.

RealReal is a platform that authenticates luxury goods and sells them on behalf of customers for a commission. RealReal recently announced a partnership with Burberry where if you list one of their branded products you get a free personal styling appointment at Burberry and a free high tea thrown in. The RealReal already ran a similar partnership with Stella McCartney.

Imagine if the entire design industry were relaunched as a public service. What would change? That question was posed by the *Great Recovery* project at the RSA, which included visits by designers to recycling and recovery centres. One example output could be that white goods like fridges are standardised so their components can be easily recovered and reused. This doesn't actually mean moving to communist-style state planning. Software and hardware IT professionals get together all the time to agree common standards. It makes everyone's lives easier when things are interoperable. In the case of physical goods, it would not only ease the recycling process but also make repair and spare parts much more affordable and available.

This circular economy idea is – in my view – best grasped as just one branch of seeing human societies as a living system. We have design, technologies, and artefacts, just as beavers have dams. Designing these so they help ecosystems around us thrive (as beavers do when they create a lake) makes obvious sense provided you start with a generative ('good for the species') intent.

The circular economy was first discussed in the 1980s, but it has taken hold to the extent that it is now official Chinese and Dutch government policy. The idea is to eliminate waste through making the output of any one process be the input of another. The famous mantra of *Cradle to Cradle* – a book that popularised this idea – was that 'waste is food'. The *Great Recovery* lists four main strategies for the circular economy, in order of preference:

Design for longevity.
Design for leasing or service.
Design for reuse in manufacture.
Design for material recovery.

These can sound quite dry. But each has been the starting point for some highly creative and disruptive new brand and business ideas.

Design for Longevity.

Howies experimented with this by creating a HandMeDown range. They sold these jackets and bags with a contract between the buyer and the company. The buyer promised to keep the object in use (and they allowed for new users taking the contract on). Howies promised to keep the legacy zips, buckles, and other parts that might be needed for repair in stock. Another way to design for longevity is to get into the servicing business. Nudie Jeans has repair shops where their jeans can be kept going. You can go to a Nudie repair shop even if you bought the jeans second hand. The service is part of the design of the jeans.

Design for Leasing and Service.

An example is the leasing model used by Interface who keep ownership of their (office) carpets and hence are able to recover and reuse fibres. Interface provide the service of covered floors. There are many sharing economy systems able to share resources better ranging from AirBnB to Freecycle. I once considered a start-up called the Prawn Shop which would pawn objects (leave your guitar & PC with us while you go travelling, to release some cash) with zero interest rates provided you sign an agreement saying we can rent it out.

Design for Reuse in Manufacture.

I worked with the Royal Mail on a sustainable innovation project and we had numerous circular economy ideas. Including turning junk mail into exercise books by collecting it in schools – something that the business (and focus groups) loved and was trialled in the South East region. Royal Mail worked with Worn Again to design coats for disassembly to be remade into cycle bags (the uniforms are high vis). Why not just sell the coats? Because the Royal Mail stopped selling uniforms after an armed gang used them to impersonate staff and raid their facilities.

Design for Material Recovery.

One company that has come surprisingly far is Apple. Their Daisy robots can each disassemble 1.2 million iPhones per year. Apple are quadrupling the number of these robots, as well as opening a dedicated Material Recovery Lab in Austin, Texas. Recovered material enters reuse cycles. For instance, cobalt from recovered batteries is used to make new iPhone batteries. Meanwhile, Apple is also refurbing and reselling around 8 million devices per year. Apple is a brand that relies on being seriously cool and clearly got the message that for the new generation making disposable electronics is not a good look.

The broader point is designing human systems compatible with living systems around us. Thinking about all the impacts we have – like the sound our ship propellers make and how distressing they must be for whales – or the impact of our ocean plastic. Seeing design like this brings not just intelligence and self-preservation, but compassion and considerateness to design. If you ignore these impacts, you are (from a broader perspective) making something ugly.

There is a new movement in the design community with this idea called Earth Centred Design.[22] The group have produced a 20-point manifesto including points like these:

> shift from a reductionist worldview that sees nature as a deterministic machine to an enlivened worldview that sees the earth as a living, intelligent organism
> no one is specifically to blame for climate change. It's also not necessary to carry the weight or guilt on your shoulders; it's the system at fault
> be inspired by, learn from and work within nature. for example, the ecology of bees has a lot to tell us about self-organising and collective consciousness.

If the hippy mindset isn't for you (or your employer), do consider that adding a dramatic new twist to a brief almost always leads to fresh thinking and big ideas.

What could an Earth-centred design look like?

Could a car start cleaning the air around it and draw some of its fuel from city pollution?

Imagine: Chinese cities could be returned to pre-industrial air quality by cars that did this.

I'm not saying it would work.

I'm saying you might not have just thought of it without an Earth-centred point of view.

The car that cleans the air to fuel itself would be behaving just like a mollusc. Ecosystems are full of actions by organisms that have a benefit beyond their own interests. Although taking a broader view it does benefit the molluscs in the long run. As any mussel would tell you, what's good for the rock pool is good for me.

A great question to ask in product design is 'what would nature do'?

1.4 Instagram, Influencers, and Brands as Folklore

Today's consumer markets are noticeably more craze prone. That's been helpful in the growth of the new greener brands and behaviours. But it is just as apparent in trends like Pokémon Go and Clean Eating. A key reason is social media. We used to have to watch TV or read magazines to discover what everyone is into these days. Now we glean this directly from each other. Young people in particular tend to share whatever they buy or are intending to buy and get feedback in the form of likes, posts, shares, and tags.

The result is that the shareable dimensions of a brand have become disproportionately important: Instagram-ready packaging design, a snappy name that's instantly meaningful, and also a great story about design, ingredients, sustainability, authenticity, the founders. We'll see this new marketing mix again and again. Instagram is the new supermarket shelf. But in a physical shop, consumers are buying alone; whereas online, the decisions are being taken together.

Soap Co. is a typical Instagram age brand. The company makes gorgeously designed ethical soap bars, handwash, and hand cream. For over a hundred years the company behind Soap Co. (Clarity) was a non-profit that employed blind people. Hence, each pack has the branding in braille as well as printed type. Previously, the charity made soap for others; now it also makes its own Soap Co. brand. Soap Co. founder Camilla Marcus-Dew left her corporate job to turn Clarity into a thriving concern and do something more worthwhile. Brands like Soap Co. are easy to share on social media. You want to spread the word because it's such a lovely premise for a company. Plus, the packaging looks so great in your Instagram feed and on your shelf.

The most successful hair product on social media last year was called Don't Despair Repair. This is a deep conditioning mask that you apply then wear their shower cap so that steam from the shower helps it penetrate your hair. Parent brand Briogeo's latest version of this cult product (containing honey) comes in a cute bear-shaped bottle that just screams *shelfie*. Brio means vibrant, full of life, while Geo refers to the bountiful earth and a natural product philosophy.

The Briogeo story started with founder Nancy Twine's grandmother who made natural soap and hair products in the bath to save money. Nancy grew up making similar products for her friends using her grandmother's recipe book. Nancy worked for Goldman Sachs for five years, but it was tough after the 2008 financial crisis. In 2014, Briogeo launched and within a year found its way into leading retailers like Sephora. Don't Despair Repair was their breakout success. On the back of this, Briogeo became Sephora's fastest growing brand in 2019.[23]

Briogeo is one of the new breed of natural beauty products. They offer natural ingredients and also high performance. Twine says it is all a matter of treating your hair just the way that you treat your skin, with natural products that hydrate, protect, and also detoxify. All of their products are free from SLS/SLES sulphates, silicones, parabens, phthalates, DEA, and synthetic colour. They are cruelty free, 'mostly vegan', and 90–100% natural.

In many markets you often see new brands like Briogeo that speak to the new generation usurping old guard incumbent brands. In the case of organic, natural, and sustainability focused brands, the new kids on the block aren't always the greenest. But they are able to grab people, be relevant, speak their language, and look good on the shelf. You see this in food and drink with the new hipster craft beer and food cart style foodie brands. And you see it in beauty.

It's interesting to compare Briogeo with Aveda. Aveda was founded by a hairdresser called Horst whose mother was a herbalist. Since the 1970s, Aveda has made plant-based hair products based on Horst's discovery of Ayurveda. Aveda is one of those *50 years ahead of their time* sustainable pioneers. They were the first to use 100% post-consumer recycled plastic packaging. Way back in the 1990s they were one of the first to sign up to the 10-point CERES principles of environmental conduct:

Protection of the biosphere.
Sustainable use of natural resources.
Reduction and disposal of wastes.
Energy conservation.
Risk reduction.
Safe products and services.
Environmental restoration.
Informing the public.
Management commitment.
Audits and reports.

That's sustainable business on a whole different level than any small eco challenger brand can manage. The deeper you look into Aveda the more impressive it becomes. They increased the organic ingredient mix of their products from 20% to 90% in weight. I met last year with an indigenous tribe called the Yawanawa (who were visiting the UK from Brazil) and guess what? Aveda has been partnering with them since 1993, growing uruku on their land to protect biodiversity while providing an income that is better than that paid by loggers.

Aveda is absolutely amazing. But brands like Aveda can easily see the new generation gravitate towards challenger brands like Briogeo who won't know nearly as well what the impacts are in their supply chain, but who know how to sell themselves on Instagram. In YouGov research, Aveda ranks as the 46th most popular beauty brand with GenX but 61st among Millennials. Compare this with Clinique, which ranks 28th among both age groups. It's clear Aveda is ageing. I asked a few friends and the consensus was that Aveda is lovely, but a bit 'auntie'.

If I were Aveda, I would look at innovating format not just messaging. Take their famous salon-based rituals and bring them to the shower in the way that Briogeo did with their cap. Aveda don't need to change fundamentals, but they do need to refresh more than the brand rhetoric. They need to find a place in the lives of a new generation and their #selfcaresaturday routines. They could do this in all sorts of ways. If you look at Korean beauty you see an incredible mix of new rituals (like their masks) and natural product innovation with fermentation, adaptogens.

This 'auntie' syndrome can be seen in lots of markets. The old hippy green is not the same as the new Instagram folklore brands which are more aspirational, hipster, and often more mainstream. Witness meat-free brands like Linda McCartney seeing Impossible Foods stealing their thunder. Prius enjoyed some time as the definitive green car, but then TESLA came along.

You don't just need new brand values in this situation, you need a fresh approach to marketing.

One way to grasp this is to see the new brands as being built by *folklore*.

In the previous century, the traditional folklore culture was eclipsed by modern schools, education, mass literacy, mass media. But now with electronic media – as foreseen by Marshall McLuhan – we are back to a global village culture. This is not because official institutions have disappeared. But rather they have been eclipsed by people directly accessing and sharing thoughts, anecdotes, photos, ideas, and of course brands. The first place we turn to discuss childhood ailments and worries is no longer the GP, it is Mumsnet and similar forums.

The clean eating craze was a demonstration of the market shifting potential of folklore amplified by electronic media. The avocado on toast wellbeing boom was tapping into a genuine public unease with processed food, contamination, antibiotics, and endocrine disrupting chemicals. But it was the hip young Instagrammers and blogs called things like *Lexi's Clean Kitchen* and *The Gracious Pantry* that made it take off as a craze.

The clean eating trend seems by now to have entered the (Gartner) Trough of Disappointment. As did Atkins a decade previously. But similar platforms and hipster personalities are now driving the vegan eating craze. As marketers it is impossible to ignore the scale and speed of these new trends. Gluten free foods grew 67% from 2013 to 2015, with 25% of consumers restricting or avoiding gluten at the peak in 2015.[24]

This folklore brand era is catching quite a few established players out. Supermarkets have rushed to stock their shelves with free from foods but are probably only scratching the surface of much bigger shifts in diet and attitude. The big one being avoiding processed foods.

Studies of traditional folklore identify four main categories:

1. Material folklore: physical objects and their design, format, categories.
2. Verbal folklore: well-worn sayings, expressions, stories.
3. Customary folklore: habits, beliefs, ways of doing things.
4. Games: the whole ritual world of play.

This stakes out the new playbook of marketing in a folklore era.

Come up with a physical format, preferably a 'Trojan horse' with the comfort of familiarity. Like a super realistic beef burger from plants. Or a TESLA car that looks just like a petrol supercar. Ideally come up with something that looks good on Instagram too.

Create catchy phrases and names, like the Impossible Burger.

Create new habits. Like wearing a shower cap to let the steam soak the product in.

Create games, customs, interactions, and rituals. Like taking your own packaging into an Unpackaged store.

Folklore draws value from ritual and repetition. Unlike a snippet of new information, folklore draws its value from being familiar: when we hear the words 'once upon a time . . .' or 'happy birthday to you . . .' or when we see a tea pot or a piece of wrapping paper we are placed into a circular time of traditions. The social media age has taken us back to a world where the currency of repetition is primary once again. It's a stark contrast from the dominance in modernist culture of the 'new and improved' formulation.

Having a phrase that is endlessly repeated can help you achieve this currency fast. Brands like Alberts (#butfirstcoffee) did this with their slogan. Briogeo went one further and did this with the name of a product (#dontdespairrepair). Marketing is no longer about attempted mind control via mass media messages. You are trying to 'catch on' in the space between people, on their level and with their help and support.

Influencers stepped into the void left by official channels. But recently got drawn into question as old world brands increasingly just paid them to post, in the same way that they bought ad spots, without really engaging in the culture and fan base. If you want to launch a clean beauty brand there are thousands of YouTube reviewers you can pay to review it. A year ago, these were the darlings of consumer brand marketing. An influencer with 100 000 followers could earn $5000 for a single sponsored post. But then marketers like Unilever questioned the widespread use of fake follows to bump up prices. Hotels started to refuse travel bloggers. Los Angeles ice cream van owner Joe Nicchi started charging influencers $8 a cone instead of $4 saying he was sick of influencers asking for free cones in return for sharing pics on Instagram.

The consensus today is that smaller influencers who people follow because they have something meaningful to say or are genuine leading figures in a community are good; bigger influencers who people follow for their celebrity, less so.

If you do something genuinely cool that people want to support, then you will build a genuine community. LEGO when I worked with them back in the 2000s built a LEGO Ambassador programme with leading figures in the adult fan of LEGO (AFOL) community. It's a 'Jazz Shop' model; where the people serving, and buying, are all part of a shared subculture of jazz fans.

Playful eco toiletries brand LUSH is increasing their reliance on influencers – while they also shocked the UK marketing community by dropping their own branded official media channels. LUSH said in their announcement:

> We are tired of fighting with algorithms, and we do not want to pay to appear in your newsfeed. So we've decided . . . to open up the conversation between the Lush Community and us instead.[25]

Word on the street is that LUSH did take a slight hit on their web traffic, but that the engagement with visitors is now deeper in terms of time on site etc.

The right way to engage in a folk culture is to be interesting and share things worth sharing.

The 'unfair' fact is that brands need to be more creative and less devious. The algorithm cannot buy you love, even if it can buy you follows. Only teams with a talent for populism who believe in what they do ever create great brands these days.

LUSH is the last brand to want to hide behind a façade, unlike many cosmetic companies. They have creative products – like Gandalf's fireworks in *The Hobbit* – made in Willy Wonka style factories and are committed environmentalists. LUSH generate meaningful engagement around causes they are passionate about, including the climate strike and (slightly more surprisingly) Spy Cops. Here LUSH windows were taped with 'police have crossed the line' over the story of policemen who had sexual relationships and even children with activists while deep undercover. LUSH's founder used to work for Body Shop and a Spy Cops campaign is the sort of thing Anita Roddick would have done 30 years ago. LUSH is well positioned as a folklore age brand and also shows how easily activism and engagement can blend these days.

1.5 Simple Marketing, Complex Sustainability

Greenwash was an early warning sign. Marketers needed to get their head around sustainability to avoid making exaggerated claims. Sustainability is a topic where there is no substitute for going through the thicket to get to simple truths on the other side. Simple answers like should we avoid using palm oil or eating meat involve complex lines of questioning. You have to go through this in order to take a sensible position for your brands. It's well worth the effort because the insights can lead to meaningful innovation and campaign platforms.

The term greenwash was invented in the 1980s by environmentalist Jay Westerveld. Jay was writing about a hotel towel scheme.[26] Westerveld suspected the hotel in question didn't care all that much about preserving ecology. Westerveld also figured that not washing towels saved the hotel money. Greenwash was a term that sounded quite like whitewash (a common term for political spin) covering over an ugly reality with a superficial lick of paint. But the word also sat well with the original case under consideration which was hotel laundry.

A 2015 study of greenwash describes it as 'communication that misleads people into forming overly positive beliefs about an organization's environmental practices or products'. A classic example was advertising in the 1980s by Chevron called *People Do*. This pointed to cute conservation projects the company funded that protected bears and butterflies. The butterfly park cost Chevron around $5000 whereas their TV advertising about it cost millions. And clearly such donations could not answer bigger questions about the oil industry and the environment.

When I wrote my *Green Marketing* book in 2007, eco-themed advertising was all the rage. Corporations from GE to Yahoo produced expensive campaigns proclaiming their commitment, boasting of their achievements and asking the public to do their bit. There was also already a fear of being accused of greenwashing. Brands like BP had already seen a backlash. Often, when giving talks to marketing teams I was asked to cover 'what is greenwash and how to avoid it?' The worry being that initiatives that backfire do more harm than good.

When Nestlé launched its Fairtrade KitKat, Greenpeace responded with a spoof KitKat commercial where biting into the snack revealed a bloody Orangutan's finger – a calculated attack on the integrity of a food brand. The underlying dispute was over Nestlé sourcing from Sinar Mas, an Indonesian company accused of illegal deforestation and peatland clearance. Unilever and Kraft had stopped sourcing from Sinar Mas, but Nestlé only responded that they were looking into it. Once the Orangutan video was launched, Nestlé found a new supplier. Palm oil is a complex issue. And here the issue of greenwash grows up. Most sustainability is in shades of grey. And choosing a least bad route does not translate into easy public headlines.

Palm oil made headlines in 2018 when UK supermarket Iceland launched a TV commercial that was originally used as an education video by Greenpeace. This was banned by the Advertising Standards Authority. And then had over 65 million views on YouTube. As a result, palm oil and deforestation shot up the public agenda. Iceland had launched the commercial to back up its promise to have no palm oil in its own label products. The BBC then accused Iceland of greenwash as they found 'goods such as fairy cakes, hot cross buns and jam tarts – all made with palm oil – available to buy online. One product carried a logo saying it was new.'[27]

Environmentalist Jonathan Porritt was furious at the suggestion that all palm oil is bad. This, he said, derailed the efforts of the Roundtable on Sustainable Palm Oil (RSPO). Porritt pointed out that 'clearing forest either for grazing livestock or for growing the feed that livestock needs is a far more serious problem than conversion of forest for oil palm – up to 10 times more serious, according to some estimates'. His key beef with Iceland's move was that all the other oils that could be used to replace palm oil have a demonstrably far worse environmental impact.

Back in 2001, Jonathan Porritt had brought a group of concerned marketers together for a project called Limited Edition. The reason being that many sustainability schemes ran aground when it came to marketing. Porritt might recommend organic agriculture. But then marketers would tell him research said consumers wouldn't pay more for it. They could have been right of course. Back in 2001, Iceland went 100% organic. Iceland claimed to have bought 40% of the world supply of organic vegetables. And it promised to forego £8 million in profits to ensure the prices were kept down. However, sales fell, and this led to a sharp fall in share price, so that eventually they had to reverse the policy.[28]

I do love Iceland's unlikely commitment to environmental causes. Iceland is not a middle-class store who can embrace organic food as yet another way to justify a premium. Iceland is the place mainstream mums and dads buy their frozen fish fingers. This feels like a genuine commitment. Their former chairman was a Greenpeace member. And they were one of the first to ban GM foods. Iceland were also the first major retailer to pledge to remove single-use plastic from own label products.[29] I would defer to Jonathan Porritt on the wisdom of their palm oil campaign, but you've got to love Iceland for making an effort?

The palm oil controversy with Nestlé has not gone away either. Nestlé were kicked out of the RSPO in June 2018 who cited breaches of its code of conduct. A month later Nestlé were reinstated as Nestlé had submitted an 'action plan to achieve 100% RSPO certified sustainable palm oil by 2023'. Nestlé went on to detail their progress and efforts on traceability:

Nestlé's responsible sourcing strategy has so far led to the company tracing 50 percent of the palm oil it buys back to the plantations and 92 percent back to the mills. In addition, 58 percent of Nestlé's palm oil is today 'responsibly sourced,' and it has achieved the status of 63 percent deforestation-free, across commodities.

Nobody wants to buy a global portfolio of brands whose ingredients are 37% deforestation based. What looks like best practice in sustainability is not much to write home about in copy. Most people would much rather they were 100% deforestation free now. I think it's one of those issues, like child labour, where public attitudes hardened fast and no matter how hard it is to police, companies have to find a way.

Numerous consumer goods organisations have pledged to be deforestation free by 2020. Again, it's kind of shocking that they weren't previously. The Consumer Goods Forum, including GlaxoSmithKline, Mondelez, and Alibaba, have pledged 'zero net deforestation by 2020'.

Note that zero net deforestation must mean they are planting trees to balance out parts of their supply chain still killing the beautiful old rainforest trees that are the guardians of our world.

Halting deforestation by 2020 is also a UN Sustainable Development Goal – although it looks a long way off, with clearance fires blazing in the Amazon through 2019. As of March 2017, 447 companies made 760 commitments to curb forest destruction in supply chains linked to palm oil, soy, timber and pulp, and cattle, according to Forest Trends.[30]

This level of controversy and factual detail is what you are walking into when you commit your brand to a sustainable future. It is tempting as a marketer to steer well clear when you start to grasp the sheer awfulness of deforestation and the devastating effect and violent conflicts this creates on the ground. And yet this same emotional force of righting injustice is what can make sustainability so powerful. Look at the impact of the *Blue Planet 2* documentary series, or the billions that tuned into Live Aid – not despite, but *because* they grasped the nettle of suffering.

The KitKat case study is an interesting illustration of what it means for a brand to engage. The accusation was one of tokenism. For chocolate sold in the UK, this Fairtrade deal amounted to 2.6% of Nestlé's cocoa sourcing. And yet the KitKat brand was a huge coup for the Fairtrade movement – by 2013 it was the second best-selling Fairtrade product in the UK.

It's a tough one. What I've heard quite a bit recently is that Nestlé is making real efforts on the sustainability front. In an independent ranking of chocolate supply chain and sustainability ethics Nestlé was middling – level with Mars confectionary and well ahead of Mondelez and Ferrero.[31]

But Nestlé was a company that activists grew up boycotting (just like McDonalds and Coke). So even if they have improved, they are going to be a ready target.

One lesson from all this is that reputations can take 30+ years to shift.

Yet another reason to try your utmost to be Not Bad.

1.6 Fifty Shades of Greenwash

Greenwash is misleading the public to make it look like the environmental performance of your company or products is better than it actually is. That can easily be unintentional.

How does it actually happen in practice?

And what are the strategies to watch out for?

I've compiled an initial list of examples. There aren't quite 50 of these (the title was a joke as well as a film reference – I liked the irony of exaggerating about greenwash). This is not comprehensive but should give some indication of the variety of ways companies can intentionally or unintentionally engage in greenwash and put their brands in peril.

Defending the Indefensible

We've just been looking at the knotty subject of palm oil, responsible and otherwise. It's a complex issue. Some argued that the kneejerk 'palm is bad' position taken by Iceland and Greenpeace does the environment a disservice. Because other oil crops do more damage. However, there is something straightforwardly wrong about the line taken by TV advertising produced by the Malaysian Palm Oil Council – hence this ad was banned in the UK:

Malaysia Palm Oil. Its trees give life and help our planet breathe and give home to hundreds of species of flora and fauna.
    Malaysia Palm Oil. A gift from nature, a gift for life.

Malaysia between 2000–2012 had the fastest rate of deforestation in Asia.[32] Palm grew to 4% of Malaysian GDP so it was natural for them to produce a campaign to defend the integrity of this key export. But it is indefensible to point to any minor benefits of the plantations, given what they often replace is virgin rainforest which has much greater benefits. Friends of the Earth say that 'palm oil plantations are linked to rainforest species extinction, habitat loss, pollution from burning to clear the land, destruction of flood buffer zones along rivers'.[33]

The Fig Leaf

This is the classic approach to greenwash and it consists of proud advertising about a little good you are doing to cover up much greater bads. This is what got BP into trouble with their $200 million (in July 2000) *Beyond Petroleum* ad campaign. You would have thought oil companies had learned their lesson by now? But consider this recent social post from Shell:

> Trees are vital in the fight against climate change. See how Shell is investing in nature in the UK as part of our broad drive to tackle CO2 emissions.

This post that appeared in my LinkedIn feed had attracted comments like 'this is blatant greenwashing and should be illegal', 'interesting this should appear the day after the *Guardian* published research naming Shell as the 7th biggest contributor to global carbon emissions'. I happen to know the head of communications at Shell is genuinely a tree hugger (I saw her talk at a conference about her family's year off volunteering in forest projects). And I don't doubt Shell are supporting some worthy initiatives. But trying to win the public debate by using tree planting as a fig leaf is a tad concerning.

In May 2019, 99% of BP shareholders passed a resolution mandating the company to align its business strategy with climate targets that are in line with the 2015 Paris Agreement. And to link achieving these targets with executive pay. So, all is not necessarily lost on the oil company front. But they are ill-served by social posts of pictures of forests. Or the post BP put in my LinkedIn feed saying: 'One big challenge, keep the world moving while lowering emissions.'

As with any greenwash, judgement is key. How much do you have to be doing as a proportion of the whole business for what you promote *not* to be a fig leaf? Toyota committed to a greener future by launching the hybrid car. This did not replace the rest of their range, which includes some massive gas guzzlers. But Toyota seemed serious about the hybrid. And electrified cars did account for more than half their car sales in Europe in 2019. There are criticisms of Toyota. And of the hybrid car. But it is substantial in terms of effort.

Getting Your Facts Wrong

Staying in one of Austria's leading environmentally friendly resorts could in some cases cause fewer carbon dioxide emissions than staying at home in the UK.

. . . according to a Visit Austria ad campaign that was highlighted for greenwash by the *Guardian*.

Unless you cycle there, I can't see any way this would work . . .

was the response the journalist got from a campaigner at Greenpeace.[34]

I had a brief from an agency working for a tech company who wanted – on the basis of their sustainability efforts – to build 'wait in line green desirability' for their mobile devices.

It wasn't hard to compare their sustainability programme with Apple's (both are good at reporting); only to find them identical on most measures but behind Apple on refurb and disassembly. Nothing against electronics giants innovating on the green front and taking consumers with them. But the absolutely greenest thing they could do is concentrate their efforts on design for the circular economy, starting with longevity and upgradability. And they certainly did not have support for selling their phones as being greener than the iPhone.

Using the Wrong Facts

We are all familiar with the politician's trick of quoting selective statistics. When you look carefully at the assumptions behind these 'facts' they often turn out to be misleading.

easyJet was pulled up on a claim that a passenger on one of its flight emitted less CO_2 than somebody driving a Toyota Prius (95.7 g/km vs 104 g/km). It turned out their calculation assumed that the plane was 100% full, that the Prius had one passenger (the average is 1.6), and other greenhouse gasses could be ignored. Overall, the emissions per passenger (according to the UK government) for a short haul flight are 254 g/km.[35] And the Prius with 1.6 occupancy is 65 g/km.

Claims without Proof

A common form of greenwash is making unsubstantiated claims. Even conscientious companies can lapse into this. Howies had an advertising standards complaint upheld in 2013 for two pieces of copy on their website:

> We make high quality, low impact clothing, for everyday life and everyday sport.
>   That's why, wherever possible, we use organic cotton – cotton grown without any of the nasty stuff.

Howies was unable to prove that their entire range lived up to the lifecycle analysis results implied by the phrase 'low impact'. They may indeed have a lower impact than other clothing companies, but there was no evidence to support this claim. Also, the ASA held that their copy 'misleadingly implied the advertiser used organic cotton in their products to a greater extent than they did'.[36]

The Stay of Execution

There is a traditional story about a condemned man who gets a reprieve after he offers to teach the sultan's (or king's, or Caesar's) horse to talk within a year. The jailer calls him a fool. It's clearly impossible. But the man replies with a wink that a lot can happen in a year.

It is common practice in sustainability initiatives to set and announce long-term goals. It makes sense when it is hard to change things overnight to ask for time to respond. But the practice can smack of teaching the horse to talk. Burger King announced it planned

> eliminating deforestation and protecting local communities connected to raw materials like beef, chicken, animal feed (typically soy), palm oil, as well as paper and other packaging by 2030.

The Union of Concerned Scientists described their commitment as 'embarrassingly weak'.[37]

Mighty Earth reported the story with the headline

> Burger King Commits to Stop Destroying Rainforests . . . in 13 Years

Hedging Your Bets

If you commit to lead your industry on a sustainable path, as KLM did with their 'fly responsibly' campaign (advertising that included advice to take the train where possible), it's a good idea to check none of your colleagues are lobbying against environmental legislation. A journalist discovered that KLM opposes a tax on aviation fuel. As KLM published on their own website: 'A national aviation tax will not improve the environment because Dutch passengers will travel by car and fly from an airport in Belgium or Germany.' KLM might have a point, but this led the journalist to conclude that KLM's ad campaign 'smells a bit of greenwashing'.[38]

From Comparative to Superlative

In 2008, Lexus had its advertising pulled by the Advertising Standards Authority. The car in question was a hybrid SUV with emissions of 192 g/km. This was better than other luxury SUVs, but similar to a standard family estate. The advertising had skipped past these relative comparisons to deal in superlatives. As the headline said:

HIGH PERFORMANCE
LOW EMISSIONS
ZERO GUILT

Also egregious was the Lexus body copy: 'perfect for today's climate (and tomorrow's)'.

The year 2008 was a bumper one for greenwash, with record numbers of complaints to the advertising standards authority. The number of complaints fell by 40% in 2009, which was hailed by the trade media as a triumph. However, the suspicion is that the global financial crisis had wiped out most brands' appetite for green and reduced their advertising activities overall. A year of belt tightening and deferred industrial growth meant that global carbon emissions fell by 1.3% in 2009.[39] Unfortunately, emissions bounced back, rising 6% in 2010.[40] So this turned out to be more of a crash diet than a change in lifestyle.

Low Standards

Forestry organisation PEFC has been criticised for giving forestry companies certification while not applying rigorous standards. They came to the attention of journalists after PEFC continued to certify an East European forestry company that others like FSC dropped following filmed evidence of corrupt deals and illegally cut timber. The journalists from France2 TV set out to test their ethical standards, mailing PEFC with applications for certificates for absurd locations:

> Most submissions were apparently approved by mail with no questions asked – sites including a pig farm, a nuclear power plant, an airport, a supermarket parking lot, and France's largest open-air night club – sites which could hardly be considered forests nor were owned by the journalists.[41]

This underlines the need to do due diligence on any awards and certifications that you will use in marketing. A key question being: does the scrutiny go beyond form filling and payment? Buying a dodgy certification or award because it's easy or cheap can be a false economy.

The Whopper

Speaking of eco labels, I was gobsmacked to discover a tin of ground coffee from Italy carrying the claim:

Lavazza Tierra! 100% Sustainable Ground Coffee

I've been using this for years in presentations as an example of naïve greenwash. How could anything sourced from the other side of the world, then processed and tinned before being shipped to my supermarket be 100% sustainable? Did they know something that I didn't?

I found out recently that actually they do.

I was researching the Rainforest Alliance certification. I had not known that the minimum requirement to use the Rainforest Alliance seal on your pack (which Lavazza Tierra! does) is that 30% of the contents are from certified sources. Not only this, but Rainforest Alliance asks that the brand state the actual percentage on the pack. In Lavazza's case this must be 100%. This might have been a simple chain of whispers: 'the client says we must say 100% . . .'.

Invent Research to Argue your Case

In the bad old world of crisis PR, one common tactic is to set up or fund a bunch of think tanks, research institutes, and so on that give a veneer of respectability to the smokescreen put out by the industry to deflect criticism and head off potential expensive regulations.

This was the tactic famously pursued by the tobacco industry.

This practice then spilled into the funding of climate change deniers by oil companies who hired the same PR firms. In the late 1990s, the Global Climate Council (funded by a consortium of oil companies and car makers) used lobbying and advertising to sow doubts about the integrity of the IPCC and about the scientific evidence that burning fossil fuels drives global warming.

The Global Energy Balance Network – with funding from Coca-Cola – promotes the argument that weight-conscious Americans are overly fixated on how much they eat and drink while not paying enough attention to exercise. Coca-Cola had a UK TV ad banned for suggesting 75 seconds of laughing out loud could burn off 139 calories. Coca-Cola commented that: 'The advert was intended to explain how people can help manage their energy balance by actively burning off calories consumed. Raising awareness of energy balance is part of our global commitment to help tackle obesity and we will continue to use our advertising to address it.'

Drinking their own Kool-Aid, perhaps?

Detoxify the Language

The Raybestos brand once was a hallmark of quality in automotive brake pads – a company that started in 1902 and grew its annual sales to $150m by the 1960s. The company changed its name to Raymark after it ceased making asbestos-based products in the 1980s. Clearly what had once been a positive scientific sounding name had become known for toxicity.

Companies detox brands because naming matters. The shift from Renewable Energy to Cleantech is one example. A venture capitalist told me this was a huge boon in pitching projects and deals to investors, comparable, she said, with when the tech industry decided that social media start-ups represented 'Internet 2.0'.

But the same means can be used to try to defer criticism. On the eve of the EU debating banning imports of tar sands crude from Canada in 2011, I was invited to participate in a Canadian news TV show to debate whether the negative branding of tar sands was damaging the image of this Canadian export product. 'Do you mean like renaming it beach oil?' I asked jokingly, 'After all, people love beaches!' The researcher said that was exactly the kind of idea they wanted to chat about on the show! (I declined the invitation.)

A real greenwash example of this is 'clean coal'. The credibility of the message probably isn't helped by statements like this from President Donald Trump:

> We've ended the war on beautiful, clean coal. And it's just been announced that a second brand new coal mine where they're going to take out clean coal – meaning they're taking out coal, they're going to clean it – is opening in the state of Pennsylvania.

Clean coal is a stupid idea. But it's not quite that stupid. It has nothing to do with coal mines, nor with washing the coal. It originally referred to carbon capture and storage: CO_2 emissions from burning coal being captured and stored rather than put in the atmosphere. Later it was also applied to (so-called) High Efficiency Low Emissions coal-fired power stations.

The costs of these technologies – even with generous subsidies from certain governments – are described by energy analysts as astronomical. Typically, they would double the capital and running costs of a coal plant. Yet their environmental performance is still worse than every single alternative. Meanwhile solar costs have fallen 85% since 2009.

So, a more accurate name than clean coal could be Costing The Earth Coal?

Natural Seeming

People intuitively feel that natural looking and sounding things are environmentally friendly. That's not always true. For instance, cotton (if it isn't organic) performs less well in sustainability terms than many synthetic fibres. Using natural cues in advertising, design, and promotion is a long-standing approach that apparently makes no definite greenwash claims. And yet clearly in many cases is intended to bolster the environmental image of a company or brand.

A classic example was the BP Helios logo, described by their design agency Landor as follows:

> A stylized sunflower symbolizes the sun's energy, while the color green reflects the brand's environmental sensitivity. With this simple shift in identity, BP staked its claim as a leading provider of energy solutions.[42]

A fascinating academic paper – *Visuality and Greenwashing* – looks at the evolving history of the BP brand. The researchers contrasted this imagery with BP's 2010 Deepwater Disaster, the largest oil spill in history. These researchers gave their own interpretation of the BP logo:

> Helios or the primordial sun is a powerful organizational archetype, important in stories of cosmogony. . . . Symbolic meanings of the sun are the sun is the center of our universe, an energy source without which human beings cannot survive; without sun (without BP), we have night, darkness, stillness and all

the things that darkness is associated with – the unknown, evil, death; and finally, the sun is an alternative form of energy toward which environmentalists think we should move. In short, the sun is life.[43]

If you believe – as BP and its agencies may have done – that you are leading the transition of your industry to a sustainable future, then it seems justified. The eco branding reinforces your efforts, attracts talent that buys into the vision, and potentially wins over consumers. I met with John Browne the CEO of BP in the 1990s when they were embarking on this journey, and had few doubts that he was sincere in this intent. But BP were called out when they launched the *Beyond Petroleum* campaign. Here are a couple of advertising headlines from the campaign:

SOLAR, NATURAL GAS, WIND, HYDROGEN. AND OH YES, OIL.
   WE BELIEVE IN ALTERNATIVE ENERGY. LIKE SOLAR AND CAPPUCCINO.

Fortune magazine covered this story with a memorable riposte: 'If the world's second-largest oil company is beyond petroleum, Fortune is beyond words.' The article then explained just how small a proportion of BP's operations were actually beyond petroleum: 'All told, BP generates enough wind and solar power (77 megawatts) to keep Boise lit for a year.'

The key point from a comms strategy point of view was *Fortune*'s final paragraph:

BP's regional president, Bob Malone, says the billboards are meant to address environmental concerns of the U.S. public and to demonstrate that the company is thinking creatively about the future of energy. 'The oil business has a negative reputation,' he says. 'We are trying to say that there are different kinds of oil companies.' As for being 'beyond petroleum,' the company's slogan since mid-2000, Malone concedes that BP is decades away. Somehow that didn't make the billboard.[44]

Years later, I met the strategist who worked on *Beyond Petroleum* and had to ask: what were you thinking? They told me that the strategy summary in the brief was Positive Energy. The trouble started when this was translated into a grabbing creative idea that redefined what the letters B and P stand for. Words are powerful. With greenwash that power can backfire.

I understand Malone's point. Somehow, we do need to help people pick out the better brands. And differentiate them from others that are lagging on sustainability.

But I'm pretty sure that exaggerating to the point of dishonesty isn't the best policy.

The trouble was that marketing had already become an arms race of immodesty.

Another good reason to put your efforts into *doing with* rather than *saying to*.

1.7 Transparency? Or Another Façade

Can virtue and visibility ever mix?

This is the question I posed at the first public talk I ever gave on the subject of sustainability and advertising. The event was hosted by Dorothy Mackenzie at design agency Dragon Rouge – one of the pioneers (along with St Luke's) of sustainability in the creative industry in the 1990s.

I started my talk by showing a clip from the movie *Dangerous Liaisons* when John Malkovich contrives to be seen handing out coins to peasants in a local village . . . at the very moment when the young woman he is trying to seduce happens to ride past. This, I suggested, is what brands are doing when they share their good deeds. The brands that did it more artfully were allowing themselves to be discovered doing good – like Malkovich – by journalists, rather than boasting overtly in adverts. But nonetheless when motivated and justified by self-interest and creating a good impression . . . you had to ask: could it ever be virtuous?

My example back then of what a true sustainable brand could look like was eBay. At the time it was the fastest growing company in the world. It was also I argued one of the greenest. Especially in America where previously people had thrown out old goods when they bought new ones. Now there was an emerging passion for bargain hunting. And the system matched buyers and sellers across the country. eBay kept old toys and sofas and clothing in use. The greenest thing of all was that eBay never talked about being green. My message for the audience being: make it work as a business and for a broader purpose. It's no coincidence that the founders of eBay both went on to further good works. Pierre Omidyar started an impact investment fund, the Omidyar Network. And Jeffrey Skoll started the Skoll World Forum.

This connected with a longer running idea I had that everything that was wrong with brand marketing had something to do with way it created a façade.

In the St Luke's days (together with Dave Buonaguidi) I created a *Not a Brand Book* for IKEA. We had been briefed to produce a brand book IKEA could use to make their global advertising more consistent. But we rebelled. Branding, we argued, was the process of making a sports shoe in a sweatshop for a dollar, hiring a basketball star to give it an image, and then selling that shoe for $100. What IKEA would do is make the shoe for $1.50 in a factory that looked after workers. And then they would sell it for $2. IKEA was not a brand like Apple, Nike, and Pepsi. It was a retailer with factories. At the start of the book was a spread with a picture of Richard Nixon and the headline ONLY LIARS NEED TO BE CONSISTENT. If they wanted to improve their advertising globally, all they had to do be bold and keep asking the question 'Is this us?'

The book never became official policy at IKEA, but somehow went viral in the organisation. Years later I met the country manager of Canada who exclaimed 'you're the *Not A Brand Book* guy!' and fetched a bootleg copy from his office.

This theory became the basis of my second book: *After Image*. My prediction, which looked premature back then, was that brand knowledge would eclipse brand image in an information age that brought transparency, lifelong learning, and empowered consumers.

The question I started that book with was: 'what is the brand personality of eBay?' My argument was that giving brands a façade of (pretend) personality was a tactic from a bygone age. A *Mad Men* era when we advertised mass-produced products whose issue in marketing terms was that they were all too similar. That façade wore thin in an era of media literacy.

Back to John Malkovich. Everything brands do that is calculated to make a good impression is a façade. The latest version of that can be faux transparency. Of course, some brands and companies are honest and open. But when companies say 'transparency' they usually mean selective transparency. Showing only the side of themselves that they are proud of. Knowing too that appearing to be transparent and honest is an attractive quality.

I'm not arguing against transparency. I just see it as having potential for fakery.

Let's look at a real-world example. There's a lovely New York artisanal chocolate called Raaka (which means raw in Finnish). And inside their label is lots of sourcing information under the heading TRANSPARENT TRADE. There is a graph showing 'what we paid for cacao' compared with the Fairtrade price and also the commodity price. The graph shows that Raaka's price paid stayed at around $5 while the commodity and Fairtrade prices declined from $3 to as low as $2. With Fairtrade being not much more than commodity. When you look on their website, you find that prices Raaka paid varied between $4.40 and $6.40 for different beans.

It sounds like they are super ethical and transparent, right?

Let's see.

As far as I know Raaka is an authentic company run by people who care. And the exporters that they buy from according to quick research on chocolate industry blogs are enabling small craft chocolate makers to tap into direct sourcing of high-quality and ethical beans.

But stating that you are paying two or so times the cacao commodity price for a premium single origin bean is not transparent. Premium beans usually cost this much or more in fact.

> Prices for fine flavour cocoa can be up to two or three times higher than those for bulk cocoa, thus providing good opportunities to suppliers in producing countries.[45]

It has taken Monmouth coffee (my favourite coffee company) 40 years to build up their ethical sourcing model. Monmouth tastes and selects the beans that the farmers grow. They originally managed this by hosting competitions. The first year in Columbia there were 86 entries, the second 360. Monmouth don't look like an eco hippy brand and they deliberately don't go in for greenwash. But they are rightly proud of their impact, as Anita LeRoy their founder explains:

> We were able to pay a significant premium and people were talking of using the money to pay off their mortgage or move their home down the hill so their children could get to school more easily.[46]

The awkward thing about the Raaka story is I suspect they are well-meaning. But technically saying you paid 2 times more than the commodity price for speciality beans is like saying you are being generous in paying 2–3 times more to buy someone's car, when the car is a Merc.

The other thing about transparency is that you are putting it out there. Because they publish their data and claims, people like me can contest them.

We do live in an age of extremes where fake news jostles with transparency-based marketing. I don't think transparency is a bad idea per se. But think of it being like food labelling where you disclose ingredients in a way that is direct, neutral, factual, and comparable.

VEJA, the ethical shoe company, are into transparency in a good way. If you go to their website you will find comprehensive details on their policies, practices, reasons why, and contracts. They publish things like the independent chemical tests they commission to confirm their supply chain is free from noxious chemicals. VEJA also publish their actual rubber supplier contracts. They even published a quotation from a Chinese factory that they used to benchmark how much more expensive it is to produce their shoes ethically (€18.21 compared to €6.55).

VEJA see transparency as the core of what they do. But it is just one part of a bigger philosophy which their founders describe as STICK TO REALITY. They see too many 'ethical' start-ups being done by someone sitting at a computer. They say that the magic in the business really happens – including the sustainability – when you visit farms and factories and meet the people. Get some Amazon mud on your boots. It was through this fieldwork that they decided to use only wild rubber tapped from trees in the Amazon (rather than rubber grown on plantations). This goes beyond conventional sustainability. It is preserving biodiversity by creating a business model for keeping the forest as it is. When you are in touch with such realities you can put consumers in touch with them too. You are healing the alienations of the world, curing its unknowingness. A sure sign you are on the right path is if the humanity of what you do shines through. Which it easily can in founder-led businesses that are good at telling their story.

Futerra produced a guide to product transparency in 2018 and sensibly, in my view, decided to call it the Honest Product Guide rather than the Transparent Product Guide. Their seven-point guide is well worth reading. According to Futerra an honest product:

- has good intentions
- makes humble claims
- always a work in progress
- goes above and beyond
- is truly helpful
- takes risks
- stands for something.

There's not much argument with these points here. But it is still possible to miss the mark. The case study that stands out is Everlane – Futerra scored them 7 out of 7 on transparency. And on this particular example, I have to say I am not so sure. Everlane is the opposite in some ways of VEJA, it is presenting a technical transparency, not sticking to reality.

Everlane is a Californian brand that has become the poster child for radical transparency. Anybody who goes to conferences will have seen them referenced as a case study. Launched in 2011, the company set out from the start to put supply chain transparency at the heart of the brand. The problem is that they are not perfect. Not 7 out of 7. More like 4 out of 7.

An independent ethical brand rating (Good On You) marked Everlane 'Not Good Enough'.

The reason being: 'there are big gaps in the information Everlane provides to the public – and on some issues, there is no information provided at all'. Everlane is probably most famous for showing photographs from their factories. Good On You commented that:

> . . . although the images provided depict good working conditions, it is difficult to confirm that they are truly representative of Everlane's suppliers as they were not provided (or audited) by an independent third party. It's also unclear which part of the supply chain is audited and how often those audits occur. And though Everlane states it has a 'Vendor Code of Conduct' unusually it does not disclose what it says – even many fast fashion brands manage to do that![47]

The Fashion Law (a blog run by a fashion law expert) similarly pointed out that H&M provides names and addresses for 98.5% of its factories and even lists those factories' suppliers. Whereas Everlane hides the names of all its suppliers as they say it is a 'trade secret'.

Everlane didn't set out to create an ethical superbrand. They were founded by a Silicon Valley entrepreneur who wanted to apply lean start up methodologies (testing designs in small batches to see what sold, rather than having planned seasons). The core idea is to be faster than fast fashion. Radical transparency was a clever way of showing the benefits of their direct to consumer online sales model. As founder Michael Preysman explained to the press, a conventional retailer would make a t-shirt for $7.50 and sell it for $50. Instead, Everlane would show transparently that a t-shirt that was made for $7.50 sold for $15. No wonder they don't live up to sustainability reporting standards. It was originally about pricing transparency.

The problem goes back to the original question – whether virtue and visibility mix well.

Everlane is clearly a successful high growth fast fashion company. They probably do 'okay' on worker welfare or they never would have started showing proud photos of their factory conditions. But they are a selective and proprietary version of transparency compared to H&M who publish the addresses of their factory and their independent audits.

It depends on your intentions (as Futerra did say).

If you want to be ethical, transparent, and trailblaze on sustainability then consider following the example of Monmouth Coffee, VEJA shoes, Natural State, and many other brands in this book by sourcing more ethically and environmentally and dealing direct with the people at each end of the chain – and at the same time resist the temptation to trumpet your good deeds.

I understand that some companies are too small to set up their own supply chain.

It's okay to be a decent company who is doing the best it can.

But be careful when you go the transparency route that you are being super transparent and not selectively showing things that try to look better than the reality. Check out VEJA's transparency page on their website and make sure that you are being at least that candid.

And do bear in mind that if you wear a halo, then you are always asking for trouble.

1.8 An Advertising Vow of Chastity?

Anita Roddick hated advertising. It didn't fit their business model, which involved putting the money into (sustainable, ethical, high quality, natural) products rather than packaging. Body Shop's range came in simple bottles in only a few different shapes and sizes. And it was natural to avoid the other main expense in building brands in her industry which was advertising.

It's the same story at VEJA, which is one of today's coolest ethical brands. Most sports shoe companies are 90% marketing. VEJA took out all of these costs and invested in raw materials, ethical sourcing, and so on. VEJA uses three main materials: rubber tapped directly from Amazon trees, B-Mesh made from recycled plastic bottles, and agro-ecological organic cotton. In 2018, VEJA moved to full transparency (for real) by providing complete and independently audited traceability statements for all of their sourcing on their website. These include the raw materials contracts, the workers' salaries, and even what the two founders pay themselves.

The other reason Anita Roddick hated advertising was its role in society. The advertising business was responsible for many of the ills in society. Why would her company pay to support that? Wouldn't that be like funding tobacco or armament companies? She worked with my agency St Luke's on the basis that we didn't do her advertising (we worked on things like in-store radio and a campaign to free Ken Saro-Wiwa). Plus, we didn't seem as 'evil' as the rest. But she didn't take our word for that. Body Shop also insisted we conduct an independent social sustainability audit into our own operations.

Someone who agrees with Roddick's view on advertising is Pavan Sukhdev. When I first met Pavan he was a banker who in his spare time developed a model called TEEB – the Economic Evaluation of Biodiversity – originally for the Indian government and later for the EU. Pavan is by now the global president of the WWF and a hugely respected figure. Pavan has this to say about the advertising business:

> By converting human insecurities into wants, wants into needs, needs into demand, demand into production, and production to profit, advertising executives are destroying the fabric of humanity and our society. I think time has come to call a halt to this, to call a spade a spade. Advertising has to be about information and communication, and less about persuasion and bullshit.[48]

I read this quote out at a D&AD meeting in London where a panel was discussing the climate strike and the mood for radical change in the creative industries. Lots of worthy points had been debated. But we didn't seem to be considering the main one, which is what if what we *do* is intrinsically unsustainable? What if fashion, advertising, design, packaging, and a bunch of other consumerist industries needed to die in order to give the planet a chance of life? Yes, these things can bring pleasure, desire, fun, aesthetic beauty, and seduction. But so does crack cocaine. Maybe it is time to confront our addiction and see advertising as the drug that we need to quit?

It's not unprecedented to restrict advertising because it harms society. Advertising to children has been banned in Sweden since 1991. It's something the EU has also been considering. Although they ended up publishing guidance to member states on children's advertising for foods that are high in salt, fat and sugar. There are few realistic prospects of a blanket ban of all advertising happening soon. An alternative is that we the creative industry take a vow of chastity. And curb the persuasion and bullshit whether clients want them or not.

I've seen pockets of this sort of thinking already. Unilever's former sustainability chief Santiago Gowland (then at Nike, then Estee Lauder, and now the Nature Conservancy) was proud of their brands promoting themselves without emotional appeals to insecurity so typical of FMCG.

My term 'vow of chastity' is borrowed from Danish film maker Lars Von Trier. This was his title for the Dogme 95 film makers manifesto. Von Trier's films are theatrical, sometimes fantastical, often awkward but never dull. The first *Festen* is a dark comedy set at a 60th birthday party where speeches reveal that the birthday boy has abused his children. Other films covered themes like grief, nymphomania, and the end of the world. Von Trier's idea was that by creating a brand and manifesto, others could make Dogme films and it could become a movement, like Bauhaus.

I like the spirit of a detailed charter urging restraint (detailing the things Dogme films cannot do); minimal lighting, no props that weren't natural to the scene, no special effects, and so on.

And I like Von Trier's idea that the very devil at the heart of creative film making – and I would say media, brands, and culture in general – is ego. Hence the last point in the manifesto:

The director must not be credited. I am no longer an artist. I swear to refrain from creating a 'work', as I regard the instant as more important than the whole. My supreme goal is to force the truth out of my characters and settings. I swear to do so by all the means available and at the cost of good taste and aesthetic considerations.

The ego is everywhere in advertising. It is in the good-looking actors, in witty headlines, wish fulfilment storylines. And it is in the 'industry' with its awards and cult of personality. We opposed this at St Luke's: we did things like flattening the hierarchy (with employee equal share holding) and refusing to enter our work for creative industry awards.

It's easy to look at somebody else's industry and say it should be curbed. That petrol cars should just not be made any more. Or junk food. But it's much less comfortable when people suggest that what you do – advertising, junk mail, packaging . . . should be canned.

If the ad business disappeared tomorrow a lot of people would think it was okay. They already filter out ads as far as possible using ad blockers or fast forwarding. They find the cultural pollution that fills our streets, websites, letterboxes quite objectionable. Cities including Sao Paulo (for a while) and Grenoble have banned street advertising. The Citizens Advertising Takeover Society (CATS) took down 60 posters in Clapham Common station and replaced them with photos of cats. The same group that made this happen – Glimpse – went on to create a CHOOSE LOVE shop where you bought goods for refugees rather than for yourself.

What would happen to the brands if advertising was banned?

As they say in clickbait headlines: the answer might surprise you.

Advertising cigarettes was banned in some countries in Europe in the 1990s. An academic study that I quoted in my first book *The New Marketing Manifesto* found that smoking grew faster among young people in countries like Germany and Denmark where it was banned than in countries like the UK where advertising was still allowed.

It wasn't hard to find an explanation. The cigarette companies in 'dark markets' had taken to more roundabout forms of promotion. Camel had a fashionable Camel Clothing line and also targeted events like Berlin's Love Parade to sample free cigarettes. This was exactly the kind of strategy that my book was about – content, community, experiences, and brand extension – the same tactics adopted by brands like Virgin, Red Bull, and other stars of 1990s *New Marketing*.

If brands stopped advertising:

- They could avoid greenwash and other sins of ego driven marketing.
- They could also drive greater brand meaning, engagement, and success.

Highly successful modern brands have been built in this way: like VEJA, one the most fashionable brands on the planet. Others use advertising in a way that is pro social; like AirBnB making a Superbowl TV advert – *We Accept* – in response to Trump's Muslim travel ban.

Refusing advertising pushes you from 'messaging' into relationship marketing, experience design, social media content. That feel less like marketing (selling) – valuable, integral, and helpful.

I have long hated the targeting and messaging paradigm of strategy. I took the Proposition box off the St Luke's creative brief because we weren't about 'saying stuff to make people buy stuff'. We were about making waves in culture, not firing 'unique selling propositions' at audiences.

It doesn't matter what you say (exactly) it's who you are, the founders' story, your credo and mission, what you bring, what you want to change, how you relate . . . USPs were an attempt to control the message, control minds even. But usually had zero effect other than making marketing look clipped, corporate, and uptight. The USP was the product of reductive narrow thinking. And these days we really need to see the bigger picture and think in a systemic and nuanced way. Brands today need to take off their masks and – as VEJA says – stick to reality.

If advertising was banned, we'd see organisations building community, launching services that are human and delightful, being innovative, authentic, and genuinely cool.

In broad terms, the sustainability opportunity in this direction is to *Redesign Life*.

This means applying the creativity, the discipline, and – as my clients at Natura would say – the *semiotic* to the service, experience, product format. Apply it to your sourcing, your deals with farmers, factories, and communities. Where you get stuff and how you ship it. What your plan is for its onward life in the circular economy. Make what you do meaningful, legible, and understood. Change things for the better. Create new ways of life and of doing business.

Formerly you were restricted by mass production to offer something utterly bland and then try to dress it up to make it interesting. Now there are thousands of ways to augment the product, experience, brand, community that can be meaningful. You can for the first time with digital create mass personalisation. That goes for your marketing too. You can increasingly meet people's needs in new ways – ones that are more efficient and less resource intensive. You can eliminate wastage on a massive scale, through design for a circular economy.

We need every product in the shop to be ethical, not just a few speciality coffees.

We need ways to maximise our wellbeing and meet all our needs without bequeathing a crippling environmental and social debt to future generations. We need to *be green*, rather than just seem green. We need to do good rather than just look good.

The first step in all this is to properly understand sustainability. Because there is no point in redesigning life if we are only going to mess it up again.

1.9 What is Sustainability?
An Ethic and an Emergency

It's important that people in marketing understand sustainability. To avoid greenwash. And to have an impact that matters. The understanding can also help in developing strategies. If you work in fashion and understand dematerialisation and the circular economy, you might be inspired to start a peer-to-peer rental service for clothes (like Hurr did).

What follows is only a brief management summary.

Brevity does have an advantage – it shows the wood not the trees. And I find that even people who work in sustainability don't always 'get it' in a first principles sort of way.

Sustainability is a terrible word for a really great idea.

As a word, Sustainability sounds like a cross between a prim old Jane Austin title (Sense & Sensibility) and the kind of gobbledegook spoken by policy wonks (Subsidiarity). Sweeping paradigm shifts ought to be wrapped up in something more bold, fresh, and snappy.

I could have titled this book *Sustainable Marketing*. But that could have sounded pretty boring? A debate with readers of my previous *Green Marketing Manifesto* was whether the word 'Green' was limiting. Because it ignored the ethical, human, social, development side of sustainability. And maybe even the climate science? It is a fair point. But I still prefer Green (and Greener) to Sustainability. When I vote for the Green Party, I expect them to be pro human rights and climate action, not just pro environmental conservation.

The way to understand sustainability in my view is on three levels:

1. Sustainability is an ethic: a guiding principle for human behaviour.
2. Sustainability is an emergency: we need to drop everything and attend to it.
3. Sustainability is ways of doing things (which we cover in the next chapter).

A new ethic can shift whole human societies. One historical example is the ethic of non-violence – *ahimsa* – a Sanskrit word literally meaning 'not striking'. This ethic is shared by Hinduism, Buddhism, and Jainism. I met this idea as a teenager when discovering yoga and one result was that I became vegetarian. Ahimsa is an ethical response to the human condition and the unprecedented (because we make tools including weapons) human potential for escalating violent conflict. How can you apply this ethic in a conflict situation? Mahatma Gandhi applied *ahimsa* to his protest against the British Raj. Martin Luther King came to stay with Gandhi and took non-violent resistance back to the US. Extinction Rebellion activists follow this today; creative protests that get attention and confront power but that are done in a loving way.

Seeing sustainability as an ethic shifts your view of the subject. It's not just another technical matter you can learn at business school or university and apply. It is something you have to believe in and express every day. Sustainability being an ethic also means it can be exciting, fizzing, and potent. Societies truly adopting sustainability as an ethic could change everything.

From a liberal, free will perspective I hope we can avoid the need to be too 'sustainabilist' with a top-down ideology that imposes control systems. Sure, we need to have carbon taxes. Regulations. We might even need some rationing. But we also want initiative, innovation, and spirited involvement. Gandhi felt this strongly with his *ahimsa* ethic. He advocated self-rule in the Hindu sense of Self; self-rule that starts with the person, the family, and the village. And he warned against setting up a top-down Congress that would replicate the British Raj.

Another ethic-led paradigm shift was the Universal Declaration of Human Rights. This was agreed in 1948 by the fledgling United Nations. It says that all human beings are created free and equal. And all have a right to dignity, freedoms of movement, association, an adequate standard of living. Philosopher Immanuel Kant promoted this idea by invoking the ethic of hospitality – the human practice of welcoming a stranger without any expectation of 'what's in it for me'. Just because it is essentially civilised to do so. Seeing others as having equal rights, regardless of gender, race, or identity has become a universal belief. Not just in the West. But held just as strongly by young people across the world. As reported in the *Financial Times*:

> Around three-quarters of young people in India, Brazil and China support equal rights for transgender people – more than in France and Japan. Overwhelmingly, young people believe that men and women should be treated equally – with the greatest support for such values in the very different societies of Canada and China. Even in India, more than nine out of ten young people support the principle that men and women should be treated equally – higher even than in the UK and the US. We can no longer generalise about conservative developing countries and more liberal developed countries.[49]

That universal global support for equal rights is what makes the legislation effective. It's not just a question of a law statutes, but something that people expect from each other and from institutions. We wouldn't have #metoo if it wasn't for this ethic.

So, what is the core ethic that defines sustainability?

In 1987, the UN produced a report called Our Common Future. This is commonly known as the Brundtland Report (after Norway's first female Prime Minister Gro Harlem Brundtland, who chaired the commission). This report is the source of the common definition of sustainability:

> Meeting the needs of the present without compromising the ability of future generations to meet their own needs.

In simple human terms, we have no right to deplete the Earth's bountiful resources and damage its ecosystem in ways that put future generations in peril. The ethic says look after future generations' needs and don't unfairly damage their prospects. Exactly what the young people behind the global Climate Strike movement are saying today.

This is an ethic you can apply at any scale. And it feels intuitive, almost instinctive: leave things as well as you found them. It applies a simple moral principle – the Golden Rule – 'do as you would be done to' to the people of the future. The Golden Rule is accepted by almost every ethical tradition and religion. It is as near as we can get to a universal human moral code.

Some also say sustainability is based upon indigenous wisdom. The Seventh Generation school claims to have descended from an Iroquois law. The historical root of their claim is contested. There are examples from prehistory of people creating the conditions for their own extinction through overhunting. But it hardly matters whether the ethic is innovation or ancient wisdom. For most of human history we usually had too small an impact to worry about trashing the Earth. There's a big difference between local overfishing and causing a mass extinction.

The question is whether it is a wise principle today – at a moment when our global population has spiked, just as we are inventing technologies, styles of farming, and industries which are seriously depleting and polluting at scale. Would it not be a good idea now to apply a principle of stewardship and take care of how we leave things for the generations that come after us? In light of the climate crisis and ecosystem collapse?

What makes this a powerful ethic is that it runs with the grain of human nature. Psychologist Erik Erikson coined the term *generativity*. His idea was that every human gets to a point midway through life where their concern shifts from establishing themselves, their identity, their career, family, and so on . . . to a concern for future generations and their legacy. Erikson felt this was the natural human response to fully realising that you are mortal. By investing in what you leave behind you can offset the dread of your own mortality. According to Eriksson the urge to be generative can be expressed in myriad ways; as a parent or mentor, starting a business, making art. Anything contributing to the stock of humanity, which you leave behind.

Sustainability is this generative urge applied to society and the whole ecosystem. And those who worry about sustainability today worry not just about a reduced standard of living for our grandchildren, but about bequeathing them a hellish global catastrophe with devastating consequences for their health, security, and life chances.

We could also link the ethic of sustainability with universal human rights. Other people have a right to enjoy a basic quality of life, health, education, food. Climate change brings two injustices. The excessive lifestyles of rich countries will most affect the quality of life in poor countries. And those lifestyles will also potentially ruin the life chances of future generations. Professor Nicholas Stern made this case in his 2006 *Review of the Economics of Climate Change*: 'future generations should have a right to a standard of living no lower than the current one'.[50]

The way this principle is turned into policy in the Stern review is through the economic practice of discounting. Economists use a discount rate to compare economic flows at different times. Discounting is a way of pricing the future effects into the present behaviours. For instance, by applying a carbon tax. The International Monetary Fund recently produced a report saying that the best way to tackle climate change is taxation to 'discourage' carbon emissions. Few would dispute the idea, but the controversy lies with the pricing. To keep the world within a 2 °C average rise in temperature, the report calculated that the carbon price which the tax is based upon needs to increase from \$2/tonne of CO_2 emissions to \$75. As a result, coal prices would rise 200%, gas prices by 70%, and petrol prices (already taxed heavily) by 15%.

Carbon taxes have already proved effective. The UK introduced a carbon tax on coal in 2013 and this led most utilities to stop using coal in energy generation because it was uneconomic. Economists favour taxes. But the *Yellow Jacket* protests in France were due to an attempt to introduce exactly these kinds of taxes to shift us away from fossil fuels. The result was the worst rioting seen in Paris since the 1960s and the intended tax being scrapped.

If we are going to get people to willingly journey down this path they need to 'get it' and agree with it. Which calls for a new shared narrative. Historically we rewrote the narrative on slavery and women's rights. Why not carbon and generational equity?

I had a chance to test this theory when working on the UK government's *Act on CO2* campaign. While developing a strategy for the mobility campaign (broadly speaking how to get people to drive less), I conducted focus groups up and down the country. One issue was how to explain the Stern Review in terms the average person would find compelling?

I found was that this was a tough message to sell. First, because 'the green-house effect' can be a difficult concept for those who don't have much sci-entific education. Second, because working-class people had an aversion to governments telling them what to do while taxing them in the process (as with smoking, drinking, sugar, and junk food). Climate change was seen by some as a conspiracy by middle-class liberals from London. And they have a point. Who, after all, flies off on the foreign holidays, eats the imported foods, heats their large detached houses? Shouldn't those people be chang-ing their behaviour? Rather than sending someone like me to see if we could persuade struggling families to go back to taking the bus? The narrative that started to win these 'hard to reach' people over went as follows:

A while ago – this is a true story – my kitchen ceiling started to drip a bit of water. It was a rented house in not great repair. And the drip was occasional. I wondered if it might be water seeping in when there was heavy rain? Or – as the kitchen was directly below the bathroom – it might be water coming through the cracked tiles on the side of the bath? But it was only occasional. And it didn't fuse the lighting or anything. Plus, it wasn't actually my house. So, I did what most people would do. I ignored it.

Two years later I came home and found the kitchen ceiling had fallen in. Luckily my seven year old son hadn't been in the kitchen at the time. But it was an unholy mess. And we spent the summer having to manage with takea-ways and inventive use of small electric hob while the kitchen was repaired. As a single dad at the time, with a struggling eco start-up to run, this was a real set back.

That's pretty much the situation that the Stern Review says we are in. We can spend 1% of GDP now to reduce climate emissions. Or we can wait for the ceiling to cave in. And permanently lose up to 20% of GDP, due to damaging effects of climate change.

I made up this story while struggling to explain the Stern Review to a group of what the research recruiter called 'codgers'; retired working-class men in the North East of England. Earlier in the focus group one had told me that he left the heating on when he went away for winter sun because the council paid for it anyway and 'it kept the place nice'. These weren't selfish people. They were decent people who hadn't grown up taking climate change into account (although they did suffer from the collapse of the coal industry). With my story of the kitchen ceiling – as a French psychoana-lyst would say – the discourse shifted. People who had been sitting back sat forward. One gave a little speech about how they did everything to ensure their granddaughter had better chances in life. And if it only took spending 1% now to avoid giving her problems down the line . . . it didn't sound that much did it?

That's an example of what I think has been missing. A simple narrative based on an ethic that intuitively appeals to human decency. I'm not sure how to get it into circulation. I am guessing the answer is probably not a government information campaign. But thousands of us 'getting it', applying it to our own lives and decisions, and then telling others about it might help.

What catches our attention and galvanises action is emergency. The modern news media is almost designed to carry and amplify crises. Whether it is Brexit, knife crime, military action by Turkey, a plane crash, or protests in Beirut. Crisis galvanises public response; outpourings of concern, attention, donation, and support. Crisis also boosts news viewing. An uncomfortable fact I once explored in a workshop with Swedish TV execs.

Extinction Rebellion and climate strikes certainly brought the news cameras.

For over a decade, some of us had been arguing that there needed to be more 'alarmism' in climate campaigns. In 2007, myself and a designer called Sophie Thomas planned a campaign called *alarmism* where at 11.11 every morning people would set off alarms, bang bin lids, chink meeting room cups, and generally take a moment to make some noise. To raise awareness that there was an emergency. We were talked out of this by peers. The counterview being that we needed to sell a positive, empowering message, inspire people to make changes, show them a future sustainable lifestyle is desirable, leading to a better more human quality of life.

I completely understand what they were saying. We need exciting, positive, and grabbing ideas that people adopt with positive relish. But we also did need some alarmism in the mix. Now that we have some – thanks to the climate protests – it is totally apparent that this was missing.

This brings us on to the second part of our definition: sustainability is an emergency. The Brundtland Report I quoted earlier spelled out (over 30 years ago) what our environmental challenges are on a planetary scale:

> There are also environmental trends that threaten to radically alter the planet, that threaten the lives of many species upon it. including the human species . . .

More than 11 million hectares of forests are destroyed yearly, and this, over three decades, would equal an area about the size of India. Much of this forest is converted to low-grade farmland unable to support the farmers who settle it . . . [51]

Just to pause for a moment's reflection – this is what came to pass. The Amazon was indeed cut down to make cattle farms; over 200 000 square miles worth – an area the size of France. And this land became unable to support the farmers, as they killed soil fertility and created a dustbowl. We knew it would happen. But we were powerless to stop it. Those forests were the brakes on climate change. Something Brundtland and colleagues also knew about in 1987:

The burning of fossil fuels puts into the atmosphere carbon dioxide, which is causing gradual global warming. This 'greenhouse effect' may by early next century have increased average global temperatures enough to shift agricultural production areas, raise sea levels to flood coastal cities, and disrupt national economies.[52]

What's missing from this account three decades ago is not the information, but the implication.

It uses the words 'threaten to radically alter the planet' but also uses the word 'gradual'.

It presents climate change as one of a series of moderate challenges – undesired side effects that are quite manageable. The report also – with equal weighting – talked about the dangers of acid rain and ozone layer depletion. Both issues that subsequently proved manageable through international cooperation. It's the difference between a doctor telling you that ideally you need to lose a bit of weight and take some exercise (good advice) . . . and a doctor telling you that you are borderline diabetic. So that without big lifestyle changes you are heading for a life-limiting permanent condition, that will on average result in you dying 10 years younger.

What the climate science is telling us today is simple: **drop everything, this is an emergency.**

Recent events like the global climate strike took the issue out of textbook terms ('intergenerational equity' and 'discounting rates') and onto front page news. People are moved by stories. Like the story of a well-informed, rational, determined Swedish girl called Greta who went on climate strike and discovered that no one is too small to make a difference. This story is intuitive and archetypal; like the *Emperor's New Clothes* it takes someone young and courageously honest to wake the rest of us up to collective delusions.

A key idea that spread from the protests is that 'we have 12 years left to act on climate change'. The source of this claim is an IPCC report from 2018 spelling out what the world needs to do by 2030 to keep temperature increases within the 1.5 °C target from the Paris Agreement. What the IPCC report says is that we need to cut global CO_2 emissions by 45% (relative to 2010 levels) by 2030. And then reduce net CO_2 emissions to zero by 2050.

Technically the report doesn't say we have 12 years. It points out how much we need to do, starting today, by 2030 and 2050. But in public mobilisation terms giving this a time limit is super effective. It is like telling a smoker that if they give up by the age of 40 they may suffer no long-term health effects. It gives an irresistible window of opportunity. And also, a deadline.

'Twelve years left' caught on as an idea. And it is entirely appropriate to act with such urgency when IPCC scientists tell us: 'Limiting warming to 1.5C is possible within the laws of chemistry and physics but doing so would require unprecedented changes.'[53]

A direct implication of this urgency is changing the language – calling it not climate change, but

CLIMATE EMERGENCY
CLIMATE CRISIS
CLIMATE BREAKDOWN

Greta Thunberg has worked tirelessly to get this message through:

It's 2019. Can we all now call it what it is: climate breakdown, climate crisis, climate emergency, ecological breakdown, ecological crisis and ecological emergency? [54]

The *Guardian* newspaper changed its style guide for writers accordingly. Katharine Viner, editor in chief explained

The phrase 'climate change' sounds rather passive and gentle when what scientists are talking about is a catastrophe for humanity. Increasingly, climate scientists and organisations from the UN to the Met Office are changing their terminology, and using stronger language to describe the situation we're in.[55]

The risks outlined in the IPCC report justify the word crisis: severe droughts, arctic ice loss, sea level rises, heatwaves, hurricanes, species extinctions, falling crop yields . . . Even English people with their love of understatement would have to agree it's more than a bit of a pickle? It is rational to describe this as an emergency – a drastic situation calling for drastic action.

Scientists introduced the term climate change to replace the phrase global warming. Amory Lovins coined the term 'Global Weirding' as an alternative that better captured what is happening; with more energy in the atmosphere you get extremes of all kinds. An analogy being that if you put more energy into the butt of a whip you see violent changes at the other end – at the most changeable extremes. These changes could be permanent. The whole of Europe may face a very cold Scandinavian climate if the ocean currents that were keeping us warm are disrupted. They could also be episodic, as with extreme weather events like hurricanes, fires, droughts, and storm surges. All of which threaten human life and can cripple food and water supplies as well as city infrastructure.

While climate change was recommended for the sake of scientific accuracy, it was readily adopted by global warming deniers. George Bush's political strategist George Luntz had his 2003 memo on this subject leaked to the *Guardian*.[56] Luntz also recommended that Republicans kept saying there was 'a scientific debate'. The same tactic was used by the tobacco industry – that there was scientific debate over the health effects of smoking – to hold off regulation for decades.

If I say 'climate crisis', the pictures I think most people would have are of storms in Florida, wildfires in Australia, desperately hungry polar bears on melting ice platforms, reefs dying, whole islands 'sinking' as sea levels rise. Those are tangible and mobilising signs of an emergency. But these are symptoms and also only early warning signs.

One abstract image that helps grasp the nature of climate crisis and how we need to tackle it is that of 'the pipeline'. Things that we did decades in the past have inexorable effects as they move down this pipeline. The climate has a lot of inertia and it is a system with a 30+ year delayed reaction. This is part of the reason for the emergency status. It takes time for the results of present actions to become fully apparent. A bit like having to brake quick enough in a car; we need to act now to avoid a fatal smash just down the road.

The pipeline means that existing carbon levels produce future heating. That's called 'committed warming' by scientists. Even if zero further carbon was emitted, a recent model published in *Nature Climate Change* found temperatures would likely rise by 1.3 °C. The researchers noted that this figure could be an understatement. Because the tiny particulates (aerosols) emitted while fossil fuels are burned actually mask the effect by reducing warming by the sun. As this smoke falls out of the atmosphere, the long-term rise from CO_2 could be higher. And that's what would happen if we switched everything off, held our breath, made the global population of one billion methane-emitting cattle magically disappear and *emitted zero further emissions*. That 1.3 °C only leaves us 0.2 °C left to play with before we hit the 1.5 degree increases the Paris Agreement and IPCC agreed as a red line we should try not to cross. What would happen if we go on exactly as we are? The models predict rises of between 2 °C and 4.9 °C.

A rise of 2 °C, according to the recent IPCC report, will have severe outcomes; like failing harvests, a food crisis, collapsing ecosystems. One report (co-authored with the World Bank) looked at projections for a 4 °C rise. It summarised these findings with the word 'devastating':

> A global mean temperature difference of 4°C is close to that between the temperatures of the present day and those of the last ice age, when much of central Europe and the northern United States were covered with kilometres of ice. A world in which warming reaches 4°C above preindustrial levels, would be one of unprecedented heat waves, severe drought, and major floods in many regions, with serious impacts on human systems, ecosystems, and associated services.[57]

So that's one thing to realise about climate. Inertia in the system creates a 30-year pipeline effect. The wildfires, floods, storm surges, and droughts we see now are related to carbon emissions at 1990 levels. And global carbon emissions rose 60% between 1990 and 2013. By today the figure is nearer 70%. And despite every climate warning, it keeps on rising.

The second vital point to 'get' about climate change is positive and negative feedback loops.

Positive feedback loops (despite the positive word) bring the worst case scenario which is runaway climate change. A series of chain reactions that we no longer can affect by changing what we do. One example of positive feedback is the thawing of the Arctic and Siberian permafrost which releases methane, a greenhouse gas 20 times more potent than CO_2. Already, huge plumes of escaping methane have been discovered and Russian scientists estimate that the thawing of Arctic permafrost has doubled in recent decades.[58] Positive feedback means processes that accelerate themselves. As methane is released this accelerates warming, and this causes more permafrost ice melts and more methane releases.

Some scientists believe that positive feedback from permafrost ice melting and methane release was the mechanism that abruptly ended the last ice age. Fifty-five million years ago there was a global climate change event – the Palaeocene Eocene Thermal Maximum or PETM – where temperatures spiked by around 5–8 degrees for 200 000 years. This was associated with a big carbon injection into the atmosphere. Theories of the cause of this event vary, but a release of methane (from seabed deposits rather than ice) is the front runner.[59]

There are a number of positive feedback effects that could create positive feedback tipping points. Another is ice albedo. Ice is white and reflects away light and heat, whereas oceans are dark and absorb heat. As ice masses melt, the Earth's total system would absorb more heat, causing further melting and, with less ice, further warming.

Given these potential mechanisms for runaway climate change, why hasn't it simply happened spontaneously before now? Some think it has, for instance the PETM. But it takes a lot of greenhouse gas and forcing to push the world past all the balancing counterforces.

Our current geological era – the Holocene – has lasted 11 700 years, since the last ice age. This covers the time of modern cities, civilisations, and farming. It is a precious balance to maintain – a Goldilocks scenario which is 'not too hot and not too cold'. Where cloud cover and ocean cycles and other benign mechanisms (within normal limits of not too much forcing) are able to hold the whole ecosystem in balance.

Our key ally holding climate change in check is forests and peatlands with their biomass and healthy soil. It is up to us whether this is a positive (deforestation) or negative (reforestation) feedback loop. As an Imperial College report notes: 'biosphere feedbacks are an inescapable part of the climate system. However, there are ways human actions influence the magnitude of the feedbacks and therefore might provide additional scope for the mitigation of climate change.' Deforestation is one of these actions. Another is avoiding overuse of fertilisers. The EU has reduced fertiliser use in recent decades by 56% without reducing yield.

Emergency aid workers are trained to give clear, emotionally neutral information about what is happening. People are stressed enough without emotionalising the issue. And having a handle on what is happening can help people to cope. We need to help everyone alive today understand why climate is in crisis. To understand the pipeline effect. And the terrifying potential for positive feedback. They also need to know that if we act fast with planet scale solutions like reforestation, we can still pull ourselves out of this steep dive with their help.

1.10 Sustainability as a New Way of Doing Business

Sustainability as an ethic was missing from the debate. Climate strikes by school children make this starkly clear. We had no right to blight their future prospects. Their protests also focused public and media attention on the emergency and need to act.

Past these realisations, sustainability in companies is best seen as a different way of doing business. A paradigm shift to new ways of thinking and doing that are mutually reinforcing. We know what this could be like as we went through a similar paradigm shift to digital business.

Digital started as an ethic in homebrew computing and hacker circles. It was never about dotcom bubbles in these early days. The ethic was about transparency, empowerment with technology, and universal free access to information. The pioneers were inspired by the radical ideas of the 1960s, by influences like Buddhism. Their ethic already had profound impacts on how we work, live, organise. This information access ethic found its home in Google, while a distributed volunteer community created Wikipedia and Wikileaks set state secrets free.

Digital has changed the everyday way that we do things. There are new processes, such as the data-rich test and learn cycles of experiment that were first used by technology firms – especially software start-ups. The original ethic continues in the Silicon Valley community to this day. Justin Rosenstein, the co-founder of the teamwork app Asana, is typically Californian in seeing the limitless potential that comes from greater collaboration and transparency:

I'm really inspired by what people can accomplish working together. I look at all of the challenges that we face as humanity, and it feels like they come down to insufficient collaboration. We have enough food to feed everyone; we're just not distributing it well. It is certainly within our grasp to develop technology for sustainable energy. Asana is a manifestation of that – trying to solve software that enables teams to work together more easily but that extends all the way to the global level of what is going to take for us as a species to collaborate effectively as one.

Roberto Unger (in *The Knowledge Economy*) argues that this agile, collaborative process is simply the most advanced form of human productivity today and should indeed be applied in every field, not just in tech firms and elites and the West. Because it is an engine for improving society through wellbeing, employment, innovation.

When you work with digital, you realise that it is a set of ideas and practices. Similarly, sustainability is a new way of thinking and doing. In this section, I will list some of these.

1. We Already Have the Solutions

Something you hear a lot in sustainability circles is that we already have all the technologies that we need. For instance, to tackle climate change. We just need to apply them.

Drawdown is the title of a book by environmentalist Paul Hawken that lists 50 climate solutions that already exist. All are practicable and economically viable. And if done together, with consistency and global scale, Hawken calculated that they are enough:

> From revolutionizing how we produce and consume food to educating girls in lower-income countries, these are all solutions which, if deployed collectively on a global scale over the next thirty years, could not just slow the earth's warming, but reach drawdown: the point when greenhouse gasses in the atmosphere peak and begin to decline. So, what are we waiting for?

The first example in Hawken's book is fridges. A 1990s piece of regulation successfully tacked ozone layer depletion by phasing out CFC and HCFC in aerosols and also refrigerants. These were replaced HFCs (hydrofluorocarbons). HFCs are unfortunately also powerful greenhouse gases. According to a recent study HFCs are already responsible for 1% of all global warming and also grow-ing at 8% a year – more than doubling their impact in a decade. And this study concludes that phasing out HFCs can avert 0.5 °C of global warming.[60]

Back in 2007, McKinsey together with Swedish power company Vat-tenfall, using similar studies to those in *Drawdown*, assessed more than 200 GHG abatement opportunities including looking at their impact on emis-sions and also at their costs.[61] This study and its key graph – what became known as The Vattenfall Curve – looks at the net costs of the deployment of these climate solutions. What the study shows is that solutions with net negative costs are quick wins that can lead the way: measures like LED light-ing, retrofit insulation, and hybrid cars, along with better practices in agri-culture. These are easy to justify but also have the least climate impact. The middle block of solutions is middling impact and cost neutral or low net cost. Measures like reforestation, organic soil restoration, and (controversially) nuclear power. Then there is a block of expensive solutions that require big infrastructure investment – but also bring the biggest benefits in terms of CO_2 drawdown. Measures like carbon capture and storage.

This chart was widely in discussion after its publication in 2007, and you can readily see why governments then applied their efforts to things like domestic energy efficiency. The policy focus now is shifting to bigger topics, such as subsidies for climate friendly farming. But a lot has changed since this original study. And a caveat to the *Drawdown* view is that while we do have solutions to get on with, we should not rule out finding better or bigger solutions.

2. Innovation Can Close the Gaps

What used to hold renewable energy back was the cost. This has fallen to such an extent that according to a 2019 report by the International Renew-able Energy Agency, nearly every type of green energy now competes on cost with fossil fuel plants.[62]

The second barrier to using more renewables was storage. Renewable energy works on nature's timetable, not ours. So, you need to store the electricity. For instance, excess solar energy must be stored from the morning until peak demand in the evening. The issue with this is that batteries are expensive. With costs of the order of $1m per megawatt. To double renewables, a report by IRENA shows that we would need 17 times more battery storage.[63] For this to become economic, storage costs would need to fall by at least 90%.[64]

This means we do have existing solutions (renewables) but we can't afford them. Which is the classic gap that disruptive innovation can play in. Two emerging solutions on storage provide examples of this. Both required a creative reframing of the problem.

The first solution is Power to Gas. This uses spare electricity that will otherwise go to waste (such as excess solar energy in Saudi, or wind power in China) to synthesise methane from atmospheric CO_2. This removes CO_2 from the atmosphere and turns emissions from fuel into a cycle. It also means the economic and environmental cost of replacing every gas engine in the world goes away. We can keep using our boilers, combustion engine cars, and gas pipelines. Power to Gas existed for decades but was only recently proved to be viable and scalable.

The second solution is Behind the Meter storage. In 2018, for the first time Behind the Meter storage costs outperformed energy utility storage. A data business can also benefit from having uninterruptible power supplies. And customers can gain economically from phasing their demand. By storing energy from cheaper times to use at expensive times one study found that 'the combination of solar and battery storage could supply an Arizona electric customer with 80 to 90% of their electricity needs less expensively than buying from their utility company'.[65]

These are just two examples of how storage (or potential energy) will be the next energy revolution. This is the big disruption market that players like TESLA are investing in. TESLA already built the world's biggest lithium battery for an Australian utility. There are numerous other grid scale storage projects on test. Projects like heavy trains rolling up and down tracks on hills; hydro that pumps the water back up hill; compressed air in old coal mines; V2G using electric vehicle batteries as energy storages for the grid.

3. Green Economy Finance

Mark Carney, governor of the Bank of England, together with the Network for Greening the Financial System wrote an open letter in mid 2019[66] giving a stark warning to banks not to ignore the dangers of climate change.

As financial policymakers and prudential supervisors we cannot ignore the obvious physical risks before our eyes. Climate change is a global problem, which requires global solutions, in which the whole financial sector has a central role to play.

The letter warns that banks must be part of the transition or themselves face extinction:

Carbon emissions have to decline by 45% from 2010 levels over the next decade in order to reach net zero by 2050. This requires a massive reallocation of capital. If some companies and industries fail to adjust to this new world, they will fail to exist.

The specific risk the bank governors point to is 'a climate driven "Minsky Moment", the term we use to refer to a sudden collapse in asset prices'. The last time Hyman Minsky's model of financial instability was all over the media was the 2008 Financial Crisis.

One promising response from the banking sector (that we meet later in the book) is Sustainability Linked Loans. Companies – ranging from Philips to Prada – have borrowed up to $1 billion for sustainable infrastructure and supply chain improvements and the terms of the loans (the interest rates paid) are linked to their achievement of specific sustainability targets. This is a new category within commercial banking but grew rapidly in its first few years. In 2018, $40 billion of Sustainability Linked Loans were made. This is good business since green infrastructure improvements are a growth lending market. It also helps banks to decarbonise their balance sheets. And starts to answer some of their *Climate in the City* and *Occupy* critics.

4. Reporting and Transparency

An American high court judge, Louise Brandeis, once wrote that 'Sunlight is the Best Disinfectant'. Just making organisations disclose what they are doing improves their behaviour. One example was the TRI (Toxic Release Inventory) law in 1987. Following the Bhopal chemical spill disaster, the US government mandated companies to disclose toxic chemical emissions. Companies like Monsanto suddenly made headlines as 'The Worst Polluter in America'. Many quickly made pledges to reduce their emissions. Monsanto promised to reduce their toxic emissions 90% worldwide by the end of 1992.

Another example was the use of total electricity use 'meters' by UK government departments. Under the David Cameron government, real time energy meter displays were put up in reception areas of public offices – the clever back end data analysis being conducted by my friends at Carbon Culture. I met Liam Maxwell, the government's Chief Technology Officer, who told me that without any other interventions this transparency and implicit competition had led some departments to make cuts of 40% year on year in their annual energy bill.

Reporting is the bedrock of corporate social responsibility departments in large companies. Tracking data on key indicators like pollution, deforestation, carbon, and wellbeing is the first step towards managing them. And the sunlight effect helps. The Carbon Disclosure Project (CDP) showed how once data is available, companies and cities can be benchmarked. CDP publishes an A-List of excellent performers which functions like a credit rating in indicating soundness and future proofing to shareholders and regulators.

Knowing that transparency drives behaviour can inspire interesting marketing campaigns. Working with a Finnish air quality monitoring company (Vaisala) one of our creative proposals was to put one of their new monitors near city hall buildings; alongside a digital poster showing live what the pollution level was in this city and how this compared with other global cities.

5. Triple Bottom Line

The idea is to account for your environmental and social impact, reporting these on an equal footing with your finances – a Triple Bottom Line (TBL) of people, planet, and profit.

John Elkington, inventor of this concept, published a 'product recall' recently in the *Harvard Business Review*, saying that businesses would move Heaven and Earth if they were missing their profit targets, but he had yet to see the same efforts applied to people and planet targets. As Elkington explained:

> TBL wasn't designed to be just an accounting tool. It was supposed to provoke deeper thinking about capitalism and its future, but many early adopters understood the concept as a balancing act, adopting a trade-off mentality.[67]

Elkington concluded that no reporting framework is enough without the suitable pace and scale of innovation to prevent overshooting planetary limits. We can't measure our way out of this crisis. My own view is that TBL still did something important in bringing sustainability inside core business thinking, where previously 'environmentalism' had been an external irritant.

The spirit of the Triple Bottom Line lives on in the B Corporation movement. This is a certification scheme; an eco-label for companies. Members are a *Who's Who?* of sustainable companies including Natura, Patagonia, Method, and Ben & Jerry's. B Corps balance purpose and profit. They are legally bound to manage their impact on workers, customers, suppliers, community, and the environment. The 'legally bound' bit works by members changing articles of incorporation. This ensures that future leadership changes, new investors or owners, or the financial pressures of a tough year can't make the B Corp in question sacrifice purpose for profit. They have engineered a solution to the trade-off issue that Elkington identified.

The B Corp movement is growing rapidly. Earlier this year when I showed B Corp to a client, they had 2600 members. Today they have 3175. And by the time you read this ... (you can check this yourself at https://bcorporation.net).

6. The Power of Risk

Lee Scott, former Walmart CEO, said their sustainability epiphany came from Hurricane Katrina. During the crisis, Walmart stores and employees had acted as community support centres providing food, shelter, essential services:

> Katrina asked this critical question, and I want to ask it of you: What would it take for Walmart to be that company, at our best, all the time? What if we used our size and resources to make this country and this earth an even better place for all of us: customers, associates, our children, and generations unborn? What would that mean? Could we do it? Is this consistent with our business model? What if the very things that many people criticize us for – our size and reach – became a trusted friend and ally to all, just as it did in Katrina? There are not two worlds out there, a Walmart world and some other world. That's what we saw with Katrina: Our associates, customers and suppliers occupy the same towns, our children go to the same schools, and we all breathe the same air. These challenges threaten all of us in the broader sense, but they also represent threats to the continued success of our business.[68]

Risk can be physical; it can also be reputational. When companies are caught out doing wrong, sanctions can be severe. Financial misreporting put Enron and accountants Arthur Andersen out of business. Emissions cheating by Volkswagen resulted in $30 billion of fines. Nike was caught out by a *Life* magazine photograph in 1996 of a child in Pakistan stitching one of their footballs and became a target (along with McDonalds, Starbucks, and others) of anti-corporate demonstrations in the 1990s. The potential for one of these scandals haunts boardroom discussions like the spectre of great white sharks must haunt divers and surfers. I've had business leaders say to me in confidence that a problem of partnering with NGOs (like they all do these days) is that it takes some of the fear out of the equation. Fear of being attacked by Greenpeace was what got sustainability taken seriously by their board.

Risk management is where sustainability always made sense to business. It is 'where the rubber hits the road'. Your future supply of raw materials could be disrupted, the public or regulators might turn against you, energy prices might spike. Directors of public companies (by law in the US) are mandated to have considered future risks, including environmental liabilities.

At a recent dinner I attended, the head of sustainability at a major UK retailer spoke about how this risk management frame may have held corporate social responsibility back. His complaint was that while risk management made it easy to argue a business case, it limited activities to tidying up the current model. And avoided the radical, transformative alternatives we need in order to respond to climate and ecological emergencies.

7. The Beautiful Coincidence

I introduced this term in *The Green Marketing Manifesto* to describe situations where doing the right thing for people and planet was a win: win business opportunity. Another natural home for sustainability in business is innovation. If there are growing profitable markets – like plant-based diets – then you can create a business case based on opportunity not risk.

When I worked with Dutch bank ING on developing green marketing, one promising finding was that green bank customers are a statistically better credit risk. So that offering green mortgages, electric car loans, funding for green start-ups is potentially more profitable. Credit risk is important to banks on numerous levels, it affects pricing and profit, but it also affects the value of their entire lending book and the credit status of the bank. Post financial crisis you find banks being very prudent and selective in who they issue credit to.

The problem with disruptive innovation is that most large companies really struggle with it.

8. The Sustainability Innovators Dilemma (and the Solution)

The Innovators Dilemma is a classic business book about why large organisations struggle with disruptive innovation. The phrase everyone remembers is 'the turkeys never vote for Christmas', which makes it sound like cultural resistance to change. But the core message of the book is that there are structural reasons why innovation is difficult to integrate.

First, disruptive innovations start small. And big companies rely on scale. Working with Philips on a sustainable innovation project, one of my clients told me it was really hard to sell his boss on anything that 'doesn't sell a billion kettles'.

Second, disruptive innovations often fit different customer segments than the company is used to targeting. Who hence probably buy in different channels, have different media habits, and have a different set of attitudes and expectations.

Third, disruptive innovations often require a new business model and bundle of value. Warby Parker, the online US spectacles company, send five pairs to try at home (you send back the four you don't want). They have an app to do an eye test, to check your prescription still works. And they also give free eye health benefits to millions in the developing world on behalf of their customers. Later on, the outlier models often converge with the existing industry. Warby Parker now has one of the most successful physical retails operations in America. But it was built on a bedrock of new, different, and better – just like Apple (one of the few retailers in the US who achieves more in $/square foot sales than Warby Parker).

Large companies aren't stupid. Far from it: they are packed with smart people. But these people can be hamstrung by these three issues. So that by the time they jump on a promising new product, service, or segment they can be too late. When I took a bunch of starting point innovations to Philips, I discovered that they had already considered and rejected most of them previously, because they couldn't work within the Philips business model.

Even trailblazing companies can fall foul of the innovator's dilemma.

Dyson recently pulled out of their electric car plans. Dyson said it had developed a fantastic electric car but that they couldn't proceed because it was not commercially viable. Electric cars (before they achieve scale) cost more to make than conventional cars and generate lower profits. Big car corporations can absorb the R&D costs while TESLA has Silicon Valley investment. Dyson had neither and hence this was a poker game where they had to fold, because they couldn't afford to keep betting.

There are three ways that large companies are managing to get over the innovator's dilemma. And each of these have promising potential applications to sustainability.

i. Ringfence innovation projects: create a skunkwork

This is the technique pioneered by tech companies like Apple to create a new generation of product without the existing systems and company culture being allowed to smother it.

Ringfencing also means behaving like an investor and giving a promising idea time to pay back.

Philips developed their Hue connected LED lightbulb in this way. Hue lightbulbs can have their colour set to any hue by app; and this leads to interactive possibilities like making a lightshow to go with your Spotify stream, tuning in to the dominant colours of a film you are watching, or different ambient pre-sets to change the mood of a room. Hue did for LED what TESLA did for electric cars. Going beyond energy savings to never seen before performance and interactivity.

Hue was the result of engineers from the lighting division being given a budget, 11 months, and their own innovation lab and told to come up with 'something that will make a splash'. Hue would have been a tough sell otherwise given the 'billion kettles' benchmark. When Hue launched it was $199 for the base kit and $59 for each additional bulb. And back in 2012 would have appealed to a niche, premium audience of interior design nuts and smart home geeks.

ii. Work with external partners

Another factor in the Philips Hue success story was that it launched exclusively in the Apple store. It would have been a stretch for Philips to do this. For Apple too. But Apple is a retailer with a concentration of creative design technology nuts willing to pay a steep premium for something new and cool. And you controlled Hue through an iPhone app. So, for Apple it is an 'ecosystem' product, just like buying external speakers or storage solutions.

Quite a few case studies in this book were born out of partnerships. Adidas is on track in 2019 to sell 11 million pairs of its ocean plastic trainers made in partnership with marine conservation charity Parlay. They sold 5 million pairs in 2018 and 1 million in 2017. No start-up could scale production of a trainer that fast. The Parlay partnership went beyond sourcing recycled ocean plastic into shared events and marketing. It made the shoe instantly credible. And Parlay also brought the ocean plastic material, sourced through their own partners in the Maldives.

iii. Let others disrupt and then adopt them

Corporates call it M&A: Mergers and Acquisition. I prefer Mergers and Adoption because if the values aren't aligned and you aren't making a good home then buying an ethical company (and trashing what it actually stands for) is a waste of money and also a waste of a good brand.

Natura Cosmetics who I worked with (alongside design agency Pentagram) are adopting companies that give them strategic access to markets and audiences beyond Latin America. Natura bought Aesop, Body Shop. Then in mid 2019 paid $2 billion to acquire Avon (who shares the same sales agent model as Natura). Natura is one of the most innovative, forward thinking, and sustainable companies on the planet – a great home for these brands.

1.11 Eco-Labels, Their Struggle and Ongoing Role

'Is Fairtrade Finished?' asked a 2019 *Guardian* article, responding to the news that some companies stopped certifying and set up their own in-house standards.[69] Two years previously, UK supermarket Sainsbury dropped Fairtrade in favour of their own standard called Fairly Traded. Just as supermarkets sell own label cornflakes, they now sell own label sustainability.

The chocolate companies also launched their own sustainability marques. I met with Barry Callebaut who process a quarter of the world's chocolate. Their sustainability scheme is called Forever Chocolate and has hard targets designed to care for ecosystems and communities. There's a lot of focus on economic development and education. Because a younger generation are otherwise leaving the farms for better paid work.

What are we to make of this? Should we see Fairtrade and other eco-labels as a transitional phase we are now leaving behind? Or do they have a greater role in future?

The story of eco-labels started a very long time ago. Clay seals were used on documents and grain jars to certify their contents and authenticity in ancient Mesopotamia. Some academics even speculate that this branding to verify goods was the earliest form of writing.

In the 1820s, anti-slavery campaigns promoted sugar from India (rather than the West Indies) with a kind of eco-label on the jars saying, 'East India Sugar Not Made by Slaves'. According to a historical account: 'it was estimated that at the height of the boycott 400,000 people had given up the use of sugar from the West Indies'.[70] Two hundred years later, we have Tony's Chocoloney – a charismatic Dutch chocolate brand that promises slave free chocolate. This sustainability promise is delivered by their processors, Barry Callebaut, who even created a Tony's vat in their factory to ensure the slave free certified ingredients were kept separate.

Fairtrade was born out of the coffee crisis of the early 1990s. I worked on a project for Café Direct, the pioneering original Fairtrade brand, and got to hear the story first-hand from trustees and partner organisations, including Oxfam and the Fairtrade Foundation. This started life as a grassroots movement partly operated by UK church groups. They bought container loads of coffee from coffee farmers at decent prices and then sold it on through their communities.

Café Direct invests 50% of its profits in Producers Direct, a charity owned and run by smallholder farmers. Divine Chocolate is 44% owned by Kuapa Kokoo, a chocolate cooperative in Ghana. I met one of the founders of Divine recently who told me Fairtrade was never about consumer economics. That was a means to an end. It was really about social justice.

For marketers, Fairtrade was a revelation. Here was living proof that people would deliberately pay more for a product in return for the promise of doing some good.

One of the failings of Fairtrade is that it could not fully address the unfairness that is baked into the system. If you pay a £1 premium for a bag of Fairtrade coffee, you probably feel like a big chunk is going to farmers. Actually, the figure is typically 3p. Most of the premium goes to the retailer, then the wholesaler, then the importer, then the processor. The premium at the farm gate is still substantial in percentage terms. But it does not buck the system.

Divine pays more than the Fairtrade premium as they also pay a dividend to farmer owners. But they are sold in mainstream channels and so suffer the same economic dilution. Divine's 2018 annual report shows a Fairtrade social premium of 1.3% of total sales revenues. And on top of that a dividend went to the farmer owners of an additional 2%. They were having a hard year and could not do more if they wanted to (one of their supermarket customers had delisted them). Divine that year only made £13 000 profit from their £15m turnover.

The unfairness in the global food system is well documented by *Stuffed and Starved* by Raj Patel. This really is a system in need of radical change. Please don't stop buying Fairtrade as a result of reading this. It needs our support and it's a hugely important idea. But we need to do better. Directly traded brands who work with and for farmers like Divine are a big part of the answer.

One market that is ripe for reinvention is coconut water: a £100 million market in the UK alone and forecast to be worth billions across Europe. It's an attractive sustainability story too in that coconut water was previously discarded as a waste product. But guess what? The brands made fortunes, but a *Guardian* article found that 'far from lifting coconut farmers out of poverty, we're left in a situation whereby farmers receive about $0.12 - $0.25 per coconut'.[71]

This is why you need to buy ethical brands like Harmless Harvest. Their founders Douglas Riboud and Justin Guilbert explain their philosophy as follows:

> Guided by the ideals of constructive capitalism, Harmless Harvest creates positive feedback loops between people and plants. By staying true to the ingredients at the source, we make better products that benefit everyone involved

in their production. The idea is that consumers purchase a product that is healthy and delicious, tasting like what the ingredients should taste like and getting that connection to the plants at the source. That purchase then promotes stable, fair wages for farming communities, organic farming practices, and decent working conditions throughout the supply chain.[72]

Harmless Harvest does use eco-labels; an organic certification and Fair for Life. At the heart of the brand is the story of the founders and their farms in Thailand growing the prized Nam Hom coconuts. It is a brand you can believe in. Something their advertising headlines nod to:

HARMLESS IS EXPENSIVE
HARMLESS IS NOT PERFECT

Doug Cameron whose creative agency is behind the campaign said,

we decided to fly in the face of traditional marketing, which boasts about low price, consistency, perfection, etc. We want to say loudly and proudly that Harmless Harvest doesn't compromise.[73]

Harmless Harvest are part of a new era of branding. One where the reality behind the brand rather than an aspirational façade is what matters.

The trouble is that our perceptions of what makes brands sustainable are often misleading. Just because it's in a farmers' market that doesn't mean they pay living wages. Even our perceptions of what materials are sustainable can be skewed. This is why in my view we still do need eco-labels, or something very like them, to verify that this is the real deal.

A century of industrial product design has manipulated such cues as the door clunk on the car, the springiness in a loaf of bread, the weight of card in packaging to make things feel 'quality'. In many cases these innovations are pure marketing. People associated quality shampoo with the foaming suds that not only have nothing to do with cleaning, but can harm hair and health. People expect organic fruit and veg to be more earthy – less evenly shaped, perhaps with mud still attached to root vegetables, or with the green stems still on the bunch of carrots. Supermarkets have learned to deploy these indicators of authentic quality, also naming the breed of chickens that lay the eggs or having a named farm with pictures on the box.

The difficulty being that there is a kind of 'greenwash' inherent in the way that design plays to perceptions; instinctively convincing, but often frankly untrue. The same goes for branding. After a childhood of enjoying treats it is disappointing to discover that: 'lovable Mr Kipling, advertising icon and master baker, is a fraud. He was invented to introduce an air of home-made authenticity to what was effectively a factory bakery owned by a foods conglomerate.'[74]

So how can you know if the product you are consuming is the real deal in sustainability terms? Labels still play a strong role as watchdogs and guarantors. Marketers just can't be trusted to tell the truth when their job is to present the most attractive version of the truth. So, my view is that we will need eco-labels of some sort in future, but that they need to evolve.

This isn't just to protect consumers. It is also vital to protect brands whose value can be destroyed otherwise when ingredient and sourcing controversies hit.

Millennial hip drink LaCroix claimed its products were sparkling water plus natural fruit flavouring. People believed them. Instagram was abuzz. LaCroix ('la croy') fans made websites like 'LaCroix Over Boys'. But then in 2018 a lawsuit was brought claiming that four of the ingredients in this drink that claimed to be 100% natural were synthetic and that (scandalously) one of them is also used as a cockroach insecticide. The owners protested their flavourings are certified by suppliers as 100% natural. But meanwhile the damage was done. The share price fell 62% and LaCroix sales are according to a beverage analyst 'effectively in free fall'.[75]

I can't think of a better example where an eco-label could have helped. One that traced ingredients along the supply chain and can't be falsified or contested. Had LaCroix chosen to label itself as Certified Organic it might have been a non-target? Any complaint would then be the fault of a supplier or a certifier, not the brand. LaCroix had been around for decades as a seltzer before the Instagram crowd picked it up. And obviously cheap fillers are often used in such industrial packaged goods. But it is a cautionary tale.

It was difficult until now to reliably attribute ethical and environmental information to products. It's fine if you sell a commodity (for instance coffee) that comes from farms or cooperatives that have a certificate. But it has proved more difficult for multi ingredient products. Which is why you only ever see organic and Fairtrade in a few aisles in the supermarket. Eco-labels have also proved fallible. It is hard when sending inspectors out in regions where corruption is endemic to ensure that there are no bad practices. Independent investigations of the reality at the other end of the supply chain all too often prove disappointing:

> A study from Britain's Sheffield University showed certification schemes by groups such as Fairtrade and Rainforest Alliance are failing to stop labour exploitation. The report found little difference in the conditions of about 600 tea workers surveyed on certified and non-certified farms in Assam and Kerala, India's major tea producing regions. All lived below the poverty line and workers on certified farms were often treated worse, facing beatings and sexual violence and having wages and benefits withheld.[76]

When it comes to plantations, there are provisions in Fairtrade that say workers should have the right to organise, negotiate with management, that there should be 'progress towards living wages' and 'guidance for workers' on-site housing'. But clearly neither the spirit nor the letter of these were applied on the sites these researchers had visited.

In recent years big data has come a long way. An example of what this could mean for traceability is the Walmart Sustainability Index, introduced in 2009. By 2019, the scheme covered 80% of all goods they sold in the US.[77] Walmart audits against external standards set by an independent NGO called TSC. The potential in this kind of scheme lies with the data. If data on sourcing were attached to the goods digitally, we would be able to shop in a smarter way. Say you have guests for dinner and three are vegan, one is gluten free, one has a pepper allergy, and another is a lawyer working on human rights. You could walk into a store and generate suggested items, recipes, and a menu reliably based on the embedded data.

Another promising technology is Blockchain. This could revolutionise supply chains and take ethical certification out of the dark ages.

Provenance is a Blockchain company founded by Jessi Baker in 2013. The scheme is decentralised, meaning that different actors in the network (farmer, inspector, customs) can access and load data. This fosters equality and open access. A farmer could even supply soil tests using a simple kit and this data could assure the organic status of the farm. The data is end-to-end so a shopper can also see data on the farm – or even digital objects like photos.

Provenance has been doing pilot projects in food, drink, and fashion. The platform is not necessarily here to replace eco-labels, and in fact has been trialling ways to improve them. Instead of annual inspections of factories, certifiers can access anything from satellite technology and social media to peer-to-peer exchanges of data via blockchain.

Blockchain can also help with specific issues like products being falsely sold as certified along the supply chain – for instance from mills to exporters. The potential for fraud in certified schemes is not just an abstract possibility. A 2006 report on the Fairtrade system in the *Financial Times* spoke to an industry source who said: 'Last year I visited ten mills. All of them had sold uncertified coffee to co-operatives as certified.'

In a world with widespread mobile phone use the possibilities of leveraging data are even greater. MPESA the Kenyan mobile phone currency was invented to reduce administration costs in microcredit loans in rural areas. By 2014, MPESA transactions accounted for half of Kenya's GDP.[78] This currency enabled a supply chain business called Twiga to connect farmers to sell directly to the people who run food kiosks in the city (with Twiga managing deliveries in-between). Before Twiga, a banana cost more in Nairobi than it did in London. The system allows Twiga to offer higher prices to farmers, lower prices to vendors and also avoid wastage as supply and demand are matched. It's a killer app. Twiga has become the biggest seller of bananas in Kenya, shifting 245 tonnes of produce a week. Twiga was even visited by Mark Zuckerberg, who came to Kenya to learn about MPESA while developing his Libra currency.

Imagine a Western Twiga. A virtual farmers market where you can buy direct from family farms and food companies. This already exists in America. Thrive Markets offers its customers 25–50% off high street prices for quality organic and GM free products. The scheme has a membership fee. Thrive Market guarantees that members make savings greater than the fee. The scheme has 400 000 members and is growing fast. It prides itself on not only giving consumers a great deal but also returning more to the farmers – typically a 15–20% premium.[79]

Back at Blockchain, one of the additional benefits of applying this end-to-end data approach is that you can continue tracking the product through to end of life. Provenance has been trialling doing this with a carpet company, who use recycled fabric in their carpets and also recover the fabrics from these carpets at end of life.

In conclusion, verified supply chain data is here to stay and independent labels can play a huge role. But they will likely evolve to take advantage of supply chain data, sensors, social media, ubiquitous mobile phones, and new technologies like Blockchain.

1.12 Let's Redesign Life

Design is central to sustainability. It can be a force for good. Or design can foster unsustainability, by creating throwaway and harmful products.

This is not a new issue. Victor Papanek wrote *Design for the Real World* in 1972:

> Advertising design, in persuading people to buy things they don't need, with money they don't have, in order to impress others who don't care, is probably the phoniest field in existence today. Industrial design, by concocting the tawdry idiocies hawked by advertisers, comes a close second. Never before in history have grown men sat down and seriously designed electric hairbrushes, rhinestone-covered file boxes, and mink carpeting for bathrooms, and then drawn up elaborate plans to make and sell these gadgets to millions of people. Before (in the 'good old days'), if a person liked killing people, he had to become a general, purchase a coal-mine, or else study nuclear physics. Today, industrial design has put murder on a mass-production basis.

Michael Braungard was an EU expert on the toxicology of materials (before he co-wrote *Cradle to Cradle* and became a sustainability guru). Michael gives horrifying talks on the hazards to human health posed by things like nonorganic meat and dairy, household printers, and the packaging of coffee capsules in aluminium. Aluminium is a neurotoxin. Over the years the packaging industry have been able to say that the science was inconclusive (haven't we heard that one before?). Recent studies from Keele University confirmed 'the findings are unequivocal in their confirmation of a role for aluminium in some if not all Alzheimer's disease'. Meanwhile we extract aluminium with hot pressured water through 11 billion capsules of coffee a year. The coffee pods can also contain endocrine disrupting plastics. And are such an environmental worry (like shampoo sachets in Asia) that the city of Hamburg banned their use in state offices. I heard from a sustainability contact in the steel industry that Michael Braungard recommended they get into the coffee capsule business to save us from this 5+ dose a day health risk.

Design, in Papanek's view, was making a conscious effort to impose a purposeful, meaningful order. Improving design would require looking beyond 'the myth of wants' with designs based on whims or whimsy. Rather it should address societal needs. These could include the needs for shelter, clean water, mobility, lighting, and so on in the underdeveloped world; and the need to stop making trashy disposable goods with built in obsolescence. One of Papanek's other observations was that mass production is a myth. If you divided the number of chairs sold in the USA in 1970 by the number of chair factories (2000) and the number of product lines, then you came to a very small number. Each chair could have been designed for 0.1% of the population. People with long legs. Or infirm hips. Exactly the way we can think today about design and value in an era of personalisation and customisation.

Another of Papanek's points that still rings true is that we are optimising when we should be innovating. His example was the dishwasher. Design efforts would be spent on minor features and upgrades to wash slightly faster or get glasses shinier. But there were alternative technologies (Papanek suggested ultrasound as one) offering breakthrough new ways to clean more effectively. I've seen dishwasher prototype designs based on liquid CO_2, such as the DualWash that won a Turkish innovation prize. Liquid CO_2 waterless washing machines are an established technology in commercial laundry. The CO_2 has very low surface tension compared to water and is recovered for reuse after every wash.

What Papanek's book calls for is a different kind of realism to be brought to design. Forget what is 'realistic' in being conventional or commercial. Think about what is really needed. It's exactly what the founders of VEJA mean with their motto 'stick to reality'.

Large companies and their agencies forgot how to do this (if they ever knew) and convinced themselves they couldn't rock the boat of industry conventions. Few asked 'why all the packaging?' Body Shop made do with only a few bottle shapes and sizes across their entire range, making huge eco savings. LUSH took this further (their founder used to work for Body Shop) and manage to sell many items unpackaged. But it took a *Blue Planet 2* consumer backlash to make the rest of the industry start to question this.

The answer to the question – why all the packaging? – is marketing. Few products need much protection. What most packaging does is compete for attention on the supermarket shelf. It turns generic products into branded goods. Any brand of modern washing powder will do the job (and they did the job pretty well 40 years ago). Through brand positioning they preserve the illusion of choice, value, and difference. Persil positioned itself as mother's care for clothes. Ariel as the science of cleaning. Much easier to justify paying more for one of these.

Consumer research might show that people will buy a sensitive teeth toothpaste, one for tartar, or one that is whitening. The brand then creates colours, naming, packaging to reinforce this perceived difference. Much of all this is pure marketing and cosmetic rather than functional. The blue or red stripes do nothing. Neither does the foaming. Or the flavour. All that works in most toothpaste is fluoride and friction.

What if you wanted to make a better toothpaste? One that didn't send billions of unrecyclable plastic tubes to landfill. That wasn't packed with chemicals. That was natural and good for you as well as effective in looking after your teeth. Lindsay McCormick did just that with a new brand called Bite. I think it's well worth delving into as a shining example of how to redesign life.

McCormick was a hard-working TV producer for an American TV show called *House Hunters*. And a passionate environmentalist. McCormick hated going through so many toothpaste tubes. She decided to make her own alternative – originally just for friends and family – and started out by researching what goes into toothpaste.

This is a huge hint for aspiring entrepreneurs. Do your research. It literally is 90% of the job. Your industry – any industry – will do things in their usual way. It's like a house of cards. If you remove cards at the bottom, then the whole stack will come tumbling down. So, you need to build a different stack from scratch and find ways to make it stand up.

First, McCormick tried everything on the market. From DIYers on Etsy, to health food shops, to big brands. But nothing was good enough. For a start, nearly all of it came in plastic. Then there were the ingredients. McCormick also wanted it to be natural and not full of chemicals. So, she took online academic courses in cosmetic chemistry. Then went to the patent office to research what exactly went into existing toothpastes and why. What she discovered was that toothpaste was like fast food. It's legal to sell but far from good for you. Fundamentally, most toothpastes are made of baking soda, water, and abrasives like hydrated silica. McCormick also discovered that if you take the water out it becomes self-preserving. That some natural tooth-pastes use kaolin clay instead of silica. And that natural sugar alcohols could be used to prevent bacteria from sticking to teeth. Add a few other ingredients and Lindsay had a natural formulation that could be a solid chewable tablet that would taste good, clean good, be self-preserving, and also be natural and healthy to put in your body. The tabs would get rid of plastic tubes and people would chew them to make them into a paste before brushing.

That was step one. The next question was how to make these tooth tabs? Remember: Lindsay's ambition at this stage was limited to friends and family. She couldn't just go to a factory. If she had, then she would have found that minimum orders and so on were blockers.

How could McCormick manufacture tablets efficiently at home? She guessed the people who make ecstasy pills must have a way of doing this. (Genius!) Sure enough, research online led to an affordable pill-making machine. McCormick ordered one from a firm in Texas and visited the company to learn how to use it. This machine made one pill at a time. So, then she ordered a bigger machine making 5000 pills in one hour. (McCormick uses the smaller machine to test out new flavours, so it didn't go to waste.)

McCormick's original toothpaste did not contain fluoride. Which meant it was classed as a cosmetic and did not need certification. She packaged Bite tabs (great name) in non-plastic containers – cardboard boxes originally. Later she used little glass bottles with a printed label. You keep the glass bottle and then get the refills in biodegradable pouches through the post. Lindsay got the word out through friends and family. Several friends had vegan and health blogs who featured the product. And the business started to grow through word of mouth.

Gradually new pieces were added to the business. A Shopify ecommerce site. Reviews by independent bloggers who discovered Bite. A deal with a factory to scale the production. By popular demand, Bite later brought out a version with fluoride. And every step of the way McCormick kept asking questions and finding better choices. For instance, Bite ships by US Postal Service. Because in carbon terms this is like hitchhiking on an existing journey rather than creating a new courier journey. It takes longer but hey, just order a bit earlier. Having control over the whole process meant that Lindsay made a profit in year one. Of course, it helps that the US media picked up the story and created huge public interest.

There are millions of home businesses that start out like Bite. Some will progress to selling in local gift shops or online. But Bite is something different. It is the product of a pragmatic mindset and of never taking 'no' for an answer.

Victor Papanek would have loved Bite.

Bite in its apothecary style bottle makes conventional toothpaste look like trash. It makes your bathroom shelf look boho chic, rather than like a poster site advertising Colgate. The product is perfect for Instagram, for passionate bloggers and friend to friend recommendations. I posted about it in social media, long before writing this case study. Just because it's a great idea.

The point is that everyone making products, services, and brands needs to be more like McCormick. We need to redesign life. In previous books I have described how a successful brand isn't a single idea. It is a molecule of connected ideas. Some of these are original. Many are borrowed from other contexts. The pill bottle, ecommerce subscription, and refill; the machine used for making ecstasy pills, kaolin clay, and chewable toothpaste tablets. None of these was new. But the Bite brand combining all these created a breakthrough that just works.

Want to start your own purpose driven successful business? Find an injustice. Somewhere corporates are giving common folks a bad deal or a rough time.

A successful business that started out this way was Warby Parker. The founders met at Wharton Business School. Dave Gilboa lost his $700 spectacles while backpacking and had to sit at the front of the class because he couldn't afford to replace them. Another founder – Neil Blumenthal – had run a non-profit called Vision Spring producing glasses for people in the developing world and knew you could make them for next to nothing. So, why are glasses so expensive? Like all good MBA students, they went to the library. And as the Warby Parker website explains:

> It turns out there was a simple explanation. The eyewear industry is dominated by a single company that has been able to keep prices artificially high while reaping huge profits from consumers who have no other options.

Warby Parker has donated over 5 million pairs of glasses in the developing world and also through Vision Spring trained entrepreneurs to give eye exams and distribute the glasses. Note that one of the founders had already worked for Vision Spring. There was genuine commitment from the outset.

The other thing Warby Parker wanted to do was set an example. As Blumenthal explains:

> So, you have this industry dynamic where there are a few very large companies who have been over charging consumers for decades and you bring in a brand that is socially conscious, that designs beautiful product and by working directly with customers, brings down the price. If more people do that, in different industries, that's the best thing in the world. And that's actually what motivates us. We want to build a great brand that can scale, that's profitable, that does good in the world, without charging a premium for that and if we can do that, hopefully we can inspire other entrepreneurs and executives to run their businesses in a similar manner.

Warby Parker were super methodical. They never overstretched. First, they did acetate frames. Their first collection had 27 frame designs and three colours. Later came metal frames, sunglasses, progressive lenses. Over time they innovated how and where they sold their glasses.

The result is another brand molecule of connected innovations and ideas:

Try at home. Warby Parker sends 5 pairs and you send back the 4 they don't like.

Virtual Try On. Alternatively use Warby Parker's app to see how glasses look on your face. Try the whole range if you like. The latest version uses augmented reality to create a super realistic real time 3D image (you can look at from all angles) in your phone.

Eye tests. Many people get new glasses when their prescription hasn't changed. Warby Parker created an app so you can do your own eye test and check your prescription.

Stores. Warby Parker opened a physical store in 2013. Now they have nearly 100. They have also tested stores on wheels and pop-ups.

Warby Parker graphic design, copy and UX are crisp. The process just flows.

Everything Warby Parker do is Instagram ready – for instance, you can share your Virtual Try On straight to social media to get advice from friends.

Make great products at great prices while doing some good. Lots of companies have charities and causes these days (inspired by successes like Warby Parker).

Keep the business honest, committed and accountable by joining B Corp.

This isn't just a random collection. A successful brand molecule (just like a protein in your body) has a purpose. Warby Parker's is summarised by their mission:

Warby Parker was founded with a rebellious spirit and a lofty objective: to offer designer eyewear at a revolutionary price, while leading the way for socially conscious businesses.

Warby Parker and Bite are both examples of redesigning life. They are not just replacing the product but the whole experience and the system behind it.

Digital technology is a blessing at a time when we need to make a huge sustainability shift in how resources, people, creativity, and technology combine. But it's not just technology that is key, it also requires evolving our ideas about business, marketing, and design.

Notes

1. https://www.theguardian.com/commentisfree/2008/jun/10/food.globaleconomy
2. https://grist.org/article/griscom-reagan/
3. https://www.environmentalleader.com/2007/02/green-marketing-could-be-key-to-corporate-survival/
4. https://edition.cnn.com/2019/06/04/health/climate-change-existential-threat-report-intl/index.html
5. https://www.ipsos.com/sites/default/files/ct/news/documents/2019-08/climate_change_charts.pdf
6. https://www.bbc.co.uk/news/science-environment-50307304
7. https://www.theguardian.com/environment/2019/apr/30/two-thirds-of-britons-agree-planet-is-in-a-climate-emergency
8. https://www.comresglobal.com/polls/comres-climate-change-poll-april-2019/
9. https://yougov.co.uk/topics/science/articles-reports/2019/09/15/international-poll-most-expect-feel-impact-climate
10. https://www.economist.com/graphic-detail/2018/05/09/climate-change-will-affect-developing-countries-more-than-rich-ones
11. Johnson, T. and Troszczynski, A. (2013). Food Price Volatility and Insecurity. Council on Foreign Relations.
12. https://www.ncbi.nlm.nih.gov/pmc/articles/PMC6572371/
13. https://www.fibl.org/en/service-en/news-archive/news/article/dok-versuch-zeigt-biolandbau-mindert-klimawandel.html

14. https://ota.com/resources/organic-industry-survey
15. https://techcrunch.com/2019/08/01/for-the-next-month-the-impossible-whopper-will-be-available-at-burger-kings-across-the-country/
16. https://hbr.org/2019/07/the-elusive-green-consumer
17. https://www.stern.nyu.edu/experience-stern/faculty-research/actually-consumers-do-buy-sustainable-products
18. https://www.theguardian.com/environment/2018/sep/10/plastic-waste-set-to-beat-price-as-uk-shoppers-top-concern-study
19. https://www.theguardian.com/environment/2019/jun/08/eco-campaigner-victory-supermarket-plastic-packaging
20. https://www.wired.co.uk/article/allbirds-shoes-on-trainers
21. https://www.inc.com/cameron-albert-deitch/allbirds-2018-company-of-the-year-nominee.html
22. https://medium.com/@TAMSINA/earth-centered-design-manifesto-beta-451e657697ed
23. https://www.yahoo.com/lifestyle/woman-behind-fastest-growing-haircare-161500748.html
24. http://www.mintel.com/press-centre/food-and-drink/half-of-americans-think-gluten-free-diets-are-a-fad-while-25-eat-gluten-free-foods/
25. https://www.thedrum.com/news/2019/04/09/lush-abandons-social-media-its-getting-harder-talk-customers
26. https://www.aol.com/2011/02/12/the-history-of-greenwashing-how-dirty-towels-impacted-the-green/?guce_referrer=aHR0cHM6Ly93d3cu
Z29vZ2xlLmNvbS8&guce_referrer_sig=AQAAAA3opx3Io2u4bgYZ-
GAASxkTEeyvNeM7gTRV20e2Kdj_GLHp_YNalqdXmBl8ASQn-
VZgeDUJMiSn9KyDCcGM2Mota_GSGY7HWkThRCkUl3bMhIFrc-
S7p8bmCvDJdJpptwjKjJJm8eFo0q2d-1lbLgSWWQtr__V655yQ9oQ-
VusZfA&guccounter=2
27. https://www.bbc.co.uk/news/uk-46969920
28. https://www.theguardian.com/uk/2001/jan/23/jilltreanor.juliasnoddy
29. https://www.theguardian.com/business/2018/jan/15/iceland-vows-to-eliminate-plastic-on-all-own-branded-products
30. https://www.theguardian.com/sustainable-business/2017/sep/29/companies-zero-deforestation-pledges-agriculture-palm-oil-environment
31. https://www.environmentalleader.com/2019/10/chocolate-makers-ranked-2019/

32. https://journals.plos.org/plosone/article?id=10.1371/journal.pone.0210628

33. https://www.ncbi.nlm.nih.gov/pmc/articles/PMC2898878/

34. https://www.theguardian.com/travel/2008/jul/06/green.ethicalholidays

35. https://www.bbc.co.uk/news/science-environment-49349566

36. https://www.asa.org.uk/advice-online/environmental-claims-recycling.html

37. https://www.reuters.com/article/us-americas-environment-landrights/burger-king-pledges-to-end-deforestation-by-2030-scientists-skeptical-idUSKBN19E0RI

38. https://www.forbes.com/sites/davidebanis/2019/07/18/is-klms-fly-responsibly-campaign-just-greenwashing/#6b00c4624a6a

39. https://www.theguardian.com/environment/2010/nov/21/carbon-emissions-fall-report

40. https://www.independent.co.uk/environment/climate-change/recession-did-not-lower-c02-emissions-6272333.html

41. https://eia-global.org/blog-posts/PEFC-fig-leaf-for-stolen-timber

42. https://landor.com/work/bp

43. https://journals.sagepub.com/doi/full/10.1177/1086026616687014

44. https://archive.fortune.com/magazines/fortune/fortune_archive/2002/09/30/329277/index.htm

45. https://www.cbi.eu/market-information/cocoa/fine-flavour-cocoa/

46. https://saffron-strands.blogspot.com/2014/06/all-about-origin-at-monmouth-coffee.html

47. https://goodonyou.eco/how-ethical-everlane/

48. http://www.ethicalcorp.com/disruptors-how-wwfs-pavan-sukhdev-went-career-banker-natural-capital-guru

49. https://www.ft.com/content/beb7ae08-ed48-11e6-930f-061b01e23655

50. Stern, N.H. (2007). *The Economics of Climate Change: The Stern Review.* Cambridge, UK: Cambridge University Press.

51. https://sustainabledevelopment.un.org/content/documents/5987our-common-future.pdf

52. https://sustainabledevelopment.un.org/content/documents/5987our-common-future.pdf

53. https://www.ipcc.ch/2018/10/08/summary-for-policymakers-of-ipcc-special-report-on-global-warming-of-1-5c-approved-by-governments/

54. https://www.theguardian.com/environment/2019/may/17/why-the-guardian-is-changing-the-language-it-uses-about-the-environment
55. https://www.theguardian.com/environment/2019/may/17/why-the-guardian-is-changing-the-language-it-uses-about-the-environment
56. https://www.theguardian.com/environment/2003/mar/04/usnews.climatechange
57. https://www.greenfacts.org/en/impacts-global-warming/l-2/index.htm#0
58. https://www.telegraph.co.uk/news/2019/10/08/russian-scientists-find-powerful-ever-methane-seep-arctic-ocean/
59. https://en.wikipedia.org/wiki/Paleocene–Eocene_Thermal_Maximum#Possible_causes
60. https://www.ccacoalition.org/fr/slcps/hydrofluorocarbons-hfc
61. https://www.mckinsey.com/business-functions/sustainability/our-insights/pathways-to-a-low-carbon-economy
62. https://www.forbes.com/sites/dominicdudley/2019/05/29/renewable-energy-costs-tumble/#4ba13d4ce8ce
63. https://www.irena.org/-/media/Files/IRENA/Agency/Publication/2017/Oct/IRENA_Electricity_Storage_Costs_2017_Summary.pdf?la=en&hash=2FDC44939920F8D2BA29CB762C607BC9E882D4E9
64. https://www.irena.org/-/media/Files/IRENA/Agency/Publication/2017/Oct/IRENA_Electricity_Storage_Costs_2017_Summary.pdf?la=en&hash=2FDC44939920F8D2BA29CB762C607BC9E882D4E9
65. https://www.solarpowerworldonline.com/2019/02/behind-the-meter-energy-storage-surges-ahead-of-utility-operated-batteries/
66. https://www.bankofengland.co.uk/news/2019/april/open-letter-on-climate-related-financial-risks
67. https://hbr.org/2018/06/25-years-ago-i-coined-the-phrase-triple-bottom-line-heres-why-im-giving-up-on-it
68. https://corporate.walmart.com/_news_/executive-viewpoints/twenty-first-century-leadership
69. https://www.theguardian.com/business/2019/jul/23/fairtrade-ethical-certification-supermarkets-sainsburys
70. http://www.quakersintheworld.org/quakers-in-action/153/Boycotting-Goods-Produced-by-Slaves
71. https://www.theguardian.com/sustainable-business/2014/aug/15/coconut-water-popularity-supply-chain-farmers-kerela

72. https://www.toryburch.co.uk/blog-post/blog-post.html?bpid=118192

73. https://www.adpulp.com/harmless-harvest-overcomes-objections-before-you-can-object/

74. https://www.telegraph.co.uk/finance/comment/4484209/Mr-Kiplings-exceedingly-good-career.html

75. https://edition.cnn.com/2019/05/30/business/lacroix-sales/index.html

76. https://www.reuters.com/article/us-india-forcedlabour-tea/exclusive-expose-of-labor-abuse-brews-trouble-for-slave-free-indian-tea-idUSKCN1IW00H

77. https://www.bloomberg.com/press-releases/2019-05-08/walmart-on-track-to-reduce-1-billion-metric-tons-of-emission-from-global-supply-chains-by-2030

78. https://en.wikipedia.org/wiki/M-Pesa#Kenya

79. https://www.forbes.com/sites/phillempert/2018/04/03/thrive-market-gets-into-perishables-and-wants-to-improve-the-way-farmers-and-fisherman-do-business/#440fe4267715

SECTION II
Net Good

What Is Net Good?

I met this idea 10 years ago at an extraordinary meeting. Once again with IKEA.

We gathered in 2010, invited by IKEA to help develop a sustainability strategy for the next 10 years. Two thirds of the attendees were from IKEA. The rest were externals like me; including people from labour rights, the UN, the manager of a factory in China.

The event took place in winter at a rural Swedish family holiday camp. I was sharing a chalet for the week with the head of retail from Holland. The event was facilitated by Marvin Weisbord and Sandra Janoff from *Future Search* (it's well worth checking out their extraordinary work and Marvin's books; I've never been to a session more like a 'group mind').

Our output was a simple vision – backed up by a detailed plan with five action points per area, from manufacturing, to logistics, to stores, to communications. The vision was this:

IKEA will be like a forest, putting more good into the ecosystem than we take out.

That's what Net Good is. Be like a forest.

2.1 Year of the Street Protest

In this section of the book, we will track how business is responding to the crisis with a shift from sustainability (Not Bad) to purpose (Net Good). This shift could not have taken hold without a dramatic shift in public mood. And the demands of a new generation. So, in this chapter we will look at this context of protest and concern.

Let's start with an extract of a speech given by Greta Thunberg at Davos in 2019:

> We are at a time in history where everyone with any insight of the climate crisis that threatens our civilisation – and the entire biosphere – must speak out in clear language, no matter how uncomfortable and unprofitable that may be. We must change almost everything in our current societies. The bigger your carbon footprint, the bigger your moral duty. The bigger your platform, the bigger your responsibility. Adults keep saying: 'We owe it to the young people to give them hope.' But I don't want your hope. I don't want you to be hopeful. I want you to panic. I want you to feel the fear I feel every day. And then I want you to act. I want you to act as you would in a crisis. I want you to act as if our house is on fire. Because it is.[1]

The *Washington Post* described 2019 as 'the year of the street protest'. French historian Mathilde Larrère described the world as being gripped by an 'insurrectionary mood'. These protests have swept across the world; a second Arab Spring in Iraq, Egypt, Syria, Algeria; a Latin American Spring starting in Venezuela and spreading to 18 countries across the region; calls for independence in Hong Kong and Catalonia; protests against austerity and taxes in France, against corruption in Malta and Lebanon. And, of course, protests about government inaction on the climate crisis and the environment – including climate strikes in 2460 cities in 158 countries. At the time of writing, 500 000 protestors joined Greta Thunberg marching in Madrid on the eve of the Cop25 talks, demanding that world leaders wake up and agree to do something. With mixed success; but it is clear there is growing public pressure for action.

The school strike protests are clearly directly about climate change. Whereas the yellow jacket protests in France were triggered by the government hiking up the tax on fuel in an attempt to tackle climate change. So, it is not a simple picture. Common features of these protests include a leaderless structure that is spontaneous and hard to repress, massive street demonstrations, protests being directed at governments, and the prominent role played by young people.

Simon Tisdall wrote in the *Guardian* that 'About 41% of the global population are under 24. And they're angry.'[2] Pointing out that although the specific grievances might range from the price of onions in India to pro-democracy in Russia, the one key factor is youth. That a demographic baby boom and the economic, social, political, and environmental stresses of the world are an explosive combination. America in the 1960s was a historical example of similar forces; a teen-dominated society in the midst of the Vietnam war, civil rights movements, and the rise of the counterculture all happened when a baby boom generation (born between 1946 and 1964) started to reach adulthood and again accounted for 40% of the population.[3]

There are three main prongs to the protests. One is protest against economic injustice, unemployment, and suffering. The second is against corrupt political establishments and for greater democracy. The third is climate change, environmental collapse, and the perception that a new generation have had their future stolen.

Social media not only amplify and organise protests, they give young generations direct access to global events and increase expectations. The What's App revolution in Lebanon follows on from Arab Spring where Facebook played a key role. I wouldn't say social media cause protests. But they do facilitate and shape protests. The protests have spread internationally like wildfire as disaffected groups in one country are encouraged by the scenes from other protests. And the protestors reference each other. When protestors in Catalan came out after the jailing of nine political leaders, they chanted 'we are going to do a Hong Kong'. Ideas about how to organise spread between the groups. For instance, learning to 'be water'; being fluid, flexible, fast moving. And learning about the use of digital tools to keep everyone involved informed.

There are lots of reports, surveys, and think tanks exploring what lies behind this.

I think that one key to the whole historical development can be seen in an Ipsos 2018 study[4] with this key question – a question that gets to the heart of the legitimacy of the political situation. Respondents were asked how much they agree with the statement:

My political leaders care about me.

Only in Saudi Arabia and India do the majority think that they do.

The global average percentage of adults who believe political leaders care about them is 23%.

In nine out of the sixteen countries, less than 20% believe this.

That is a *massive* crisis of political legitimacy.

It is this issue that looks to be predictive of both the protests and also the rise of populism (reactionary 'strong man' leaders promising to tackle a broken system). And when the promises aren't delivered – and the nasty sides of populism become visible – protests return. As they have in Italy where the Sardines movement is currently packing public squares.

The Edelman Trust Barometer[5] has been tracking a global crisis of faith in leaders and institutions for many years. One interesting finding of their survey is that there is a growing gap between informed publics (college educated, follow the news) and the mass population. Their trust index (the average percentage who trust NGOs, business, government, and the media) has always been higher among the educated minority. But the gap has grown from 9 points in 2012 to 16 points in 2016, and interestingly this is not because of declining trust in the general population but the rebuilding of trust among the informed elites. Trust in business is improving for all groups.

Looking at different industries, people most trust the Tech sector (78%); the least trusted are Fashion (65%), Energy (65%), Consumer Packaged Goods (64%), and Financial Services (57%). It's interesting how much of the noise about sustainability comes from these last four. It starts to paint a picture of companies feeling public pressure to demonstrate a positive role.

The killer question came when Edelman asked people: 'is the system working for you'? Only 20% agreed among the general population and 21% among the informed public. High proportions of people in both groups felt a sense of injustice (72% and 74%) and expressed desire for change (70% and 76%).

Back to the question of 'why all the protests'?

It doesn't seem to be that much to do with a generation gap in terms of attitudes and concerns. The Ipsos MORI global study compared youth and adult attitudes and they were very similar – young people's only outlying attitude was much higher concern about education.

It doesn't seem to be only about climate change either. Although you could make an argument that all of this is due to climate change, because the economy is a subset of natural ecosystems. And chaos in one drives the other.

According to surveys, the following four ideas seem to be driving protest globally:

political leaders do not care about me;
the system does not work for me;
I feel a sense of injustice;
I have a desire for change.

We've seen several global surveys showing that roughly 80% of people agree with each of these. And I think that this cluster of core beliefs is the real story of the crisis of our age.

The people want what Thunberg and others call system change.

I imagine that if you had surveyed the Russian population in 2016 or 1988, the French population in 1787, or Algeria in 2009, you would have found similar attitudes and ideas.

One other key indicator is whether people are engaged with the news. Edelman found a huge uptick here. In 2018, 50% read or followed the news weekly. In 2019, that figure increased to 72%. News is not necessarily a cause of protests, but it is likely that if you live in Hong Kong or Beirut or indeed anywhere you will be glued to the news of existing protests.

If you do read the news, another theme near the top of the agenda is economic inequality.

According to Oxfam the number of billionaires doubled in the last decade and their fortunes continue to grow at $2.5 billion a day. Gro Brundtland (former Norwegian PM behind the UN report quoted earlier) in a foreword to this report pointed out that 26 individuals own as much wealth as the bottom 3.8 billion of the global population. This bottom half of the population mostly live on less than $5.50 a day and saw their income fall by 11%.[6]

The thing that shocked me about the $/day figures is that (I guess like most people) I used to think that $1 might actually go quite a long way in a poor country. But that's not what is being reported here. The figures are *equivalent spending power.* The $5.50/day figure is people with the spending power in their own country that an American would have with only $5.50 a day. If you have travelled in the developing world, you will know exactly what that looks like.

It's not just the developing world. In the USA in 2018, 11% of all households were classified as food insecure by the USDA ('uncertain of having or unable to acquire enough food to meet the needs of all their members because they had insufficient money or other resources for food'). That's actually an improvement on 2008–2011 when the figure was 15%.[7] One in seven American households going hungry is quite shocking. The political wunderkind Alexandria Ocasia-Cortez is a prominent advocate of tackling such a growing gulf of inequality:

> What kind of society do we want to live in? Are we comfortable with a society where someone can have a personal helipad while this city is experiencing the highest levels of poverty and homelessness since the Great Depression . . . a system that allows billionaires to exist when there are parts of Alabama where people are still getting ringworm because they don't have access to public health? I think it's wrong that you can work 100 hours and not feed your kids. I think it's wrong that corporations like Walmart and Amazon can get paid by the government, experiencing a wealth transfer from the public, for paying people less than a minimum wage.

Ocasia-Cortez has proposed raising the upper tax rate for those earning $10m or more to 70%. (In the 1950s and 60s, after all, the upper tax rate was as high as 90%.)

And guess what?

In a poll by HarrisX, 59% of the US public said they supported this policy.[8]

It goes straight back to the mantra we found from opinion polls:

political leaders do not care about me;

the system does not work for me;

I feel a sense of injustice;

I have a desire for change.

Nobel prize winning economist Joseph Stiglitz has argued that we live in a 'rigged economy' and that this is a problem for everyone, not just those it is rigged against:

economies with greater equality perform better, with higher growth, better average standards of living and greater stability. Inequality in the extremes observed in the U.S. and in the manner generated there actually damages the economy.[9]

Stiglitz points to a sudden and recent appropriation of wealth. In 1985, in most advanced economies the richest 1% earned 7–9% of national income. In 2015 in France, Italy, and Japan, the figure was still under 10%. In the UK, Canada, and Germany it had risen to 12%. But in America it had increased to over 20%. This is not a natural situation. It is sudden, dramatic, and new. A raid on national wealth by the elite, comparable with Russia and its oligarchs.

Perhaps the most interesting chart from a sustainability point of view in Stiglitz's analysis is the percentage of children in the US who earn more than their parents. This fell from 92% for those born in the 1940 to 50% for current generations. A 2016 survey found that 76% of all Americans expected to be 'much worse off' than their parents when they retired. It's direct evidence that we are moving away from having regard for the needs of future generations.

All in all, there is a plenty to protest and a public mood that is ripe for system change.

For businesses finding a new sense of purpose, it also helps that trust in business in improving, and people are increasingly well informed and engaged.

2.2 The *Blue Planet* Effect

Any system under this amount of stress is prone to buckling. That explains the prevalence of protests. It also may explain sudden market changes, like a revolution against single use plastic.

Blue Planet 2 was a BBC documentary series released in October 2017. The show was a global success. In China the number of people streaming the show simultaneously (8 million) was said by the *Sunday Times* to have slowed the internet.[10]

The UN succeeded in getting 200 countries to sign a resolution to eliminate plastic pollution in the sea only a few months after the *Blue Planet 2* aired. The United Nations Environment Programme (UNEP) cited research stating that if plastic pollution rates continued, there would be more plastic in the sea than fish by 2050.[11]

In October 2018, after a global outcry over ocean plastic that the media dubbed the 'Blue Planet Effect', the European Union voted for a ban of all single use plastics that can readily be replaced. This means items like plastic cutlery and plates, cotton buds, straws, drink-stirrers, and balloon sticks. Other items judged not easy to replace must be reduced by 25% by 2025.

Europe is not responsible for most plastic in the oceans. The EU's research showed that 150 thousand tonnes of plastic were thrown into European waters every year – 2% of the 8 million tonnes entering the oceans globally. Waste management infrastructure in the developing world is key. A report by the Helmholtz Centre for Environmental Research found that 10 rivers are responsible for 88–95% of plastic waste reaching the sea. Eight are in Asia (Yangtze, Indus, Yellow, Hai He, Ganges, Pearl, Amur, Mekong) and two in Africa (Nile, Niger). These rivers have two things in common. A high population. And poor waste management infrastructure. China, the country with the largest throughput of plastics, stopped importing foreign waste plastic and set targets for much higher recycling rates. According to the UN Environment Program head Erik Solheim: 'If there is one nation changing at the moment more than anyone else, it's China. The speed and determination of the government to change is enormous.'[12]

India announced in 2019 that it will phase out single use plastics by 2022. The government was said to have been considering an immediate ban but was persuaded by lobbyists who said that low-price products sold to poor people in sachets would be wiped out. These cheap sachets have been exploding as multinational corporations used them as a way to target the 'bottom of the pyramid'. It started with shampoo, but spread to other products in affordable small quantities, like soap, talcum powder, and salt. The Philippines with a population of 105 million consumes 60 billion sachets a year. An environmental organisation (GAIA) calculated that this is enough to cover the capital city of Manila in a layer of plastic one foot thick. The same organisation found that over 50% of waste in the Philippines was branded packaging from just a few multinational companies.

What can you do when you find that your genius scheme to make your products available to the world's poor has an unintended consequence? Unilever has made commitments to tackle the plastics crisis head on: 'to halve our use of virgin plastic in our packaging, and to collect and process more plastic packaging than we sell . . . all by 2025'. Unilever in Manila introduced an incentive programme where people can trade in sachets in return for discounts. That's fine in a crowded city like Manila, but is hard to translate to the 7600 Philippine islands, or to rural areas in India and Africa where the infrastructure just isn't there.

Long term, Unilever is working on refill stations, increased use of paper, and enhancing its waste collection efforts. How Unilever intend to do this is a mix of strategies; multi use packs (refills and reusable packaging); naked products with no packaging; alternative materials; investing in waste management infrastructure and collection partnerships; and buying and using more recycled plastic. According to Unilever CEO Alan Jope:

> We can only eliminate plastic waste by acting fast and taking radical action at all points in the cycle. This demands a fundamental rethink in our approach to our packaging and products. It requires us to introduce new and innovative materials, and scale up new business models, like reuse and refill formats, at an unprecedented speed and intensity.

The unprecedented speed and intensity are down to the galvanic effect of consumer, media, and political pressure. Unilever was already forward on its sustainability ambitions. But even at Unilever a sudden turn against plastic must have caught them out. This is a consumer packaged goods company. And the packaged bit was mostly plastic. But the world has now turned firmly against this model. As in any transition those that move faster can make fresh fortunes.

None of the solutions can work unless they attract consumers. The favourite packaged goods example in my own household is the bamboo paper and sanitation project-funding loo roll company Who Gives a Crap? The brand was low on plastic from the start (the loo rolls are wrapped in paper), but they have been working hard across 2019 to eliminate every last bit of plastic from things like packing tape. Every few months we receive another bulk box of brightly coloured funkily designed loo roll packs. The messaging is punchy and grabbing:

> Good for the world. All of our products are made without trees.
> Good for people. Helps build toilets for people that need them.
> Good for your bum. We don't use any inks, dyes or scents.

The Who Gives a Crap? brand is endless fun. They have an app where you can read jokes sitting on the toilet. They sent a message about World Toilet Day featuring a video of a man tap-dancing on a toilet (celebrating the fact that toilets have added 20 years to the human lifespan). Most importantly, 50% of profits go to sanitation projects.

The Who Gives a Crap? packaging is as cool as a trendy chocolate or juice brand. It shows how the service system pioneered by Dollar Shave Club, allied with a cause marketing, can disrupt the world's most boring category. Forget 50 years of ads featuring puppies to communicate softness. Telling the truth is so much more fun. As is daring to use words like 'crap' and 'bum'.

The plastics crisis has been a frenzy of discoveries and innovations.

In London we learned that what had been called a 'fatberg' blocking our sewers was actually due to wet wipes. There are 300 000 sewer blockages per year, and these cost the UK £100 million.[13] No wonder, as apparently we go through 11 billion wet wipes a year. One of these 'fatbergs' in East London was a quarter of a kilometre long, weighed 130 tons, and took 9 weeks to remove.

In one day, volunteers removed 23 000 wet wipes from a foreshore of the Thames, the other key constituent being tampons and sanitary towels. Researchers described wet wipes in the Thames as a second riverbed.

The issue with all of these products – along with tea bags and other everyday items – is that they look like paper but are made of plastic. This makes a dramatic difference once the product is disposed of. A plastic nappy sent to landfill can take 300–500 years to biodegrade. One made with plant cellulose such as Kit & Kin can biodegrade in 3–6 years. Note that word 'can'. Industrial composting as available in Holland can biodegrade non-plastic products quickly. In the UK they will likely end up in landfill where things take much longer. But biodegradable is a step in the right direction – I'm sure waste management infrastructure will catch up.

Kit & Kin launched (like Who Gives a Crap?) as a subscription by post service. It was co-founded by former Spice Girl Emma Bunton who was frustrated at not finding nappies that didn't trigger her children's allergies. Like Jessica Alba with Honest, an A-List celebrity mum passionate about causes as a founder does a world of good publicity-wise. Kit & Kin have a cool design (children love the animal pics on the nappy), a good mix of eco materials, and also fund the purchase of 1 acre of rainforest through the World Land

Trust for every 10 subscriptions. The range expanded to cover biodegradable wipes and is available in Tesco as well as online.

Some brands choose change. Others have had change thrust upon them. Major high street brands like Walkers Crisps and PG Tips were held to account by consumer boycotts and petitions over their continued use of single use plastic. According to PG Tips website:

> We've been GREEN and RED since 1930. But we thought – how can we be even GREENER? So, we're on a mission to make all our pyramid tea bags with a new fully plant-based material. And having already produced 1 billion we're well on our way!

PG Tips had already used plant-based alternatives to plastic in their tea bags in Canada, Indonesia, and Poland. So, they may have been planning a switchover already. But the BBC reported that the announcement was made in response to a consumer protest:

> Mike Armitage from Wrexham started a petition after finding white residue from teabags in his garden compost. The petition called on manufacturers, including Unilever, to stop producing teabags with polypropylene and to date has attracted over 232,000 signatures.[14]

The UK drinks 62 billion cups of tea a year, so this white residue soon mounts up. Co-op stores announced they were shifting to plant-based teabags after finding out they were responsible for 150 tonnes of tea bag plastic contaminating food waste compost or going to landfill.

This is the new cycle of innovation that is driving mainstream marketing.

There have been petitions, boycotts, and campaigns for companies to change as long as there has been environmental activism. What has changed is the galvanic, tipping point time we live in. A protest can blow up into a full-scale crisis of public confidence, with serious implications for share price, distribution, and sales. The public mood is full of frustration, urgency, and anxiety. It takes relatively little – the use of plastic-based glue in your teabag – to put you in the firing line. People get (rightly) worked up about an issue like plastic. Companies are forced to respond. In some cases, they do so convincingly. Others try to argue the problem away, announcing vague targets. Then challenger brands launch alternatives and consumers vote with their wallets.

Plastic has only been used in consumer products and packaging since the 1950s: 50% of plastic ever made was made in the last 13 years.[15] Only 9% of plastic ever produced was recycled. It is a fast increasing issue that overwhelmed waste infrastructure. So, what is to be done?

One answer is turning back the clock.

There is a movement in soap 'back to the bar'. Award-winning beauty bar company Ethique pioneered this trend in New Zealand, along with the UK's LUSH. It's an obvious way to avoid plastic packaging and it happened spontaneously. I met Mumsnet founder Justine Roberts and she told me switching back to bar soap had been a hot topic of discussion in her community.

A second answer is taking plastic out of products where it has been added.

Roberts told me Mumsnet was getting behind a plastic free sanitary protection brand. This is the perfect place for a frank conversation about personal habits. There are no taboo subjects on Mumsnet. It's also the kind of place where people choose new brands, as they trust other mums a thousand times more than digital advertising in their Facebook feed.

A third answer to look at the whole system. See it afresh through a circular economy lens.

There could be new and valuable uses of plastic waste. Our roads could be made of what is called 'plasphalt'. Plastics can be processed to produce fuels (for instance hydrogen gas) and many other byproducts. There are more than 500 000 landfill sites in Europe. And each holds ample building materials and enough energy to supply 200 000 homes for 20 years.[16] We may end up mining landfill for these valuable hydrocarbons, as well as precious metals in electronics devices like mobile phones. eWaste contains 40–50 times higher concentration of precious metals than the natural deposits in goldmines.

The main solution to plastics has to be reducing production and use. Whether by regulation, taxation, consumer pressure, or corporate innovation. Or all of the above. Restricting the supply, acceptability, and affordability of plastic forces innovation of alternatives.

The bigger solution to plastics is to change the way that we shop and consume. There is little need for such a staggering variety of cleaning products in the first place. Commercial shampoos, soaps, and household cleaners are made from the same base surfactant (detergent) with only cosmetic differences introduced to differentiate them. One soap factory boss told me that they use the same (high quality, organic, biodegradable) base to make washing up liquid and premium branded shampoo. Only cosmetic additives for scent, colour, and viscosity differentiate them. The reason for dozens of different bottles in your home was the need of soap giants to justify sales. In a wartime you would have one base cleaning liquid and add your own scents or salt (the main thickening agent). And we are in an environmental crisis. Go figure! Another easy opportunity is concentrates. We've had concentrated detergents for laundry for years – leading to less shipping weight, less CO_2 in transport. And much less plastic.

A long-established way to avoid plastic packaging waste altogether is the milkman model. Create a delivery system with reusable packaging designed in. The UK milkman used electric delivery vehicles 50 years ago. Well ahead of its time. And quiet too. Following the *Blue Planet* documentary, the BBC found dairies across the UK reporting a huge increase in milkman customers: in Carmarthen, Nigel's Dairy increased their glass bottle deliveries from 4000 to 9000 a week. 'We feel like we've won the lottery', the owner Nigel Dragone said.[17]

In 2019, Terracycle launched Loop which I always explain to British people as 'like the milkman but for groceries'. Terracycle is a recycling firm working with big American companies like Walmart to increase recycling rates. They put distinctive recycling centres into Walmart carparks and even created upcycled products (ranging from toys to stationary) out of old packaging. Loop goes beyond recycling or even upcycling. It takes the waste out of the system. And it does this by applying the milkman model. With reusable containers – for instance Haagen Dazs ice-cream in tins – collected the next week, washed, and refilled.

Loop couldn't work unless they got a significant proportion of the packaged consumer goods companies on board. A few years ago, this would have seemed unimaginable. But now with the plastics crisis snapping at their heels it seems every company wants to play, including Unilever, P&G, Nestlé, Body Shop, and Danone. Trials started in France and the USA, then the UK.

When I first saw Loop, I thought it must be expensive. But Terracycle's CEO Tom Szasky says the opposite:

The key for us is affordability because the consumer doesn't own the package so effectively doesn't have to pay for it, just their use. The convenience to us is very important so when the package is empty it doesn't need any cleaning, nothing, they can simply chuck it back into the bins they received it in and then it gets picked up.[18]

Loop costs less, but it looks premium – what Terracycle calls 'elegance'. Previously ice-cream, oil, and nuts only came in glass and metal in upmarket outlets like Harvey Nichols. Plastic said mainstream and cheap. It is literally trashy. The behaviour change feels fairly easy too as many have already made the transition to new models like subscription (veg box), home delivery (Ocado or Amazon Fresh) and click and collect, or self-scanning in store.

The Loop scheme uses another staple of reusable packaging schemes, which is that people pay a deposit to incentivise them to return the pack. Reverse vending machines have long been popular in markets like Germany and Norway where deposit return and recycling laws are much tougher. The UK has been looking at introducing them to tackle the plastic bottle epidemic. They would tax the drinks companies to pay for these.

Reverse vending is an example of how Blockchain can also play a role in system change. The German government was once defrauded to the tune of €8 million by gangs in East Europe making cheap counterfeit plastic bottles in order to feed them into reverse vending machines and claim the deposit. Which means there is a business case for ways to identify a bottle is genuine. There have been pilots in recycling using Blockchain, like the UK Recycle To Coin. Others trialling similar platforms include Plastic Bank in Canada, Circularise in Holland, and Empower in Norway. Traca is enabling producers, recyclers, and regulators to share information like inspection data and even photos. The association behind Traca say it cuts paperwork down from hours to minutes, while making sure all parties see the same trustworthy information.[19]

One worry about the plastics frenzy was that we might be blowing the public appetite for system change on a minor issue. Looking at the ocean there are bigger problems like the 'deadly trio' of acidification, warming, and deoxygenation (caused by climate change) along with overfishing and pollution of all sorts including sewage, fertilisers, chemicals, and oil. As previously noted, only 2% of plastic in oceans originates in the EU. So, if it became the *main thing* consumers worry about, could this be a distraction from much bigger issues like climate change?

Plastics intuitively seem a less carbon-emitting use of oil than burning it in cars. But a scientific lifecycle analysis found that 'Plastic production, use, and disposal all emit prodigious amounts of greenhouse gases.' According to this study in *Nature Climate Change* by researchers at University of California, Santa Barbara:

> Plastics have surprisingly carbon-intense life cycles. The overwhelming majority of plastic resins come from petroleum, which requires extraction and distillation. Then the resins are formed into products and transported to market. All of these processes emit greenhouse gases, either directly or via the energy required to accomplish them. And the carbon footprint of plastics continues even after we've disposed of them. Dumping, incinerating, recycling and composting (for certain plastics) all release carbon dioxide. All told, the emissions from plastics in 2015 were equivalent to nearly 1.8 billion metric tons of CO_2 . . . On the current course, emissions from plastics will reach 17% of the global carbon budget by 2050, according to the new results.[20]

Naturally the plastics industry has their own story. One claim that the British Plastics Federation (BPF) make is that 'Plastics reduce the consumption of oil elsewhere. They reduce the weight of vehicles, aircraft, ships, packaging and products, meaning that less fuel is burnt, and CO2 emissions are lower.'[21] The BPF don't quote a source for this claim (nor any of the other stats that they quote on the same page) which technically means that it is greenwash.

It is true that when looking at sustainability you need to look at all the impacts and side effects. It is also true that reusable plastic is a different question than single use disposable containers. But when peer-reviewed science says plastics are on track to become 17% of the global carbon budget, it is hard to argue plastics are not something we should prioritise.

2.3 Plant-Based Revolution

We've seen how public outcry on plastic brought sweeping change. And how this cut deep into supply chains, disruptive innovation, and carbon budgets. Another much publicised impact of modern lifestyles on climate change has been eating meat. It features heavily on lists of things people can reduce (along with flying) to do their bit. The plant diet trend was well underway when blockbuster documentary *The Game Changers* on Netflix arrived on the scene.

But I met a parent at my son's school yesterday who told me her teen stopped eating meat as a direct result of seeing this. So it has clearly amplified the trend.

Another person who announced they were going vegan after seeing this documentary was Roger Whiteside the CEO of Greggs, a food company famous for its sausage rolls. Greggs already hit the headlines earlier in 2019 when it launched a vegan sausage roll in time for Veganuary. Piers Morgan railed against this on Twitter: 'Nobody was waiting for a vegan bloody sausage, you PC-ravaged clowns.' Greggs replied and in the ensuing social media frenzy was judged to come out ahead (some commentators did point out that Piers Morgan and Greggs share a PR company – and wondered whether this was all a tad staged?).

Game Changers is a fascinating exercise in myth-busting. It looks at the mistaken association of eating meat with sporting prowess and physique. One of the sporty celebs behind *Game Changers* was racing driver Lewis Hamilton, who also recently opened a vegan café in London. I met some clients there and have to report their vegan take on burger and chips was pretty tasty. A far cry from when I started out as a vegetarian in my teens when 'nut loaf' made it onto restaurant menus (for similar reasons: aiming to mimic meat dishes).

This has not been an overnight phenomenon. The Vegan Society quotes Google Trends data showing that Veganism as a search term increased sevenfold between 2014 and 2019.

Their research also showed that the number of vegans in the UK is also growing steeply:[22]

2014	150 000
2016	276 000
2019	600 000

More widespread change is seen in the adoption of meat-free meals and the so-called flexitarian diet. Research for supermarket chain Waitrose[23] in 2018 found that among UK adults:

3% are vegan
9.5% are vegetarian

21% are flexitarian

33.5% of the population cut down on or cut out meat.

Another big trend is dairy free milks: these now account for one quarter of Waitrose 'milk' sales. Oat milk sales grew +116%, Coconut milk +60%, and Almond milk +26%.

In surveys people give a variety of reasons for these changes. Those avoiding meat altogether cite animal welfare as their number one concern. People eating less meat tend to emphasise health and weight. The Waitrose survey found that 38% cite environmental issues.

Why now? A complex set of factors like celebrities, vegetable forward trends in fine dining, exciting new brands with something different to say – like Impossible Burger and Oatly – and media hype . . . all combine with a galvanic time when people are looking for system change. Previous clean eating trends were mainly about wellbeing. But the vegan trend is more than that. There is a lot in the media about cutting down meat to save the planet.

Skeptical Science[24] picked up on a typical media claim:

Animal agriculture and eating meat are the biggest causes of global warming. Becoming Vegan or cutting down on your own personal meat consumption could be the single most effective action that you can do to help reduce green-house gas emissions.

Skeptical Sciences goes on to 'debunk' this claim. But I think they may have been a bit harsh. I followed up and found that, to be fair, the original article was referencing reputable sources:

The UN Food and Agriculture Organizations have reported the meat industry is 'one of the most significant contributors to today's most serious environmental problems.' In Al Gore's handbook, Live Earth, it says that not eating meat is the 'single most effective thing you can do' to reduce your climate change impact.[25]

Skeptical Science does admit that animal agriculture globally accounts for 18% of climate emissions. This is more than the emissions caused by transport. But much less than the 64% of all global emissions caused by the burning of fossil fuels.

The key point is where the emissions are happening. Deforestation due to animal agriculture – cutting down the Amazon to make way for cattle farms – is a huge issue. One study found that 71% of deforestation in South America was linked to cattle, compared with 14% due to planting crops.[26] However, most meat in your supermarket does not come from South America. South America's meat exports mainly go to China (35%) and the Middle East (17%) while only a small fraction end up in the EU (5%) and the USA (1.5%).

If you look at the footprint of animal farming close to home, where deforestation is not a factor, then Skeptical Science says:

> In the United States, fossil fuel-based energy is responsible for about 80% of total greenhouse gas emissions as compared to about 3% from animal agriculture. [27]

The UN FAO predicted in 2012 that meat consumption would increase by 76% by 2050.[28] A 2018 report in *Science* drew attention to the effects of growth in meat consumption in rapidly developing countries like China: 'It is difficult to envisage how the world could supply a population of 10 billion or more people with the quantity of meat currently consumed in most high-income countries without substantial negative effects on the environment.'

Hence it is heartening that China (the biggest importer of beef from forest risk countries like Brazil) has joined the plant-based diet craze. The Chinese free from meat category grew 33.5% to $9.7 billion according to Euromonitor. Zhenmeat brought out a pea plant-based substitute joining established players like Whole Perfect Food. China has a tradition of non-meat options such as Tofu and the new trend is less about 'meatless burgers' (as in the US) and more vegetable dumplings. The Chinese government, meanwhile, issued guidelines recommending individuals reduce meat consumption by 50% by 2030. Chinese consumers who are eating less meat cite health as the main reason (63.5%) and also environmental concerns (40%). The same survey found 60% intend to eat more vegetables and 39% are reducing meat.[29]

The impact your diet has on emissions depends on where food comes from and how it is farmed. A study by an Oxford University and Swiss team published in *Science* found that:

> High-impact beef producers create 105kg of CO_2e and use 370m^2 of land per 100 grams of protein, a huge 12 and 50 times greater than low-impact beef

producers. So, if you are going to eat meat choosing local sustainably farmed options makes a huge difference. Low-impact beans, peas, and other plant-based proteins create just 0.3kg of CO_2e and use just 1m² of land per 100 grams of protein.[30]

The study concludes that 'plant-based diets reduce food's emissions by up to 73% depending where you live'. That does sound like a big impact, in answer to the Skeptical Science critique. However, you can achieve three quarters of the same impact according to the same report by avoiding animal products from high impact producers. In conclusion, the climate science does support meat free and also supports responsibly farmed meat from local sources.

As marketers, we know that perception is what matters most. The BBC noted that

> IPCC presents a complex and nuanced discussion about many aspects of land use, but most news organisations boiled all that down to 'eat less meat and save the planet'.[31]

This meme gets reinforced by charismatic millennial vegan bloggers, delicious 'dirty vegan' food carts, vegan menus at venues ranging from Wagamama to the Ritz. There are Meatless Mondays, Veganuary, and other campaigns too. The trend has also spilled from food into drink. Guinness went vegan by stopping using fish guts as a fining agent. Vegan beauty brands are a hot trend – high end like Le Labo or Lime Crime and mainstream brands like Soaper Duper.

Edited research found a 75% increase in UK products describing themselves as vegan.[32] The biggest category for new vegan products was beauty. They also found that in the US vegan shoes grew from 16% of the footwear market in 2017 to 32% in 2018. Like those made by our friends at POZU, who use Appleskin fake leather (and who also made the boots in the Star Wars movies). Gucci, Chanel, Burberry, and others have pledged to no longer use fur.

Let's take a look at two of the key trends for system change brands: meatless meat and non-dairy milk. How did these suddenly become so hip?

Soymilk was introduced to the US in the 1890s. Quorn launched in 1985. Linda McCartney launched her meat substitutes in 1991; golden nuggets, cheese pie, pasties, lasagne, toppers, and beefless burgers made with textured vegetable protein. Why make such familiar dishes? Why not just popularise daal or tofu? The argument (going back to Linda McCartney's range) is that you need to make food that meat eaters accept and serve it in formats that mainstream families accept and recognise. Whether it is soya mince pies or the Impossible Burger.

The thing that most excited *Wired* about Impossible Burger – their use of genetic modification – horrifies some Greens. Impossible Foods discovered that one molecule called 'heme' is responsible for the taste of cooked meat. So, they genetically engineered yeast to produce a heme (leghemoglobin). Impossible claim this molecule is identical to one that humans consumed for millennia. That it satisfies the cravings of meat eaters without the planet impact.

Whole food advocates such as Jon Mackay (founder of Wholefoods) criticise Impossible for being processed. Others are against the GM ingredients. Moms Across America produced research showing – as a result of using GM soy – the Impossible Burger tested positive for glycosphate. This ingredient from Monsanto herbicide Roundup was classified by the WHO as 'a probable human carcinogen'.[33] Mom's Across America say they are 'concerned that consumers are being misled to believe the Impossible Burger is healthy'.[34]

Is it too good to be true? (If so 'Impossible' have gifted headline writers with a way to write their obituary.) I was glad to note that the UK equivalent Meatless Meat only uses non-GM soy.

People adopting a less meaty diet give health as a top reason. So Impossible do need to counter the criticisms – along with those about salt and saturated fat levels. The sudden turn against vaping in the US shows how even mighty trends can crash on health concerns.

Impossible Burger, like the hybrid car, was designed to attract people to a substitute with lower emissions, but zero compromise. They do seem to have delivered on this part. Many on the climate campaigning side welcomed Impossible as an iconic example of creating new lifestyles. The United Nations even gave them a Global Climate Action Award in December 2019.

There are no health caveats with our next case study – Oatly. Not only is oat milk a good tasting dairy substitute and one that makes excellent foam in coffee. But studies have shown that drinking oat milk rather than cow's milk results in 'significantly lower' cholesterol levels.[35]

Oatly was founded by Rickard Oste, a researcher from the University of Lund in Sweden who had been researching both lactose intolerant populations and the role of dairy in climate change. Rickard found a way (using an enzyme) to turn fibre rich oats into a nutritional drink. He teamed up with his brother Bjorn (a seasoned tech entrepreneur) to build a company. And they never stopped innovating. Bjorn and Rickard's latest invention is called *Good Idea* – a sparkling water (containing five amino acids and chromium) clinically proven to reduce the blood sugar spike after a meal.

The Oste brothers got Oatly off the ground as a product, worked out how to manufacture and distribute it. But they credit the CEO Toni Petersson (hired 10 or so years later) with the craze the brand created. According to Bjorn, Toni Petersson 'took Oatly from being a food brand among others to being *the* lifestyle brand'.[36] That's the story I want to focus on.

When Peterssen joined Oatly he took his long-time collaborator John Schoolcraft as creative director. Schoolcraft describes how the organisation had started out visionary and entrepreneurial, but ended up behaving like any old consumer packaged goods company:

> In terms of the brand, I used to say it looked like a Dutch multinational, just indistinguishable from anything else on the shelves.[37]

Petersson's presentation of his new vision to the board was in the form of a brand book. The front cover simply had the word CHANGE printed on a wooden cover. As Schoolcraft reports, this manifesto has stood the test of time:

> Years later, all we've done is execute the book. If you start at Oatly today, you get the same book from 2012 and we haven't changed a word.

The CHANGE book sets out a cultural manifesto for actions inside and outside the company. Pages say things (in CAPITALS) like:

WE HAVE VERY BIG GOALS
AN EMOTIONAL EXPERIENCE BASED ON SCIENCE
IS THAT EVEN LEGAL?
PEOPLE DON'T NEED BRANDS
THEY NEED SOMETHING MORE REAL
WHATEVER YOU DO PLEASE BE HUMAN
AND NOT A LOGO

In other words, they educated the whole company in how to build an authentic brand.

From this kernel (to use an oat term) they developed the key ingredients of the brand. First of all, the packaging. As Schoolcraft explains: 'because we don't have these US or UK size advertising budgets it's really our main media'. With authentic brands this is so often the case. Your packaging is your biggest opportunity if you are bold with it.

The Oatly packaging reminds me of Dr Bronner's (long form manifesto copy) . . . crossed with the punk visual language of Brew Dog. It's an essay in storytelling branding. And in not being a (fake) brand. Oatly talks to you as a human being, just like their CHANGE principles say. This approach and graphic style continued into their ads. With headlines like:

WE MADE THIS MURAL INSTEAD OF AN INSTAGRAM POST.
WAITING FOR SOMEONE?
JUST BE COOL AND PRETEND TO BE READING THIS.
IT'S LIKE MILK BUT MADE FOR HUMANS.

This last line ran in the UK in 2018. It was advertising copy Oatly previously ran in Sweden. That had resulted in them being sued. And yet they went ahead in the UK. Oatly explained: 'Although we lost a lawsuit from the Swedish dairy industry in 2015, we still believe in the line, it's still the truth, which is why you're seeing it across the UK.'[38] John Schoolcraft has described Oatly as a company that is 'fearless when other companies are scared shitless'. This seems a good example of what that looks like in practice.

The line 'It's like milk . . .' originally featured in 2014 TV commercials by legendary Swedish agency Forsman & Bodenfors. Toni Peterssen starred in these. In one he is in a field, playing a vintage synthesiser, singing a song he wrote himself with the words 'Wow! No Cow'. In another ad 'Nonchalant' he talks about 'selling in a non-selling way'. Oatly constructed its brand by being human, telling the truth and being charming in the process. It isn't naïve, dull, or worthy, it is knowing and hip. Some Oatly posters simply talk about them writing posters so that people will read them.

Oatly built their business through third wave coffee shops in the US and the enthusiastic adoption of their product by baristas. They marketed a Barista Edition made specially to be foamed. In the process, Oatly contrived to be adopted by hipsters. For their next adventure Oatly are in China, coming full circle back to Rickard's original research and marketing to a population who are lactose intolerant. Once again Oatly are starting in third wave coffee shops which are a huge trend in China. (Toni Petersson claims there are more third wave coffee shops in Shanghai than New York.) The brand created a new Chinese character (letter) combining the words plant and milk. Oatly started strongly with a presence in 3400 outlets, is looking to double its sales there in 2020, and is opening an Asian production facility in Singapore.[39]

Four things to take away from this case study. Apply some real science. Get on the right side of history. Build your brand on truth and stripping away the façade. And every revolution starts on the inside, transforming your own culture and way of working. The other thing that shines out from this case is the importance of having a purpose. As Michael Lee from Oatly explains:

> For us, there is a much more grounded purpose of why this company exists, why we chose oats, why we think this is an important and big idea. It's not grounded in a trend or a fad, it's grounded in making a really nutritious product that doesn't tax environmental resources in the process of making it.[40]

2.4 Capitalism. Time for a Reset

There's a lot of talk these days about needing a paradigm shift.

John Elkington describes this using an analogy from studies in perception. In the 1890s a scientist called George Stratton wore a pair of goggles that inverted his view of the world. The first day he felt nauseous and disoriented. But after seven days it had become 'the new normal' as his brain was compensating, so that when he stopped wearing the glasses it took days to adjust. Elkington points to the middle phase of this transition where there is an oscillation between seeing the world one way or the other. We are in the middle of a transition; at times we see climate change and the adjustments we need to make clearly, and at other times we revert.

The term 'paradigm shift' comes from a book by Thomas Kuhn called *The Structure of Scientific Revolutions*. Kuhn studied how new radical ideas took hold in science. What he noticed was that proponents of a new theory inevitably clashed with incumbent professors and the institutions they led. This clash was seldom resolved. Rather it typically took a generation for a paradigm shift. The length of time it took for old professors to retire and new ones to gain tenure.

One academic field in the middle of a paradigm shift right now is economics. In 2011 during the Occupy protests, Harvard students walked out of the lectures of Professor Gregory Mankiw. Their protest was about his economics course presenting social justice and economic efficiency as competing interests. The organisers of the walkout pointed to Professor Mankiw claiming that minimum wage legislation causes unemployment. And that Mankiw wouldn't admit that the 2008 financial crisis was a direct result of the free market philosophy he espoused. Mankiw wrote in response that 'The recent financial crisis, economic downturn and meager recovery are vivid reminders that we still have much to learn. Widening economic inequality is a real and troubling phenomenon, albeit one without an obvious explanation or easy solution.' Mankiw couldn't resist also having a dig, saying all the protestors had was 'a grab bag of anti-establishment platitudes without much hard-headed analysis or clear policy prescriptions'.[41]

Kate Raworth's *Donut Economics* could be read as a response to Mankiw (and she mentions this episode in the opening chapter). This is a thoroughly researched, clearly articulated, and radical alternative to the free market orthodoxy. George Monbiot described Raworth as 'the John Maynard Keynes of the 21st century: by reframing the economy, she allows us to change our view of who we are, where we stand, and what we want to be'. Raworth's theories have been taken up in places ranging from Occupy and Oxfam to the UN General Assembly.

Raworth's core diagram – the donut – has an inner 'social foundation' circle (the minimum needed to sustain a good quality of life for all) and an outer 'ecological ceiling' circle (hard planetary limits). Somehow, Raworth says, we have to find our way into the doughy donut in-between.

Ten years ago, these ideas seemed radical and speculative. Today they seem like a sensible way forward. Even the *Financial Times* has called for a 'reset' of capitalism. The year 2019 was not just one of street protests, but also one of pronouncements from the heart of the capitalist establishment calling for reform. Their key prescription? Every business needs a social purpose.

This recent canonisation of purpose in business raises a central question. Are we using purpose to re-describe the 'good bits' of the current system to justify its continuation? Or are we describing a more radical vision of businesses that will be reconstituted around this purpose? I am reminded of Gorbachev's warning to the Soviet Communist Party when he unveiled *Perestroika* (restructuring) and *Glasnost* (openness) in a speech in 1986:

> Previous Leadership. For a number of years, the deeds and actions of party and government bodies trailed behind the needs of the times and of life. The problems in the country's development built up more rapidly than they were being solved . . . The situation called for change, but a peculiar psychology – *How to improve things without changing anything?* – took the upper hand. But that cannot be done, comrades.

The liberal capitalist model is at a similar crossroads. Some seem to hope to *improve things without changing anything.* Others see the need for real change and deep reform.

Let's start with an extract from an open letter from the editor of the *Financial Times*:

> The liberal capitalist model has delivered peace, prosperity and technological progress for the past 50 years, dramatically reducing poverty and raising living standards throughout the world. But, in the decade since the global financial crisis, the model has come under strain, particularly the focus on maximising profits and shareholder value. These principles of good business are necessary but not sufficient.
>
> The long-term health of free enterprise capitalism will depend on delivering profit with purpose. Companies will come to understand that this combination serves their self-interest as well as their customers and employees. Without change, the prescription risks being far more painful. Free enterprise capitalism has shown a remarkable capacity to reinvent itself. At times, as the historian and politician Thomas Babington Macaulay wisely noted, it is necessary to reform in order to preserve. Today, the world has reached that moment. It is time for a reset.

It's interesting that the *Financial Times* chose to launch this campaign in the middle of the climate strikes. And yet chose not to mention the climate emergency in their declaration. Perhaps they worried that siding with XR might risk losing their audience? We also maybe need to bear in mind that the *FT* is no longer a UK title. It has 1.2 million registered readers in China.

The *FT* did, however, produce a stunning video on climate in partnership with the Royal Court theatre. The monologue takes the form of a newscast from 2050. A future where the world responded too little and too late and must now face the consequences. The newsreader speaks graphically about wars, riots, bio terror, 'dengue fever on a world tour'. It is too hot to go outside for more than an hour in Doha, Austin, or Manchester. The message is one of regret that we couldn't have had a better conversation about this in 2019:

> We needed to make this as everyday as bath time, as graspable as pre-packed sandwiches or your loved one's hand. And we didn't. Every time we tried to make the defining statement, we thought, maybe this is the one. Maybe this is the one that gets through. We didn't need data or heroes. We didn't even need voices pretending to be from the future. We're in the same place. It's not about our children or our grandchildren anymore. The future's come to meet us. Most of the people watching this will be there when it happens. We needed to understand quietly every day that this is the future, now, Every single second.

Stirring stuff.

When organisations like the *Financial Times* put their name to statements like 'it is necessary to reform in order to preserve' I am reminded of historian Alexis De Tocqueville writing in 1856:

> Experience teaches that the most dangerous time for a bad government is usually when it begins to reform.[42]

Several revolutions in Russia serve to illustrate De Tocqueville's thesis. In 1916 the Tsar instituted a mock parliament. In 1989 the collapse of the Soviet Union was preceded by Gorbachev's well intentioned Perestroika and Glasnost. Give protestors an inch . . .?

The *Financial Times* can influence the debate and report its leading voices but is not in a position to reform capitalism. Larry Fink the CEO of Blackrock probably is. He started his 2018 open letter to CEOs by recognising that the real problem is the legitimacy of the whole system:

> In 2017, equities enjoyed an extraordinary run – with record highs across a wide range of sectors – and yet popular frustration and apprehension about the future simultaneously reached new heights. Since the financial crisis, those with capital have reaped enormous benefits. At the same time, many individuals across the world are facing a combination of low rates, low wage growth, and inadequate retirement systems. We also see many governments failing to prepare for the future.

Then Fink comes to his concrete prescription for companies:

> Society is demanding that companies, both public and private, serve a social purpose. To prosper over time, every company must not only deliver financial performance, but also show how it makes a positive contribution to society. Companies must benefit all of their stakeholders, including shareholders, employees, customers, and the communities in which they operate. Without a sense of purpose, no company, either public or private, can achieve its full potential. It will ultimately lose the license to operate from key stakeholders. It will succumb to short-term pressures to distribute earnings, and, in the process, sacrifice investments in employee development, innovation, and capital expenditures that are necessary for long-term growth.[43]

Blackrock manages around $6 trillion in assets. Big enough to have influence with the CEOs whose stock they hold and with central banks whose bonds they buy. After the Lehman Brothers crisis Blackrock became known as 'the Ghostbusters of Wall Street' – adept at the analysis and containment of toxic debt. Some critics say they have become too powerful.[44] Blackrock calling for profits with purpose makes the *FT*'s 'communist manifesto' moment more explicable. The logic of Blackrock's letter is that corporations need to move with the times and reform. Because short termism – pandering to speculative equity markets who want you to burn your furniture to make them a few cents richer – won't deliver wealth creation and resilience.

The idea that business needs a positive social purpose and should serve the needs of diverse stakeholders (not just shareholders) is catching on with business leaders too.

2.5 Corporate Citizens

In August 2019, 181 American CEO members of the Business Round Table (BRT) signed a declaration under the heading: *An Economy That Serves All Americans*.[45] The declaration starts with a credo reaffirming their belief in free market capitalism:

> Americans deserve an economy that allows each person to succeed through hard work and creativity and to lead a life of meaning and dignity. We believe the free-market system is the best means of generating good jobs, a strong and sustainable economy, innovation, a healthy environment and economic opportunity for all.

The declaration goes on to detail what – over and above their own commercial purpose – the companies are committing to with each stakeholder in society:

Delivering value to our customers.
Investing in our employees.
Dealing fairly and ethically with our suppliers.
Supporting the communities in which we work.
Generating long-term value for shareholders.

Sustainability comes under the communities heading:

We respect the people in our communities and protect the environment by embracing sustainable practices across our businesses.

The idea of business serving multiple stakeholders has been around a long time. Why come out and say it right now? BRT chairman Jamie Dimon (and CEO of JP Morgan Chase) commented:

the American Dream is alive but fraying. These modernized principles reflect the business community's unwavering commitment to continue to push for an economy that serves all Americans.[46]

Their proposed solution could be interpreted as what Gorbachev described as 'how to improve things without changing anything'. Of course, it's a small miracle that they got any statement down on paper that 181 leaders of major businesses could agree to.

The hard truth is what Dimon said. The American dream is in tatters. Trump came to power promising to *Make America Great Again*. In line with the free market ethos these leaders affirmed, Trump then handed massive corporate tax cuts to the very same companies who signed this declaration. Larry Fink mentions this windfall in his 2018 letter about purpose:

In the United States companies should explain to investors how the significant changes to tax law fit into their long-term strategy. What will you do with increased after-tax cash flow, and how will you use it to create long-term value?

This was a moment when purpose could have been turned into investment. Unfortunately, what actually happened was a Vegas-style shareholder jackpot with zero long-term investment.

Trump cut the corporate tax from 35% to 21%. AT&T received an immediate tax benefit of $21 billion; a sum comparable with their entire operating profit of $26 billion. Like most corporates who lobbied for tax cuts, AT&T promised to create jobs and invest. Since the tax cuts, the *Guardian* reported that AT&T did the opposite of what it promised, reducing capital expenditure by $1.4 billion and cutting 23 000 jobs. It wasn't just AT&T. A Washington research organisation found that only 4% of workers saw pay increases as a result of tax cuts. Wells Fargo made a statement that they increased minimum wages to $15 an hour. The *Guardian* reported:

> The bank's 2018 tax savings were 47 times more than the costs of its minimum wage increases. Rather than invest in its workforce, Wells Fargo bought back shares in early 2018, worth about $22.6bn, increased CEO salary by 36%, and announced plans in September 2018 to eliminate at least 26,000 jobs in the US over the next three years.

Blowing the largest tax windfall in American history on share buybacks (that hand the cash to shareholders) and bonuses was a monumental lost opportunity. The tax cuts could have been used to fund green infrastructure investments. Investments that will pay back in the medium term but take capital expenditure up front. Creating long term value and climate progress.

Analysts found that while a small fraction (1/30th) of the tax proceeds did go into pay increases there was zero benefit for investment. The independent, non-partisan Congressional Research Service found that, 'net investment as a share of GDP stayed below its levels in 2014. The tax cuts did not accelerate investment as promised by supply-side advocates.'[47]

One company that steered a different course is Patagonia. They were due to receive $10 million in tax windfall thanks to the Trump 2017 corporate tax cuts. A drop in the ocean compared to the billions handed to companies like AT&T and Wells Fargo. But still a bonanza. What did Patagonia do? They gave it to the planet. As their CEO Rose Marcario shared in an open letter:

Based on last year's irresponsible tax cut, Patagonia will owe less in taxes this year – $10 million less, in fact. Instead of putting the money back into our business, we're responding by putting $10 million back into the planet. Our home planet needs it more than we do. Our home planet is facing its greatest crisis because of human-caused climate disruption. All the extra heat we've trapped in the earth's atmosphere is not only melting the poles and raising sea levels, it's intensifying drought and accelerating the extinction of species . . . Mega-fires. Toxic algae blooms. Deadly heat waves and hurricanes. Far too many have suffered the consequences of global warming, the political response has so far been woefully inadequate, and the denial is just evil.

You have to applaud Patagonia for a move that was wholly consistent with their core purpose:

Patagonia is in business to save our home planet.

This purpose has clear direct benefits to their business. For instance, according to Glassdoor:

91% of Patagonia employees say this is a great place to work.
95% say 'I feel good about the ways we contribute to the community'.
94% say 'I'm proud to tell others I work here'.

If they ran engagement surveys they'd be off the charts. But they don't, according to Dean Carter head of human resources, because 'it's not important to know if employees are 97 percent or 98 percent engaged'. Good for Patagonia.

According to Gallup, in 2018 'The percentage of engaged workers in the U.S. – those involved in, enthusiastic about and committed to their work and workplace – is now 34%.' This is a sad indictment of modern capitalism. Two thirds of all employees not enthused or committed.[48]

There was a telling survey by the Global Wellness Institute in 2016.[49] In America around half the employees had workplace wellness programmes. The key question GWI asked was *why does your company have this programme?*

25% of employees think it is because their company genuinely cares about its people.
75% believe it is only there to reduce insurance premiums or increase productivity.

The study shows that these two views massively determine responses on every other measure:

Employee Response to Survey Among	25% Who Believe Company Cares	75% Who Believe It's Insurance/Productivity
Rate their health/wellness high	57%	39%
Rate their health/wellness poor	8%	21%
Report very high stress	17%	41%
Report their work as satisfying	52%	25%
. . . exciting	33%	16%
. . . interesting	66%	30%
Proud to be associated with the company	68%	16%

Correlation is not causation. But this does show a polarisation into great places to work vs companies that don't care for employees, making them sick and disaffected in the process. Global Wellness CEO Susie Ellis commented:

> The findings surprised us: we saw significant, diverse and positive implications when a company is perceived to care about an employee's personal wellness, and extremely negative outcomes when it was perceived as a non-caring company.

It doesn't seem that surprising to me.

Surely it is significant that the CEOs of Amazon, Walmart, General Motors, IBM, and JP Morgan acknowledge business needs to have a social purpose and serve the needs of all?

But does it go far enough?

The World Resources Institute (WRI) gave the Business Round Table a withering review:

> Let's face it: We are in urgent need of transformative, disruptive change at a global level. We don't need just more of the same – we need innovative, sustainable business models. And the best some of the largest corporations can offer is a plan that was considered cutting-edge in the 1990s? It is equivalent to Apple announcing a new portable cassette player.[50]

More constructively the WRI put forward three proposed additions to the BRT manifesto:

Delivering customers environmentally and socially sustainable products and services. This means embracing circular economy models, such as designing for longevity and reuse, and being willing to rebalance product portfolios away from unchecked consumption and damaging products toward full sustainability.

Using corporate brands and political influence to support systemic changes that ensure equitable opportunities for all. This means lobbying for climate-positive legislation and increasing corporate transparency; using brand and advertising to lead customers from unsustainable to sustainable behaviors.

Acknowledging that the resources upon which businesses depend are limited, and business models that thrive within the available resources of the planet are needed. This means setting and acting on emissions-reduction and other sustainability targets that are science-based and meet the needs of all human society, not just the corporate world.

We covered most of those ideas in the first section of this book.
I would make three further suggestions:

1. Commit to their responsibility to future generations, to leaving a lasting positive legacy. One way to keep this honest and relevant would be to assemble an advisory board of younger people with a keen interest in both planetary limits and social development.
2. Commit to long termism and tackle the root causes of short termism. Frame plans and proposals in 5-year (urgent, significant, and immediate enough) and 50-year time frames.
3. Define a meaningful purpose that drives your core strategy, is additional or different to what you did before, is a big stretch and is a Net Good on social and planetary benefits (And, as WRI notes, do check these targets against the science and external frameworks to ensure they are radical enough).

Does that all sound super idealistic and unrealistic?

Unilever did not think so. Keith Weed, former CMO, has often spoken out for including young people and disruptive innovators in the heart of business decision making: 'Business leaders – bring young people into your organisations and let them shape them from within with their fresh ideas.'[51]

As for the second and third points, those were arguably the key achievements of Keith's boss, the former Unilever CEO Paul Polman.

Polman started out by challenging the short termism caused by the time horizons of investors who held Unilever stock for an average of only 17 weeks. (No wonder they were focused on this quarter's results. Most weren't even planning to hold the stock for a second quarter.)

Polman did what so few CEOs dare to do. He took a stand:

> One of the things I had to do was to move the business to a longer-term plan. We had become victims of chasing our own tail, cutting our internal spending in capital, R&D, or IT to reach the market expectations. We were developing our brand spends on a quarterly basis and not doing the right things, simply because the business was not performing. We were catering to the shorter-term shareholders. So I said, 'We will stop quarterly reporting, and we will stop giving guidance.'[52]

Shares fell by 8%, as short-term investors dumped the stock and rejected this plan. But others (like pension funds) with a longer-term view stayed and grew their holding. By 2017, Unilever's top fifty shareholders had an average holding period of over seven years. This gave Polman the remit to develop a long-term vision. Ten years later as he passed the baton on to the next CEO, Polman was able to tweet 'It's been a great honour to lead this team for the past 10 years and together build a #sustbiz that has made a difference to millions of lives.'

Polman's radical strategy was the Sustainable Living Plan, launched in 2010. This promised by 2020 to grow the company to twice its size, while halving (relative to size) its environmental impact. It also promised to help a billion people take action to improve their wellbeing. And to enhance the livelihoods of millions of people. There are detailed metrics under each ambition. A 2018 review showed that Unilever had met some targets, for instance a 52% reduction in emissions from energy use. However, it was behind on others, such as only 56% of agricultural products being certified (the target was 100%).

The Unilever Plan had decent overall goals. But the cutting edge of its plan – where social purpose came in – was individual brands and their ability to shape lives, habits, and mindsets.

Unilever rolled out a Brand Imprint programme. The typical format was a two-day workshop with several external speakers (I attended some of these sessions) and a team drawn from across the business, including brand management but also production, logistics, sustainability, and so on. The aim was simple. Come up with three new actions relevant to the brand that would contribute significantly to the overall Sustainable Living Plan.

The case study that you used to see a lot on the sustainability conference circuit was the Lifebuoy soap story. A 2019 report on the brand's impact claims that over the last 10 years of handwashing education programmes – like World Handwashing Day – the brand reached 458 million people. The recent Lifebuoy report says that globally (UNICEF estimated) there has been a '36% reduction in childhood deaths from diarrhoea from 2008–2016, equivalent to over 265,000 lives saved'. Something Lifebuoy contributed to. The brand purpose is 'to help parents ensure their children fall ill less often'. The absolute numbers hardly matter; if they saved even a few lives, it's a noble cause. Unilever has pointed out that social purpose went back to their founder Lord Lever being concerned to make cleanliness commonplace.

Some brands in Unilever had a defined purpose before the Sustainable Living Plan. Like the Dove *Campaign for Real Beauty* (empowering women and girls by tackling media representations and body images), or Persil's *It's Not Dirt* (encouraging parents to get their children to play outdoors more, get dirty, play away from screen time).

Their brand which most changed its spots during the Sustainable Living Brand era was Lynx/Axe. Previously their advertising told men to 'spray more to get more' and was known for glamorous commercials packed with objectified images of women. This was always incongruous next to Dove in the portfolio – prompting commentators including yours truly to ask: is Unilever feminist or not?

More recently the Axe brand has set its core purpose as Redefining Masculinity. The thought being that men still use fragranced deodorants in the hope of being attractive, but that what women really find attractive is men who are comfortable with themselves. So, the brand set out to empower men to express their individuality. This helped them identify some interesting NGO partners to work with like: Ditch the Label, Promundo, and The Representation Project. It also helped Lynx stretch into new grooming products and appeal beyond the teen market.

Another Unilever brand that redefined its purpose was Hellmann's. Hellmann's is known for sauces like Mayonnaise and Ketchup. These ultimately come from farms and farmers. A new generation has grown up with no sense that food comes from anywhere except a supermarket or the fridge. Hellmann's set out to change that by championing real food and the people who grow and harvest it. They of course also set sustainability standards for the eggs, tomatoes, and so on. But then it's an opportunity to reach mainstream families and involve them in food again – something Hellmann's did in imaginative ways, like live streaming from tomato farms in Latin America and inviting families in Canada to come visit rapeseed farms.

Unilever bought the longstanding eco brand Seventh Generation in 2016 and this brand (along with Ben & Jerry's) enabled Unilever to test just how far it could go with brand activism and a deeper sustainability vision. Seventh Generation is named after the idea (credited to the Hopi) that big decisions should always be taken with the seventh generation in mind. Unilever's redefinition of its purpose was to bring the brand to mainstream consumers and grow the audience. It's often the case that the more socially positive a brand is intrinsically, the more commercially minded its marketing strategy tends to be.

Seventh Generation succeeded in expanding the brand by using humour and humanity to broach subjects like sustainable tampons. Comedian and rock star Maya Rudolph starred in hilarious commercials titled things like 'and now an important message about vaginas'.

The year 2019 brought a different theme as Seventh Generation got behind the climate strikes. Making content where young people explained the movement (seriously – if you want to see how badly Pepsi got it wrong with Kylie Jenner, watch the online videos to understand what the lost opportunity was for brands to engage with the protests).

Seventh Generation then handed their entire ad budget to 350.org and closed their offices to join the climate strikes in person. It's what you would have expected Seventh Generation to do – just like Patagonia and other brands who really take a lead on environmental causes. But it's also totally in line with their (post Unilever) brand vision. And makes commercial sense too. Environmental sustainability is going mainstream. And Seventh Generation have excellent products to promote, like their washing detergents made purely from plants, not petroleum.

The ad was created for 350.org by my friends at Futerra and shot by Rankin (founder of *Dazed & Confused* magazine). The script features climate activists explaining themselves as follows:

Hi I'm out of the office
Because I'm out of patience
And we're out of time
This is a climate crisis
So I'm out on strike
In the streets
For climate justice
For all our futures
Join the Climate strike
Are you with me?

A multinational corporation made this happen. And to their credit they didn't even put their name to it. This shows (to paraphrase Greta Thunberg) that you can make a difference, no matter how big you are.

2.6 Every Business a Social Venture

Harvard Business School professor Michael Porter (with co-author Mark Kramer) in 2006 put forward the concept of Creating Shared Value (CSV). This was presented as an alternative to traditional business strategy that positioned corporate social responsibility (CSR) and charitable giving as an afterthought:

> Shared value is a management strategy in which companies find business opportunities in social problems. While philanthropy and CSR focus efforts focus on 'giving back' or minimizing the harm business has on society, shared value focuses company leaders on maximizing the competitive value of solving social problems in new customers and markets, cost savings, talent retention, and more.[53]

The radical idea here is not the one about solving social problems with a commercial venture. The idea of a social venture was well established. Early examples included Grameen, The Big Issue, and Toms Shoes. According to research by GEM in 2018, one third of the companies started globally were social ventures.[54]

The radical idea here is that *every* company should be a social venture.

This means having a commercial mission that drives revenues, growth, and profit. But making this money through products and services that solve social problems, unlock opportunities, and in so doing bring a net positive contribution to society and the planet.

Say you were a sports apparel company. Like Nike. If you are honest with yourself, you are currently a fashion business, used by a minority of customers for sport.

I said this once to the global marketing director of Nike. He insisted that they are a sport company and told me they banned the mention of 'fashion' from internal discussions. But the facts speak against this. According to NPD Group data, 25% of those buying athletic shoes said they would actually use them for athletics and sports. The figures varied by brand. ASICS were two thirds bought for sports. Under Armor around half. Nike and Adidas around one third. About two thirds of Nike revenues come from trainers (and one third from clothing). So, half of Nike's business is people buying trainers to wear as fashion with no intent of doing sport.

From a sustainability point of view, using performance sports shoes for fashion is problematic. It's a bit like buying a tractor to use as your car around town. A study by MIT found that 'A typical pair of running shoes comprises 65 discrete parts requiring more than 360 processing steps to assemble, from sewing and cutting to injection molding, foaming and heating.'[55]

Technical running shoes are hard to make sustainable. VEJA launched an attempt at a post-petroleum running shoe in 2019. The upper is 100% recycled plastic bottles, midsole is 55% rubber and 45% bio-based materials (banana oil, sugar cane, and rice husk). VEJA admit there's a long way to go, as it still uses virgin plastic in the sole. VEJA co-founder Sebastien Kopp commented: 'A running shoe has to have flexibility, strength, and memory; plastic is the best and cheapest material to do that.'[56] Overall this shoe is 47% virgin plastic. Whereas VEJA's overt (made for fashion) everyday sneakers are much simpler to make and are designed to be sustainable from the ground up.

As well as the waste of wearing performance shoes for everyday walking, there is the wasteful nature of fashion per se. Around 24 billion pairs of shoes are sold every year. The average woman in the UK owned 24 pairs of shoes in 2017; 80% said there were shoes in their collection they had bought and never worn.[57]

So, here's the issue. People who buy shoes for sport actually need the technical performance and the eco footprint that goes with it. But they buy only a few pairs for specific needs. And it is good for society if they are fit, healthy, and engaged in sport with all its benefits. People who buy shoes purely for fashion buy more pairs and buy them to keep up with trends, match new outfits, or just on a whim. VEJA try to counter this by making shoes in classic styles that you can wear season after season. But it's a stretch to describe fashion as a social benefit.

One greener marketing strategy could be to hack the shoe buying process. Ask about intended use and then provide an identical looking shoe with the right level of performance and an eco-footprint and price to match. I would argue we already apply this logic to computers. Here, if you want performance (which uses more energy) for gaming or multimedia production, you do have to pay a lot more. People don't buy computers with high end GPUs because they light up or heat the room. They buy them for the better framerates and smoother gameplay.

The idea I once suggested to Nike (that they hated) was to charge people for technical running shoes based on fitness. Run on a treadmill. We'll then measure how long it takes your heart to return to its resting rate. If the next Mo Farah walked in the store, they'd get shoes for nothing. But a couch potato could pay $500. Nike rightly pointed out that this was discrimination. But you could also limit technical sports shoes – on prescription – to those with a letter from their coach or sports club. And do a mid-range shoe for those who just need a cross trainer to run and go to the gym in.

What could a CSV (creating social value) strategy look like?

What if instead of accepting that you sell performance trainers and apparel as fashion you instead tried to get the people who buy your shoes to take exercise?

This would ensure that your technical efforts were not wasted. But also, you would be aligning your business model and strategy with social good. Of the world's population, 30% is obese or overweight. Resulting in health problems like heart disease, diabetes, high blood pressure, and stroke. The problem is getting worse. The WHO estimates that the proportion of the population who are obese more than doubled between 1980 and 2014. If trends continue half the global population will be overweight or obese by 2030. The WHO also quantified the economic cost, totalling $2 trillion or 2.8% of global GDP.[58] That is a huge social problem worth solving. And if it takes some virgin plastic and stitching, so be it; we can cut carbon elsewhere.

What could a company born out of a desire to tackle adult inactivity look like?

Actually, we already know the answer. It would look like Nike.

The legendary sports coach and co-founder of Nike, Bill Bowerman, wrote a bestselling book in 1967 (five years before the launch of Nike) called *Jogging, Running for Fun*. The word jogging was his invention. The ensuing keep fit craze catapulted Nike into a different league. They had originally set out to make technical running shoes for athletes. Nike's original business plan had anticipated sales of $1 million. But with the jogging craze they soon exceeded $1 billion. The waffle iron running shoe that was perfect for road races was also perfect for joggers running a couple of miles every day. Bowerman once said: 'if you have a body you are an athlete'.

Today history is repeating itself. A brand called Outdoor Voices (OV) promotes #doingthings (their open and inclusive answer to Nike's 'just do it').

As the Outdoor Voices slogan says:

Doing Things Is Better Than Not Doing Things.

Outdoor Voices make the kind of fashionable athleisure that millennials wear to yoga class. OV is determined that their take on athleisure is not fashion, but designed for people to sweat or stretch in. OV organises things like dog walking and yoga in the park as well as running with friends, which is founder Tyler Haney's favourite thing in life. The designs are feminine and fashionable – helpful in popularising everyday non-competitive exercise. The inclusiveness extends to body size and OV win regular praise for featuring plus size models. Their 2019 summer collection featured a model in a wheelchair. Haney commented:

We put real people at the centre of everything that we do, so it was a no brainer to include Aaron. She is a key player in this campaign because of the energy she exudes and the strength she carries, and we are excited to have her on Team OV.[59]

The *New Yorker* described Outdoor Voices as blurring the lines between working out and everything else; 'in the absence of quantified results and competitive pressure, physical activity will feel like play'. Playfulness saturates the brand. The OV name comes from the Haney's childhood when her mother would shush her with the expression 'use your indoor voice'. One of Haney's first product designs (when a teen working in the holidays at her parents' sportswear company) was a t-shirt saying, 'Famous People Wear This Shit'.

The conclusion? Not Bad means trying to make less unsustainable sports shoes and apparel. Net Good means getting people who buy them to do more exercise.

For Porter, setting a purpose for your company or brand is not just a vision statement exercise. Purpose means shifting to a new business model. In a 2018 presentation on how to put Shared Value into action[60] Michael Porter pointed out that the largest markets are often those where social needs go unserved. Porter listed some examples:

energy efficiency
environmental improvement
water use
education and skills
health
worker safety
affordable housing
economic development
jobs for low income citizens.

Tackling these will involve stepping out of conventional consumer markets and entering spaces of market failure traditionally occupied by the public sector and charities. Porter says that the choice to play in these spaces is strategic – not to do with personal or collective values or 'doing good' but building competitive advantage. It involves designing a value chain and defining a value proposition. It is serious business.

Porter cites IKEA as an example. IKEA's visionary purpose from day one has been to *improve the everyday life of the majority of people*. Their value proposition is offering affordable furnishings to people with limited budget and space, who are design conscious. The value chain – how IKEA operates to achieve this – is utterly distinct from the rest of the industry in its scale, scope, efficiency, and innovation. This is the company that invented out of town shopping and flat packs and continues to reinvent itself for the digital age. All because (in the words of their classic ad slogan in Sweden) IKEA is *for the smart, not for the rich*.

Based on his understanding of how organisations develop an effective strategy, Porter put forward a process for Creating Shared Value with three buckets of distinct activity:[61]

1. Reconceiving Needs, Products, and (unserved or underserved) Customers.

   An example is Max Levchin (former PayPal co-founder) whose start-up Affirm offers credit to buy things to underserved segments in the US, such as young adults, single mothers, and immigrants. Levchin innovated with big data analytics behind the scenes looking at how to only lend when the consumer should be spending and also how (unlike credit cards) to create an institution that 'doesn't benefit off of its customers screwing up'.

   In late 2019, Affirm raised a further $1.5 billion of capital so clearly this is a big market. The scheme is not without critics. But Levchin seems to be trying to build a great business in markets most banks won't touch. His fellow PayPal alumni include Elon Musk the TESLA founder; also a Shared Value company with its mission to *accelerate the world's transition to sustainable energy*.

2. Redefining Productivity in the Value Chain.

   A good example is Interface carpets. I saw their CEO Ray Andersen speak at a sustainability event in the early 2000s. He told us how he went on holiday, read a book, and realised he had to do something about the environmental crisis for the sake of his grandchildren. Andersen's original idea was to leave Interface, his family-owned office carpet business, and go work for Greenpeace. But he realised that his core skills were in carpets not campaigning. So, Andersen resolved instead to make Interface part of the solution. The result was one of the first modern circular economy businesses. The first step was leasing carpets rather than selling them, so that Interface could manage the sustainability of carpets and reclaim materials at end of life.

   I met someone who had worked at Interface during this transition and they told me that what people seeing this case study don't appreciate is the *Herculean effort* it took to bring colleagues at Interface – a conservative business to business organisation – around to Andersen's way of thinking. If Andersen hadn't owned the company, it might not have even happened?

3. Improving the Local Business Environment.

An example is Natura Cosmetics and their business programme in the favelas of Rio. I worked (with Pentagram the design agency) on the brand strategy for Natura. As part of our induction we went to see their favela project. If you want to understand what life was like in favelas before the army moved in, watch the Oscar nominated *A City of God* (2002) based on a true story and set in a real favela called *Cidade de Deus*. Wikipedia defines a favela as:

Unregulated type of slum neighbourhood in Brazil that has experienced historical governmental neglect; in present day Rio about one in five people live in a favela.

We were guided on a tour of this particular district by Beto, a former member of the special forces involved in the 'pacification' of the favelas (the army moved in and criminal armed gangs made a sharp exit). Beto was a cool dude in shades and a CSI T-Shirt who had starred in a TV documentary and taken a PR role.

It was Beto who first convinced Natura to come and create a sales network business in the favelas. It wasn't easy. Natura came in several years before the army. And the Natura management repeatedly insisted when we talked to them that 'this isn't charity, it is business'. The favelas, we learned, were mostly populated by women and young children. Many men and older boys were in prison for drugs and arms offences. These women had jobs in the city and worked hard to bring up their families. Natura had come in and recruited them as sales agents.

Beto had gone to Natura and given an emotional speech a week after a close friend and colleague had been shot dead. He told the story of what life was like there. With children on street corners carrying war guns. Beto told Natura that he could never solve the problem of violence with yet more violence. Only bringing the promise of a better life could improve things. Natura themselves had issues with the favelas, like their trucks getting hijacked. But the argument that won them over was this: 'you cannot make a healthy business in a sick society'.

Natura is not the only large company to tackle employment and social development. Diageo – owner of drinks brands like Guinness and Johnnie Walker – has a scheme called *Learning for Life*. This started as a programme in Latin America and the Caribbean and spread worldwide to 40 global countries and 140 000 participants. *Learning for Life* takes unemployed people and teaches them the skills they need to work in the hospitality sector, including providing work experience. *Learning for Life* trains a new generation of bartenders, baristas, and restaurant waiters. It is putting back into the ecosystem that Diageo relies upon.

When you look closer at companies who do things like this you find a consistent pattern. Diageo were Britain's most respected company in 2018. They were one of the first companies to adopt science-based targets – a movement that has grown by now to 819 companies committed to 'driving ambitious corporate climate action'. Diageo ranked 31st in the 50 Best Places to Work UK by Glassdoor – the only beverages company and only FMCG to make the list. Anglian Water was #1 (while Google tumbled from first place to #13 in a year when staff had staged walkouts over #metoo issues). IKEA also made the list. As did the BBC.

Diageo is a company focused on doing the right thing. It's not as showy in its commitments to sustainability as Unilever. But the company has deep roots in this way of doing business. Guinness in Ireland or Desnoes and Geddes (the Red Stripe brewery) in Jamaica are well known for supporting their community. Of course, Diageo makes alcoholic drinks and if you were tallying net contribution to society that would be a debate. (Diageo are also active investors in the low and no alcohol category, acquiring Seedlip in August 2019.)

What Diageo bring with *Learning for Life* is not just training but the dignity and prestige of their brand. I once ran a workshop for Microsoft with retail sales professionals in mobile phone shops. As part of this we tested concepts their agency had come up with to incentivise salespeople to sell more Microsoft devices; typically, things like 'win free music festival passes'. The concept which won – by a mile – in the workshops was:

WIN A JOB AT MICROSOFT

Young sales reps saw this as a dream job for a company that is defining the future of technology. And it wasn't just these workshops. Glassdoor in the US found that Microsoft ranked #6 in the companies millennials would most like to work at.

Microsoft is another prime example of a large company successfully adopting a purpose led strategy. And unlike the previous examples, they chose to do this without targeting the underserved – but rather recognising the potential of their core offer to create social good.

The strategy was set by their new (in 2014) CEO Sataya Nadella. He's nowhere near as brash and aggressive as previous generations of leadership. But during his time at Microsoft the share price has quadrupled, significantly outperforming even their archrival Apple.[62] I worked on a brief for Microsoft when Nadella was new in the job, coming up with an initiative to get the whole company together. Our idea was originally called *One Day* (it later became *One Week*, a shame as 'one day' also referred to the future). Nadella seemed a new kind of leader; an Obama to his predecessor's Bush.

Five months into the job, Nadella sent an all staff memo defining a fresh purpose for Microsoft:

Empower every person and every organization on the planet to achieve more.

It's an artful encapsulation for a company that had grown super diverse. Originally known for Windows (the operating system), Microsoft now included Skype, Xbox, Office, Nokia, Azure (Nadella's previous job), the cloud platform, and many more. But while the purpose statement is all embracing, it's also quite tight. The logic of this statement is to:

do what empowers people and organisations, not just what suits us.

A signature action in his first year was Nadella announcing you could now use Office on the iPad. Preventing iPad users from accessing these programmes was a bad decision for empowering the user, even if it favoured Microsoft devices and those powered by Windows.

The Microsoft family continued to grow – but with the acquisition of what are clearly empowering platforms like GitHub, LinkedIn, and (in a different way) Minecraft.

Microsoft did also make an effort to extend their reach. Including underserved populations.

For instance, there is their 4Afrika programme:

investing in start-ups, partners, small-to-medium enterprises, governments and youth on the African continent. Our focus has been on delivering affordable access to the internet, developing skilled workforces and investing in local technology solutions. Africa has the potential to lead the technology revolution – and so we're empowering those with the right ideas to drive economic development, inclusive growth and digital transformation.[63]

Academics reviewing Michael Porter's Shared Value idea have suggested that the key line of thinking which led up to it was not Sustainability, but rather Development – for instance the 'bottom of the pyramid'. Business guru C.K. Prahalad urged this approach in 2002 saying:

> For companies with the resources and persistence to compete at the bottom of the world economic pyramid, the prospective rewards include growth, profits, and incalculable contributions to humankind. Countries that still don't have the modern infrastructure or products to meet basic human needs are an ideal testing ground for developing environmentally sustainable technologies and products for the entire world.

One of Prahalad's case examples was Unilever's laundry business in India which – spurred on by a local competitor – had developed a profitable business selling sachets of detergent designed for people who wash their clothes in rivers and public water systems. Total sales of their new brand Wheel had reached $100 million (compared to $180 million in sales from the premium products Unilever traditionally sold to the Indian middle classes). Their return on investment from the fast-growing Wheel brand was 93% (compared to only 22% for their old portfolio).[64]

Unilever went on to replicate this success in Brazil with a similar brand called Ala.

We saw in the section on plastic that this success story brought unintended consequences. But it was still an important chapter in the development of corporate business thinking.

Prahalad pointed out that the real challenge for managers is not technology, innovation, distribution, or finance. It is having the imagination to see a market where currently you see only abject poverty. The benefits of a scheme like this are not only the better lives with cleaner clothes (and hopefully less polluted waterways) but also the jobs created in distributing and selling the products. I worked with Coca-Cola in the 1990s on a potential soft drink social business for sub-Saharan Africa. This would need no fridges and would cost pence in local currency (whereas a bottle of Coke in equivalent local spending power terms was $25). But the big potential win was creating work in delivery and collection of bottles (for deposit return) by local entrepreneurs in the *Jua Kali* (African informal economy). A decade later this same population was home to MPESA, the world's first successful mobile currency. The bottom of the pyramid isn't just about scale, it is about disruptive innovation born out of tough conditions.

The Shared Value concept can also have a sub-purpose. We've seen Unilever applying a different relevant purpose to each brand. You can also have a purpose that tackles only one aspect of your operations. For instance: 'Vodafone aspires to be the world's best employer for women by 2025'. This doesn't mean that Vodafone will only hire women or only sell phones to women. It is a sub-objective that is good for the world and also for attracting the best talent.

A corporate purpose doesn't have to be social. It can be directed at tackling the climate crisis.

In 2019, 99% of investors backed a resolution calling for BP to prove its business plan was in line with the Paris climate agreement. A sub-clause of the same resolution calls for executive pay to be linked to this target. BP are being held to account by the very shareholders who were previously implicated in short termism. Carbon Disclosure Project research showed the number of shareholder resolutions about climate issues doubled over the last five years.[65]

In fashion, a growing movement of 30+ brands were joined by Condé Nast (the magazine group that owns *Vogue*) signing the UNFCC Fashion Industry for Climate Action. This commits the signatories to set science-based emissions reduction targets in line with the 1.5 degrees trajectory set out in the Paris Agreement. Condé Nast has also joined the Ellen Macarthur New Plastics Economy Commitment, meaning it has until 2025 to remove all non-recycled plastics.

The Condé Nast move was welcomed because fashion and media have a disproportionate influence on culture and lifestyles. The UNFCC's press release revealed that Condé Nast will work with industry partners to promote 'the re-use of clothes, sustainable fashion, innovative materials and technologies' and that 'Condé Nast intends to empower and educate consumers on how to lead more sustainable lives through the different lenses of the company's leading media brands including *Vogue*, *GQ*, *Wired* and *AD*'.

The idea of Shared Value may have been published by business school professors, but it was also being pioneered 'out there' in real businesses.

Indra Nooyi, PepsiCo CEO from 2006 to 2018, introduced *Performance with Purpose*:

> delivering top-tier financial returns by making more nutritious foods and beverages, limiting our impact on the planet, and supporting the people who live and work in the communities we serve. [66]

Not only did this deliver 80% growth in revenues, but they also increased what Nooyi describes as 'more nutritious offerings' from 38% to 50% of PepsiCo sales. This strategy led to significant acquisitions like Naked Juice. They identified water as a key issue – in a world with increasing water stress and risk – and announced a positive water impact strategy. In recent results, the current CEO highlighted their new brand Bubly – a fruit infused water offering a healthy alternative to sodas – that he said was on track to be their next billion-dollar brand.

If you want to tackle obesity as a world issue, you need to start where Pepsi starts, with the consumers they reach. McKinsey looked at 47 interventions that can solve the obesity crisis. The top three (in years of life saved) were: portion control, reformulation of food products, and (limiting) availability of high calorie food and beverages. All things that PepsiCo can tackle. Dr Karl Morten, a leading expert in diabetes research at Oxford Uni, once told me that the obesity crisis came down to 'a biscuit a day' – a constant 'drip drip' of too many calories. When Pepsi launches flavourful alternatives to sodas like Bubly, or when Cadbury and Heinz reduce their sugar content, it can make all the difference. Governments can also play a role by introducing a sugar tax. But ultimately, to tackle the obesity crisis you need to shift that 'biscuit a day'.

The modern way to think about creating Shared Value is the concept of impact investing – measuring the social benefits of a business just as rigorously as the financial metrics. A former colleague of mine, Ramona Liberoff, used to run the Spring Accelerator. Their scope was defined by just one impact measure – empowering teen girls:

> An estimated 250 million adolescent girls worldwide live in poverty, unable to pursue learning, build assets or safely raise the income needed for a more prosperous life.

Impact investors need to be as lateral thinking as entrepreneurs in spotting commercial opportunities that also drive social benefits. An example in the case of Spring was a floor coating company in Rwanda called Earth Enable.

In Rwanda, 75% of homes have dirt floors. Concrete floors are expensive, costing an average of two months' household income. Earth Enable floors are much cheaper, costing on average $80 per home. Dirt floors are bad for health, harbouring microbes, mosquitos, and parasites. Healthy floors reduce childhood diarrhoea by 50% and parasite infections by 80% plus conditions like asthma. Earth floors are also much better for the environment than the alternatives. Concrete has a big carbon impact due to the energy cost (5% of global emissions). According to the Earth Enable website, their floors have 90% less embedded energy than concrete.

Earth Enable are also (despite the earthy sounding name) the result of a technical innovation. Compressed earth floors are already growing in popularity in the West. But these use linseed oil to seal them which is too expensive for Rwanda. Earth Enable found another solution:

> With the help of chemistry PhD Rick Zuzow from Stanford University, a new oil was created which could seal the floors properly and safely at a cost of 90% less than linseed oil. The oil permeates the fine earthen mix and forms a waterproof and plastic-like resin on top. This is also the layer that gives the floor its shine, makes it easy to clean and incredibly durable.

What on earth does this have to do with impact investing to empower teen girls?

Easy to clean and healthy both mean more time to study. Spring is a VC fund. They are looking for stellar returns as well as a clear quantifiable impact on teen girls' lives. Flooring is a smart commercial investment in a product that – while small now – is aiming to replace 2 million dirt floors by 2025 and in the long term replace the estimated global 300 million dirt floors. If they succeed, the Earth Enable business will have revenues in the billions of dollars. Earth Enable started life at a Stanford programme called Design for Extreme Affordability. Other projects include cooking, (solar) refrigeration, energy, agricultural, and fishery innovations.

As well as their impact, social purpose businesses can also have a big influence.

'Setting a positive example' is a key motivation that I have heard from many entrepreneurs. One example is Eric Ryan, co-founder of Method (and now a vitamin company called Olly). Method was never about to take over from the soap giants in revenues, but they created a debate about chemicals in the home; what is safe (or 'clean') from an environmental and health point of view. And they showed how eco could be human, sexy, mainstream, and aspirational.

The Warby Parker founders Dave Gilboa and Neil Blumenthal also talk about how influencing other businesses was a core part of their mission from the outset:

> . . . we hoped to demonstrate that it was possible to build a business that grew quickly, was profitable, and did good in the world - and that our example would inspire other entrepreneurs and executives to use their businesses to make a positive impact.[67]

Impact investing is obsessed with metrics. Warby Parker measures itself using the Global Reporting Initiative (GRI). It is unusual for a small private company to go to those lengths.

GRI is a rigorous framework used by most of the largest companies in the world. The important thing being that third parties such as journalists, NGOs and regulators can compare your GRI performance with others using common measures and standards.

Metrics matter. But the important thing to understand about leadership in companies like Warby Parker is that they are all about qualities, not quantities. They are led by values and principles. Just like a human being who conducts their life based on values:

> In the early days of Warby Parker, we gathered our first 20 or so team members and asked them, and ourselves, to reflect on the principles by which they lived. Work aside, just think about what gets you up in the morning and what keeps you going (no pressure). These first employees were the nucleus of Warby Parker, and their personal values helped inform the company's values. They wrote down over 200 ideals – many of them overlapped – and every employee voted on what would become the organization-wide standards of accountability, our core values. Nearly 10 years later, these remain the key pillars against which we weigh every decision.

If your organisations haven't done this exercise, I can highly recommend it. We did something very similar back when starting our journey at St

Luke's. Wherever I have seen trailblazing leadership and innovation it often starts with this kind of reflection on why? and how?

2.7 Is it a Purpose (or Just a Pose?)

In the 1990s, only a couple of brands stood out for mixing politics and commerce. Body Shop who we worked with at St Luke's was one. Another was Benetton. Benetton were known for brightly coloured Italian wool jumpers. Hence their famous United Colors of Benetton campaign. Which makes lexical sense. But it was (and still is) an odd juxtaposition of mainstream fashion and edgy activism.

In 1984, creative director Oliviero Toscani started casting multiracial models in ads. United Colors of Benetton then developed into a conceptual theme about uniting opposites; a black woman breastfeeding a white baby, living friends gathered around a man dying of AIDS, a nun and a priest kissing.

Benetton founded Fabrica, an art school with a radical social agenda. And published *Colors* magazine where design and politics mixed. *Colors* was about visual anthropology. It would use visual essays to show things like human hair culture; from African indigenous people to pubic hair grooming in America. This was not about the 'latest look'. It was about looking at ourselves. What it means to be human. Toscani and Benetton didn't only advertise their brand, they also applied that brand to useful things like selling condoms.

Toscani was often asked why his advertising was so political. All fashion advertising is political, he responded. It showed women as objects; valorised white middle class genetically perfect (but thin) models. His advertising was also political, but it represented the diversity value of the company and its audience rather than the homogenising dictatorship of globalised culture.

The core Benetton value is tolerance. A human universal message that few would argue with in theory. People seemed to object more to the challenging way it was presented. When Benetton showed a multiracial lesbian couple with a baby, they did not make it 'sexy' or exotic in an orientalist way, they made the subjects look strident. When Benetton tackled race, they did so in visceral ways – like the three bloody hearts with the label: WHITE BLACK YELLOW. Benetton would not have felt out of place in an art gallery. What was unusual was its repurposing of the advertising space to critique society and discomfit the viewer.

The controversy caught up with them in 2000. An advertising campaign *We On Death Row* prompted a backlash in the United States. The campaign included a 100-page magazine supplement featuring photographs, profiles of prisoners, and their human stories. The stories were deeply affecting; one prisoner was so lonely he just wished someone would write to him, another was refused art materials so resorted to using coloured M&Ms to draw with. There was a chilling interview with a prison warden who said he only held prisoners' hands while they received a lethal injection if they repented first.

In Europe many would have agreed with the campaign; that capital punishment dehumanises a whole society. This is arguably an easier message here than Catholic hypocrisy, the politics of AIDS, or racial unity. In America clearly it is a different story. Several State governments sued Benetton (for breaching the terms under which they were given access to prisoners). Others called for a national boycott. Publicists deployed families of the victims in the media to whip up conservative hysteria. Sears Roebuck then tore up a franchise agreement and removed Benetton goods from their stores.

Toscani was unrepentant. 'I don't have to justify myself. Controversy is very useful. It's up to the other side to justify the shit they do. It is almost a Third Reich in these prisons.' But his boss at Benetton decided this had gone too far. And so, Benetton parted company with the visionary behind the brand.

The story has a footnote; in 2017, Toscani came back to Benetton. Benetton had already returned to the theme of intolerance with its *Unhate* campaign featuring world leaders kissing (the pope and an imam, the leaders of Palestine and Israel). And now Toscani returned to the fold in a move reminiscent of Apple rehiring Steve Jobs in 1996. *Vogue* interviewed Toscani and asked if he would return to the political advertising that he was famous for? Toscani replied:

> Why would you want to see clothes in an advert? You can just see them in our shops. On a billboard, I can show you how a company thinks, what it believes, what it represents. Advertising is primitive and powerful – it is more than art.

Sure enough, by June 2018 Benetton was back in the headlines for a poster featuring migrant boat people in life jackets. Right wing Italian politician Matteo Salvini tweeted: 'Am I the only one to find this despicable?'

Salvini is known for being anti-immigration. His reaction came as no surprise to Toscani, who commented to the BBC this 'makes me realise I'm right'.[68]

Today Benetton advertising like this seems far from shocking. We are now used to brands taking political stands. In the 2000s mainstream brands started finding a political voice.

Dove preached feminism and made YouTube videos viewed billions of times about subjects like the photoshopping of models.

Persil promoted the idea that children should get dirty while their laundry detergent would deal with the consequences. Their campaign *Dirt is Good* won awards for its combination of chilling facts (the average child goes out-doors less hours per day than a prison inmate) and creativity (a book with images that appear when you rub with dirt).

Ben & Jerry campaigned on social and environmental issues – for instance supporting same sex marriage celebrated with ice-cream (renaming *Chubby Hubby* flavour *Hubby Hubby*) and holding wedding ceremonies in store.

All three of these examples are from Unilever.

By 2019, 28 brands in the Unilever portfolio (including Dove, Knorr, Persil, Sure, Lipton, Hellman's, and Wall's) were included in the Sustainable Living division which means they are brands with a bigger social purpose than clean laundry and tasty food. Even Vaseline has extended its remit from chapped skin to disaster relief.

According to Unilever these brands are growing 69% faster than the rest of the business. Alan Jope, incoming CEO, described the results as showing: 'clear and compelling evidence that brands with purpose grow'. Adding that: 'Purpose creates relevance for a brand, it drives talkability, builds penetration and reduces price elasticity.'[69]

Jope went even further at the Cannes advertising festival telling journalists they would dispose of brands that don't stand for something. He revealed that Kantar are auditing all Unilever brands to see if consumers perceive them as having purpose driven goals. Those that fall short will be reviewed:

> There won't be a set deadline; it'll be a gradual process. But I would imagine in a few years' time we will look at our portfolio and the dramatic majority of our brands will be competing with a clear view on what little good they can do for society or the planet.[70]

The threat of disposing of brands that don't measure up is not an idle one. Unilever already sold off its spreads (margarine) division. This made sense commercially as it was a low growth category. And Unilever needed some cash to reward shareholders after seeing off the attempted takeover bid by Kraft. But the reason spreads were low growth was that health opinion had turned firmly against trans fats (and processed food in general). For an organisation dedicated to improving wellbeing, selling margarine had become incongruous.

Disposing of brands that don't suit your overall ethic proves you are serious. Might the Guardian Media Group struggle to be so supportive of Greta Thunberg and Extinction Rebellion if they had not divested fossil fuel investments in 2015 and sold off *Auto Trader* in 2014? Strictly, if you were pursuing benefit to society, perhaps you should shut it down rather than sell it off. But in the real world of balance sheets, at least if you don't make money from it that's something.

A trickle of ethical indie brands, then the mainstream brands from Unilever, has now become a torrent of packaged goods brands wearing campaigning hearts on their sleeves. We are at the stage with brand purpose that we were 15 years ago with greenwash. We are figuring out what is working (for the business and the cause), what is credible, what is jumping on the bandwagon.

What does it even mean for a brand to be purposeful? I've seen that phrase in numerous corporate briefs recently, asking agencies to come up with a relevant cause or purpose campaign. Here is an anonymised extract from one such brief that I was given:

> ___ has begun to define their purposeful positioning as a brand unlocking a more emotional space in people's minds. Creating distinction for the brand and consideration with their key target audiences. With a fresh and dynamic point of view on the world of ____ that people can really lean into. With their purposeful positioning locked down we now want to explore what that implies for the role the brand could play in addressing societal/environmental issues in a meaningful and credible way.

Fair enough. The brief says that the brand owner wants to have a meaningful, credible purpose.

Isn't it great that we are getting briefs like this rather than just one asking us to apply our creativity to helping _____ sell more? But there are dangers too, as when celebrities decide to boost their image by adopting charities. It runs the risk of tokenism. And of the greenwash issue where the virtuous image of your campaign far outstrips the truth of the company.

From the cause point of view – with celebrities or brands offering free publicity – what's not to like? There is a side of cause-related marketing it is hard argue with: generous corporates willing to give marketing to causes who will benefit from their budget, reach, and ability to grab people.

This kind of brief has become the new normal in 2019.

I met a design agency recently that had failed to win a pitch. They had pitched the idea – beyond the scope of the client brief – that the brand adopt a social purpose. The pitch intermediary mentioned in the feedback that all five agencies pitching had taken exactly the same approach. It had been hard for the client to choose, as the submissions were so similar.

We used to say to clients at St Luke's that if you don't stand for something you don't stand out. These days it might be more that if you don't stand for something you don't keep up? Or don't get kept in the portfolio at Unilever, since the CEO Alan Jope stated:

> We will dispose of brands that we feel are not able to stand for something more important than just making your hair shiny, your skin soft, your clothes whiter or your food tastier. [71]

The debate now is not whether it is possible for brands to espouse politics and social causes, nor even if it is advisable, but rather: by what criteria should we decide 'do they work'?

Adage magazine hailed Nike as their Advertiser of the Year in 2018.[72] The *Adage* headline proclaimed that the:

> Colin Kaepernick ad is a textbook example of how a marketer can change a conversation.

And the next line of the piece (the caption under the photo) adds what for *Adage* was the clincher:

> Love it or hate it, the Kaepernick ad just did it for Nike's bottom line.

This wasn't an aside, the article goes on to say:

Nike ended up right where it needs to be: in the middle of a debate that drew attention, admiration and – most importantly – sales from the urban millennials it needs to keep the swoosh strong.

That 'most importantly' sounds cynical. Most importantly for who?

I must admit I made a similar argument in defence of Nike. At a conference (in Brazil) another speaker had criticised the Nike advertising for causing a backlash and a boycott in the US. Implying that it had a negative effect on the brand and the business. They were using this as an example of why brands should leave causes alone.

In response I pointed out that Nike sales the following quarter had actually gone up 10%.

But is this the right way to look at it? Should we ultimately measure the success of advertising which takes a political stand, or that which links up with a worthy social cause or charity, purely in terms of how much extra merchandise it shifts: 'People loved the tree planting campaign – sales shot up – but didn't like domestic violence so much.' Can brands afford to be that mercenary? Sure, you want to choose popular causes that are relevant to your audience. But if you decide to shape the debate and take a stand, surely you should do so whatever the cost?

What if Nike sales suffered because trolls who burned their Nike trainers in social media succeeded? And what if this had outweighed positive support from those agreeing with Spike Lee that siding with Kaepernick put Nike 'on the right side of history'? Would Nike still be *Adage* advertiser of the year?

We do need to celebrate examples of doing well by doing good. So that people in other companies can justify marketing for social good. The fact that Nike showed increased revenues after the controversy can be used in this way in pitches and proposals. It is a nice proof point.

But there are a couple of things wrong with this argument.

First, we don't know that the Kaepernick controversy caused these results.

And second, even if we did, I'm not sure we should judge its success in those terms.

Let's reduce the first argument – the controversy caused the changes in sales – to absurdity. In 2016, Samsung was forced to recall Galaxy Note phones. It was a public relations disaster. I heard their US CMO at the time describe himself jokingly as 'the chief recall officer'. But guess what? Their brand was just fine. Samsung filed a 50% increase in profits the very next quarter. The reason was strong demand for their chips and screens (used in competitor devices) and from favourable currency exchange rates. Nothing to do with the mobile recall. Nobody would buy an argument that said: 'What you need is a product safety crisis. Just look at Samsung. They recalled 2.5 million exploding phones. And their profits were up 50% the next quarter.'

But that's exactly what *Adage* is arguing for Nike. I suspect the real sales gains were in new digital channels, new product ranges, better forecasting and merchandising . . .? I do understand that salience can drive brand share. But Nike has plenty of awareness and goodwill to go around. I might be misreading it, but I don't think this actually transformed Nike's brand enough to account for a 10% increase in sales. It's hard for me to judge because I wasn't there.

The second point is tougher: *should* we judge political advertising against increasing sales?

I'd happily buy Ben & Jerry's because I agree with and support their activism. If I lived in the US, I probably would have bought the Resist anti-Trump flavour. But the deal is I'd expect others who like Trump not to buy this. And probably not to buy the brand. Being rational, Trump must have appealed to a lot of people to have won an election. To Ben & Jerry's credit, they didn't care about the numbers. They made a stand as they thought it was important to do so.

So did AirBnB – who made an ad in direct response to Trump's Muslim travel ban. They spent their 2017 Superbowl ad budget on a commercial that said *We Accept* featuring people of diverse backgrounds. It wasn't a one off. The brand also responded to Trump's comments about 'shit-hole countries' (Haiti, El Salvador, and 'Africa – all of it') concluding 'let's open doors, not build walls'. These are not brand purpose statements. AirBnB has decided that it is important to the company. Numerous tech companies including Apple, Google, and Facebook joined forces on the travel ban because of its impact on talent, employment, and the economy. In 2016, 30% of new start-ups in the United States were started by immigrants and 51% of the start-ups worth a billion or more.[73] You could almost call this lobbying rather than marketing.

To the debate about judging the results, Kim Rubsey – head of social impact at AirBnB – revealed that they don't track the results of these marketing activities in the usual way:

> For us, this is the one area where we're not so metrics-obsessed. There's just a whole bucket of things where it's the right thing to do and that drives the decision-making.

Rubsey also revealed that they do receive negative comments on social media but:

> If they don't believe in the ethos of our form of travel and our form of hospitality, they're probably not going to be great guests or great hosts. So, for them to make other choices when they travel is absolutely fine with us.[74]

Nike is a trickier one to read. Way back in the 1970s, Nike hired John McEnroe, the bad boy of tennis (known for angry outburst and the phrase 'you cannot be serious'). Nike's headline was 'Rebel With a Cause'. Over the years Nike has stuck closely to this theme and sided with the outsider, the underdog, and the rebel. Kaepernick conforms to this pattern and appeared in an ad that was made to celebrate 30 years of the *Just Do It* campaign.

When Kaepernick appeared on screen in the Nike ad, his voiceover said, 'Believe in something, even if it means sacrificing everything'. This was just one scene in a spot about sporting heroes who overcame adversity – disabled, female, refugee . . . It also features Serena Williams and the line 'and if you are a girl from Compton, become the greatest athlete ever'. The reason Kaepernick's line was so controversial was he had claimed to have been side-lined by the NFL after refusing to stand during the national anthem in 2016.

Whatever you think of the Kaepernick case, this is clearly 100% on brand. Nike in my view definitely, deliberately chose to make a point. The ad was shown in the opening game of the NFL. They are not naïve and must have known it would create a debate. They would have weighed the pros and cons and decided – probably on the principle 'we are a brave brand not afraid of risks'– to just do it. Assuming it wasn't just a cynical ploy designed to reinvigorate a flagging brand, then good for them. And great that their business is going so well too.

Colin Kaepernick made his protest in support of *Black Lives Matters* – a campaign of demonstrations against police shootings of unarmed civilians. At one of their protests in Louisiana, a 35 year-old nurse called Ieshia Evans stood calmly while police in riot gear arrested her. The photograph of this event called *Taking a stand in Baton Rouge* went viral. It was compared by some with the image of the man in front of the tank in Tiananmen Square. Evans was named Afro America Network Black Woman of the Year and also was named one of the BBC's 100 Women of that year. If you are having a bad day, I'd recommend Googling and contemplating this image. It's an uplifting moment of human dignity and equanimity.

Enter Pepsi's marketing team who decided to recreate this scene with Ms Kendall Jenner.

There were instant denouncements in social media posts of Pepsi for trivialising the issue. Pepsi pulled the commercial one day after it aired. Although they had initially tried to defend it saying, 'this is a global ad that reflects people coming together in a spirit of harmony'.

My own main problem with the ad is that it is cheesy and superficial. It trivialises the issue because it is just a really bad film. I wouldn't have any problem with PepsiCo or any other company saluting people who take to the streets to protest. We already saw in a previous chapter how Seventh Generation gave their platform to climate strike protestors. This was a cool thing to do (*and* they did it quietly without a big fanfare or trying to take any credit).

Let's deconstruct what Pepsi is communicating: *here is a celebrity – she's a role model – she is having her photo taken – she sees a group of young people joining a protest – on a whim she joins them – everyone loves her because she is beautiful and/or a celebrity – she hands a can of Pepsi to a nice young policemen – everyone cheers.* If I saw that script, I might have thought it was a spoof commercial for a product called Narcissist Barbie!

There is an attitude somewhere at Pepsi and/or their agencies that the way to appeal to a new generation is through celebrity culture – and what they deduce are the codes of reality TV.

It isn't (the way). And those aren't (the codes).

A survey by the Varkey foundation asked young people globally what would be their most important criteria in deciding a future career. Globally the top answers were skills, pay, opportunities, and travel; 13% also said it was important that the organisation they work for makes a positive impact on the world. Only 3% said what was important to them was celebrity or fame. Results were similar in the US; celebrity scored 3%, social impact scored 17%.[75]

If Pepsi got this, they would realise that what was important to people was declaring support for things like *Black Lives Matter* (like Nike did, implicitly) not celebrity aspiration.

The ad also arguably does a disservice to *Keeping Up With The Kardashians*. This show may be about wealthy, famous, and glamorous women. But it is also is a warm and involving human account of life in a close-knit family. (Okay, I don't watch it, but everyone has seen clips.) If you wanted to tap into this phenomenon and their power as role models, then get Kim or Kylie to talk about how they built billion-dollar business empires, perhaps?

There's a lot of what went wrong that just comes down to execution and sheer superficiality.

Fearless Girl – in my view – landed on the right side just because it was such an apt and timely symbol, whoever made it and for whatever brand. This statue opposite the bull of Wall Street was created to memorialise an initiative by an American financial services company to get companies to have more women on their boards – the SHE fund which invested in gen-der diverse companies. They unveiled the statue on International Women's Day. There were criticisms, calling out State Street Global Advisers on their own diversity and an investigation found they routinely paid men less than women. (Ouch!) But in marketing terms, a company that needed to launch a diversity themed fund found a way to promote it that generated millions in free media coverage. What's not to like? According to State Street, numer-ous women now appear on boards as a result of the SHE fund; 152 boards they contacted now have a woman director who did not previously and 34 more committed to add one soon.[76]

Another campaign that attracted mixed reviews was Gillette's toxic mas-culinity spot. This was a well-crafted Superbowl spot highlighting some bad things that males do, like kids bullying other kids, men touching women in business (okay, on the shoulder, but it's an American TV commercial), and dads saying, 'boys will be boys'. The ad came in for a mix of criticism and praise. Responding to the criticism, Gillette's brand director told the *Wall Street Journal*:

This is an important conversation happening, and as a company that encourages men to be their best, we feel compelled to both address it and take action of our own. We are taking a realistic look at what's happening today and aiming to inspire change by acknowledging that the old saying 'Boys Will Be Boys' is not an excuse.

Within the ad industry the collective reaction – what I heard at an event the week the campaign aired – was WTF? Just because you had 'the best the man can get' as your slogan, you don't get to lecture people on gender politics. It seemed almost like strategy by thesaurus.

This could be a good base principle for purpose marketing. Make sure that any cause-led marketing campaign stacks up in strategy terms.

Why are they telling me this?

Who are they telling?

Who is the brand to say this?

What are they asking me to do?

So that there is a logic behind it, just like any other advertising.

Another campaign that raised the same – why are they telling me this? – debate was Burger King's mental health awareness. They produced some special 'unhappy meals' (geddit) with names like SALTY and DGAF and a nicely made rap video where people sang about #feelyourway and the fact that not everyone is happy every day.

Personally, I liked the creative elements of the campaign. They were simple and well executed. And if the aim was to raise awareness of Mental Health Awareness Month, perhaps you could argue that it worked. There is some value in normalising an issue, getting people talking about it, hopefully getting some help. Their charity partner Mental Health America commented that:

> The conversation about mental health starts to become much more normalized when a big brand like Burger King comes to an organization like ours and wants to partner in providing our resources to this audience of young people that we share and, not only that, put their marketing genius behind it.

But the backlash tweets, articles, and posts made some good points:

• the charity link (Mental Health America) is in the background, it just says that Burger King supports them, did they even donate some money or just make the ads?

- it's not integral to what Burger King are about, their stated mission – it just looks like an idea someone had for a creative campaign having a dig at McDonalds' Happy Meal;
- the campaign does good for Burger King by selling some special edition meals and raising top of mind awareness, it's not nearly as clear what it does for the cause;
- mental health issues aren't about being in a bad mood due to facile external causes (there is a difference between being dispirited by circumstances and being depressed);
- Burger King doesn't do too much to support its own employees with mental health issues – and past employees tweeting about this did not look great in PR terms.

Overall it looks like the client asked an agency to come up with a relevant cause for their audience, the agency did a pretty good job and made a nice campaign, but deep down the company isn't really that passionate about this issue. Also, the campaign (with 'unhappy meals') can look like it is exploiting a painful social issue just to sell a few more burgers.

Compare this with the UK mental health charity CALM's campaign with Lynx. CALM (Campaign Against Living Miserably) is a new charity with limited means and reach. The charity managed to increase awareness of male suicide (as the top cause of death under 45) from 19% to 43%. And they mainly did this with brand partnerships. Their *Bigger Issues* campaign with Lynx reached 23 million people and even led to a parliamentary debate. Andrew Brown, CALM's head of partnerships said the association also benefited Lynx:

> Before this campaign they were stuck in a rut of being for 14-year-old boys that were looking for a girlfriend. Their ambition was to move into a broader audience, operate in a more sophisticated space. As a brand they needed to make a big leap, so they used association with us and their engagement with the debate to make them a more progressive brand, in tune with contemporary male thinking.

That actually sounds like a strategy. Combined with the fact that Lynx belongs to Unilever that mandated its brands to have a positive social purpose. It just makes sense. Lynx were growing up the brand by supporting young men, helping them be more themselves.

Heineken made a series of social norm-challenging commercials from 2011 onwards. One asked men to be a hero and drink in moderation. The underlying message being that women wanted to be around men who weren't drunk, which makes sense. Some people hated this ad for reasons ranging from 'why do all the girls have to be pretty?', to 'some women drink more than men', to 'stop telling me what to do'. Personally, I thought it was the first (regulator appeasing) Drink Responsibly ad I'd seen based on a real insight and consumer benefit.

Another ad – 'open your world' – paired people with starkly opposing views and gave them a task to do together before at the end they sat down for a beer, by which time they had clearly connected as human beings. I'd say this was Heineken promoting a Dutch take on life. They were well constructed ads too. But more to the point they genuinely reflect the culture at Heineken (in my experience).

Heineken dropped this campaign and their reasons for doing so were interesting too.

> Heineken says the insight that 'to progress in life you must cross your border', was no longer interpreted as inspirational but pressuring. They believe that the previous generation broke the world in many ways – from climate change to the economy – and they feel the responsibility of having to save it. 'You must cross your border' was simply another a layer of pressure that we were putting on top of them.[77]

I'm not sure. There are so many brands out there from Samsung to Land Rover telling us to cross our border, maybe people just got sick and tired of it?

But perhaps it truly is a different thing for a brand to work with a cause or purpose today. We are at a critical point in history – many do feel we are at a breaking point. There are protests in cities all over the world every week. It is a great time to make a positive contribution. But do choose carefully.

And consider *doing* something good, rather than just doing something that looks good.

Preferably something that is a proportional response to the crises of our age.

2.8 Brands Doing Good

Tesco were masters at the old kind of charity partnership. I used their *Computers for Schools* promotion back in the early 2000s as an example in a talk in the City. At least three banks in the room were among the top 10 corporate charity givers in the country. Whereas Tesco at that time did not even make the top 100. Yet it was consistently rated in surveys as one of the top companies doing good; whereas the banks didn't get a look in. Why was that? My thesis was that it was due to Tesco's insanely popular collection scheme with a simple hook (hand in this voucher and we donate computers to schools) that was just so engaging and meaningful.

Tesco, the biggest retailer in the UK, now looks like a defining example of what a 2020 charity partnership can and should look like. One that achieves substantial change. Tesco has partnered with the WWF in a four-year ambitious programme called

CHANGING THE FOOD SYSTEM TO SAVE THE PLANET

That is immediately in tune with the times. The ambition of the partnership lives up to this title with the goal to

Reduce the environmental impact of the average UK shopping basket by half.

Tesco aim to do that without increasing prices. And to have an additional knock-on impact by influencing consumers and others in the food industry to follow suit.

To know if they are succeeding, the partnership is developing a new way to measure the total environmental impact of food. Here, Tesco are on a similar path to Walmart in developing a measurement framework (in their case the Walmart Index).

The partnership covers three main areas:

- Helping everyone eat more sustainably.
- Restoring nature in food production.
- Eliminating waste (both food waste and packaging waste).

The partners backed their launch announcement with new research showing that 80% of UK shoppers say they want supermarkets to do more to reduce the impact their food purchases have on the planet. Dave Lewis, the Tesco CEO, made all the right noises:

I'm pleased we're making progress, but we want to go further to achieve our goal of providing customers with affordable, healthy, sustainable food. Partnering with WWF will help us make our customers' shopping baskets more sustainable. Our shared ambition is to reduce the environmental impact of the average shopping basket by half. By working with farmers, suppliers, colleagues and other experts we hope to develop innovative solutions so shoppers can put affordable, tasty food on their plates today, confident they are not compromising the future of food for generations to come.[78]

One immediate outcome is a food waste programme. Tesco partnered with Jamie Oliver to teach community centres to cook delicious healthy meals from the surplus sell by date food that the supermarket provides. To achieve this, they launched a Tesco Community Cookery School teaching Jamie Oliver's specially designed recipes to 1000 community centre chefs.

Tesco have also released videos covering their soil and farming initiatives, working with Tesco farmers and WWF experts to subsidise practices like using cover crops.

Dave Lewis – previously from Unilever – is credited with bringing Tesco back from the brink. When Lewis took over in 2014 the group had a black hole of debt, an ailing brand, and was losing shoppers while facing competition from new players like LIDL and Amazon. Lewis started his tenure by taking the leadership team to a remote farm in Norfolk where they had to shop and cook together. They had a rough first few years with a £6 billion loss in 2015. But the group now has 15 quarters of healthy sustained growth and seems to have won confidence back from shareholders and also consumers. A perfect time to launch a category leading sustainability programme and bring in a reputable partner to help see it through.

I think we will see more and more of these partnerships in future. Companies with sustainability and social impact ambitions can take them much further with a qualified NGO partner. There is also some humility implied in admitting that you can't go it alone. The Paris Agreement calls for unprecedented shifts in climate and environmental impacts; Tesco with 25% of UK groceries can make a decent dent in this.

With the public mood at the moment, we will likely also continue to see brand charity tie ins of the more traditional sentimental type. I think the key question here is about being not just credible and relevant but quite frankly generous enough.

Charities rely on these partnerships to generate awareness and income. I can't think of a reason not to push one of these partnerships if you as a marketer have a passion for the cause and sense that your customers will too. However, the right charity partnerships can bring significant revenues as well as 'making us look good'. The key thing with this model – as with greenwash – is that the credit taken, and the money given, should be in some senses proportional.

Let's start with a generous example: innocent's *Big Knit*. One of the founders heard a news story on the radio about fuel poverty in the UK affecting many old people. So, in 2003 they started a scheme where volunteers knitted woolly hats to put on top of the drinks. And in the process donated 50p per smoothie to Age Concern. The scheme continues to this day. I did notice that in the Coca-Cola era the donation per pack has been quietly reduced to 25p. But it's still a fair whack on a product that typically costs £1.79. Last year 1.5 million hats were donated – and since 2003 the brand has collected 7.5 million hats and donated £2.5 million.

Compare this with the popular and successful Pampers' baby immunisation promotion. The snappy hook here is that the brand donates 'one life saving immunisation per pack'. If you read into the details (for 2009 in the US): 'a total donation of at least $2.2 million, which will help UNICEF purchase more than 30 million vaccines'.[79] That's a donation of only 7 cents per pack. Sizes and prices vary, but a medium sized pack of Pampers nappies on Amazon.com costs $48. Meaning that Pampers would have donated $2.2m on sales of $1.44 billion. It's a subjective call, but I suspect many mothers who switched brands from cheaper own label nappies to buy 'one life saving immunisation per pack' had it in mind they were donating more than 7 cents?

The Pampers promotion on a $48 pack of nappies is 125 times less generous than the innocent woolly hat promotion. You have to buy five expensive Pampers packs to match the donation of just one £1.79 smoothie. Both the promotions are creatively well executed and appealing. But one is simply a lot more generous.

If you look at causes through a marketing lens today, you are likely to see them as a way to make your brand stand for something, stand out and gain trust, loyalty, and engagement. Which is fair enough. The charity sees you as a means to gain large revenues and awareness with almost no effort of expense on their part. Both parties are 'adults' and know what they are doing. Consumers are buying a quick fix of 'feel good'. Provided the benefits are proportionate to the commercial gains, it's hard to find fault in any of this.

It may be that greater transparency in future means we can compare charity donating brand schemes just as easily as today consumers can compare airline point promotions or calories. As consumer markets become more transparent, brands won't be able to live on the perception of doing good unless they are making substantial contributions.

The above are examples where a brand has selected an external cause. What if you created your consumer brand in the first place as an engine for doing good?

One example of this new kind of cause brand is Karma Cola.

Karma started out within a Fairtrade organic fruit importer in New Zealand. The founders decided that soft drinks were ripe for an ethical makeover. They sourced cola nuts from Boma, a village in Sierra Leone. Karma then hooked up with Albert Tucker, a seasoned supply chain development whizz (one of the co-founders of Divine Chocolate). Tucker is originally from Sierra Leone and helped the Karma team work with Boma villagers to set up not just a trade agreement, but a foundation that shares in the profits of Karma. And it is important to all involved that the farmers and community decide what to do with the money.

Simon Coley – creative brains behind this exquisitely designed set of brands – tells the story of when they went to visit Boma. A long journey from city, to town, into the Gola forest. As they got closer to the village, they could hear drumming in the distance. When they arrived, they found the whole village waiting in welcome on the bridge that was funded by the Karma Foundation. Makennah Bridge joins the old Boma to new Boma and boosted their economy.

Coley always reminds people at Karma Cola about the bridge: 'it's what we are selling, our brand, it's the story of the good that we are doing by doing business in a better way'. The journey hasn't been easy as the country was recovering from a civil war. And then later was hit with Ebola. Simon told me that at this time the farmers had a simple request – 'please stay, stick with us'.

Over the years, Karma have worked with Boma and seven more communities in the Tiwai region. And more good uses have been found for the Karma Foundation share: scholarships for more than 60 school places, funding five school teachers in a community run school; two rice-processing centres to secure food supply; an educational HIV/AIDS theatre group; meeting-houses (barri) and a guest house to rent out to visitors; medical supplies during the Ebola outbreak; rehabilitated rainforest farms; a seed bank for future seasons; helping a group of entrepreneurs start small businesses; an adult literacy programme; training community organisers and leaders.[80] That's a lot of good to come out of a small craft soda company.

At this end of the chain, Coley and his co-founders have steadily built a modern business and hip brands. They only sell direct to likeminded cafés and stores (because like VEJA they realised you can only be ethical if you make decent margins). The packaging and design is amazing – Gingerella was one of my favourite brands even before I met Karma and heard their story.

If you are going to build this sort of business, you have to build it with your bare hands. And it also helped that one of Simon's co-founders is a financial wunderkind with an MBA that used to work for the New Zealand treasury, while Simon was an accomplished creative director. The company keeps innovating with new drinks, new farmers, and supply chains and is expanding in the UK and Australasia with an eye on the US next. It must be one hundred times more effort than just ordering a product from a factory and putting your wrapper around it (like most small food and drink brands do) but as the story of the bridge shows, it is 1000 times more worth it.

Karma started with an experienced leadership team and as part of an existing wholesale business. As did some other ethical brands like Green & Blacks. What's perhaps even more impressive are the brands that started from nothing. Jess McMenemy started out by selling her mother's delicious 100% Natural raw vegan brownies in Brighton Market. Later, Jess realised that you couldn't trademark the term '100% Natural' so renamed the brand Natural State. By now their brownies are stocked in impressive places including Harrods and Sourced Market.

Jess is from the generation that won't take planetary death and social injustice lying down. She's hugely spirited and funny (and reminds me of Anita Roddick, including the determination). Jess, like Karma Cola and VEJA, believes in real relationships and knowledge of every step, especially farming. Jess is so obsessed with the farming bit that in her spare time she has been visiting a regenerative farm and recording a podcast. I took the opportunity to ask Jess to set something down in her own words, so you can get a direct sense of the mindset behind the next generation of brands that have doing good baked in.

<u>Tell us a bit of the story that brought you to this point...</u>

When I was 8, we moved to Somerset from Portobello road. I remember looking out of our window and seeing a truck filled with pigs drive past. Something about this and my mum's explanation that they were being driven to a distant abattoir as there wasn't a local one, triggered enough of a reaction in me to write to the Minister of Agriculture.

My young mind started to question the food system and piece together where it comes from and how it's grown. Over the years the injustice of our broken food system became more and more evident. My mum's delicious brownies, these little squares of raw chocolate deliciousness seemed like the perfect little protest. A chocolate placard campaigning for transparency in food.

We set out on a mission to reconnect ourselves and people to food, committed to buying ingredients directly from farmers and meeting them to understand how and why they farm. But the way our food system is set up created hurdles; orders too small to buy directly from farms, third party distributors unwilling to disclose their sources, huge processors dumping cacao in ginormous silos, so transparency is lost.

It has taken us 7 years to create a network of suppliers with full traceability to the farm. I have been lucky enough to meet lots of them and the connections made from meeting them directly can't be matched from a phone call or email. Staying with Orlando and his family in the Mayan jungle, driving out to remote villages to collect freshly picked cacao and going back to Jose's house to look at his record collection after a day in the almond orchards. These are experiences which remind us that our food is grown and picked by people, with faces and stories.

The brownie's journey has been an interesting series of serendipitous twists and turns.

As I'm writing this, I have just arrived in Sri Lanka on a mission to find vanilla and coconuts. I took a 3 hour train journey to Kandy from Colombo last night and stayed in a little guest house on a quiet hillside above the city. The guesthouse owner, a hipster guy called Vindika is keen to help my mission and as luck would have it, his uncle owns a coconut farm and a friend of his cousin's is a member of a vanilla cooperative. Little breadcrumbs on the trail to show me that I'm on the right track.

<u>What in a few words would you say is your purpose?</u>

To regenerate the planet with delicious, irresistible food and to reconnect people to the land it comes from and the people who grew it.

<u>If someone gave you a billion pounds to make change, what would you do with it?</u>

1. Give kids in schools window boxes to grow their own food. Seeing a plant sprout up is magic enough. To then see it produce food which you can pick and eat is like a little miracle which creates a connection and a sort of respect to how food is grown and where it comes from. We need the young generations, the change makers to have this understanding from an early age.

2. Buy land and give it to farmers so they're not beholden to rents. Our farming system is based on a mass of stressed out farmers, working round the clock to pay off rent and loans to tractor + chemical companies. If farmers had a bit of breathing space without being so worried about yield, our soils and eco system would be a very different place.

3. Create a processing hub within a 10 mile radius from each farm. Power and money has been taken away from farmers by oversized commodities brokers. Our food system needs to be smaller and localised. It's nonsensical that food can be grown on small, beautiful farms and shipped sometimes across the world to be processed. Farms need local hubs with small scale machinery where they can process ingredients themselves and sell directly to buyers. More money for them, power back in their hands and less transport emissions wasted.

<u>What's your product philosophy?</u>

First and foremost; deliciousness. There's no point producing anything that people wouldn't want to eat. We have spent hours in the kitchen adjusting the recipe to make the brownies rich, chocolatey, with a bit of fudgieness here, a sprinkle of salt there. Minute grams of cacao nibs added to give an extra layer of crunch, teeny bits of cacao added to make it slightly more rich. We won't produce anything that we wouldn't want to buy daily ourselves.

Second ingredients. This is also related to deliciousness because you can taste the difference between those sourced well and those not.

We don't buy anything we wouldn't want to put in our own bodies. And we don't work with farmers who do anything we wouldn't do ourselves. I personally could never bring myself to spray, to put any chemical inputs on the land or to pay workers any less than a wage they deserve.

The brownies stand for truth and doing all things with love. They wouldn't be doing their job if any step of the ingredients didn't support this. And the only way we can ensure that every step of the journey is filled with goodness is to visit the farms ourselves and to meet the people who are growing each ingredient.

<u>What are some of your 'sustainabler' decisions?</u>

To hunt down small scale farmers. The ones with forest gardens, culturally practising organic because it's in their DNA and because they could imagine no other way.

To source as much from the UK as possible. Next year we are partnering with a farm to grow our own flax, hemp, buckwheat and oats.

To find producers with processing facilities in the country/region so the added value remains within that place of origin.

To add ingredients into our brownies which are as good for soil health as they are for us; buckwheat and hemp are amazing nitrate fixers.

To use home compostable packaging. This isn't cheap and we have worked for years to try and find the right material. It isn't perfect, but it is home compostable, and it feels good to be wrapping in something which will naturally degrade in 26 days if left exposed to moisture + air.

The new branding looks so cool. Why are charisma, design & words important?

We have never wanted to preach. There's serious undertones to what we're doing, but at the end of the day, it's a brownie. We wanted the branding to bring the character of the brownies to life. Someone once described them like a hug in a packet. For whatever reason they seem to make people happy, so the branding is a bit of colourful joy, with a sprinkle of the stuff we really care about.

Do you think of yourself as reaching like-minded people, or switching on a bigger public?

Switching on a bigger public. The brownies aren't exclusive, they're accessible and since day one the people who have eaten them have reflected this. 78 year old John from Tunbridge Wells who used to get a train to Brighton weekly to buy his brownies from Infinity Foods, the Queen of Qatar; Sheika Mozah, teenage girls overcoming anorexia and realising treats can be healthy, people with diabetes, UK Olympic athletes.

Regenerative farming. What is it and why does it matter?

Regenerative farming gives back and replenishes the planet rather than merely extracting. Since the industrial revolution we, mainly in the West, have been intensively farming the Earth to satisfy our insatiable greed for growth. Farmers, corporations and organisations across the planet are now realising that we have almost pushed the soil to its limits and in some areas have just 10 harvests left. Regenerative farming seeks to work in harmony with nature, to mimic her naturally occurring patterns rather than claiming dominion over her and applying ever more inputs to push for greater and greater yields.

It is our biggest hope for rescuing our food system. Regenerative farming practices drastically improve soil health which is vital for a number of reasons; for nutrients, biodiversity, prevention of soil erosion and carbon sequestration.

It is most needed in the West.

This might seem like a controversial statement, but when you speak to small scale farmers in Sri Lanka and Belize, you realise that they are already practising 'regenerative farming' and have been for centuries. What is deemed as standard cultural practices in Sri Lanka (composting, mulching, intercropping, cover cropping) falls under definitions which have more recently arisen in the West (Permaculture, Regenerative, Organic, Biodynamic). The regenerative farming movement is the biggest development in farming since the agricultural revolution.

2.9 Consumer Behaviour – Snakes & Ladders

Behaviour change was a hot topic when I wrote *The Green Marketing Manifesto*. Everyone was at it. Ariel asked us to 'turn to 30'. Sky, Yahoo, and others asked us to change lightbulbs. Twelve years later, this approach has become discredited – associated with companies shifting the onus of guilt and responsibility onto consumers. The pendulum may have swung too far in the other direction, but that seems to be 'where it's at'.

In my view this topic is ripe to be revisited. Circular economy models often depend on behaviour. Consumers have to choose to go to the Nudie repair shop and to keep jeans in use.

We'll look at a lot of the qualifiers and pitfalls. But first let's look at why behaviour change should still be top of many green marketers' agenda. As always with sustainability, let's start with what research tells us has the most impact. A 2018 report by a team of academics in *Climate Policy Journal* concluded that:

> Consumer initiatives can have a big effect on embodied carbon imports. We connect a portfolio of 90 green behaviour changes to a global supply chain database to model impacts holistically. We estimate that with reasonable levels of adoption green consumer actions can reduce the EU CO_2 footprint by 25%.[81]

Reducing the total EU CO_2 footprint by 25% certainly does sound worth pursuing. The study points out that behaviour change initiatives thus far had focused on in-home behaviour (like turning down the thermostat, changing lightbulbs, and taking devices off standby), whereas consumer choices can have much bigger impacts along the supply chain:

In Production: choosing low GHG products.
In Trade & Transportation: buy local.
Buying: change the level and composition of demand.
Use Phase: change/reduce use, sharing economy.
Disposal: choose durable goods, reuse and recycle.

It doesn't follow that the smallest changes in behaviour have the lowest impact. An academic study found that teaching eco driving reduced CO_2 emissions (and fuel consumption) by an average of 32%.[82]

If you are a car company, you can teach people to drive more eco. Toyota of Sweden did this by putting a glass of water on the dashboard and telling the driver: if you don't spill it you are driving eco. Originally, they used real glasses of water, handing them out in Stockholm summer traffic jams. Later they transitioned to an app with a virtual glass of water.

There are other ways to achieve big reductions within everyday driving habits.

Eliminate short journeys: 24% of journeys in the UK are under 1 mile.

Working from home days and lift sharing schemes that reduce the commute emissions.

Servicing (full tyres), taking off the roof rack, and keeping windows shut all reduce fuel consumption.

DriveGain analysed data from 10 000 journeys and found that limiting maximum speed to 60 mph reduces fuel consumption and CO_2 emissions by 10% but only adds 2 minutes to the journey time. So, watching your speed makes a big difference.

These figures have not been lost on the car industry. I saw a speaker from Ford presenting their eco driving initiatives and he claimed that achieving the same gains in fuel efficiency through engine design as consumer behaviour might take 10 years.

Unilever once published a figure from their own research saying that

Over two-thirds of our greenhouse gas impacts and 85% of our water footprint is associated with consumer use.

Meaning the shower and the washing machine were a significantly greater part of their total footprint than sourcing, manufacture, packaging, transport, warehousing, and so on. Unilever have since removed this claim. This reflects the shift in Unilever's strategy as more of their brands embed sustainability, rather than relying us taking shorter showers.

I worked in the past with Unilever on some of their brands. One brand team I met with was PG Tips/Lipton. In my research for this assignment, I discovered that household kettles use 34% of cooking energy.[83] And that kettles tend to be overfilled which is a waste of this energy. My proposal was that PG Tips could communicate this to consumers and ask them not to overfill their kettle. The Energy Savings Trust later promoted this same idea:

More than nine in ten people boil a kettle every day and 40% boil water five times a day or more. However, three quarters of households boil more water than they need, costing households £68m a year in energy bills.[84]

My other suggestions to PG Tips were first that they popularise moving back to leaf tea. Only 4% still make their tea this way (mostly grandmothers and upmarket tea shops). Another idea was that they normalise composting with a PG Tips branded composting bins, composting lessons and clubs. I didn't know at the time that their teabags contain plastic glues so leave a nasty residue when composted. Although thanks to a public petition that is now due to change.

My argument was that involving people in such activities would build brand love as well as reducing environmental impact. Tea is a quaint, nostalgic drink. The local 'I'll pop the kettle on' chatting over the garden fence kind of environmentalism suits the brand really well. They could have sponsored the Big Lunch – street parties designed to rebuild community, started by the Eden Project and now attended by nearly 10 million people a year.

The opinion in sustainable marketing has turned against changing consumer behaviour. I think this might be a baby/bath water sort of situation. We do want to avoid advertising behaviour changes as a substitute for meaningful action. Consider this example:

Coca-Cola is launching a marketing campaign to encourage people to recycle its bottles as it attempts to reduce its environmental impact.

An article in *Marketing Week* noted that:

While the move was broadly welcomed, critics raised concerns over how much plastic waste the company is responsible for, with the company selling more than 100 billion single-use plastic bottles a year.

Their advertising copy also veers into greenwash when it says: 'single use plastic bottles are only single use if you throw them away'. I'm not against companies asking consumers to recycle. I think it's a great idea. I loved Coca Cola's campaign in Belgium which said bluntly:

DON'T BUY COCA-COLA IF YOU DON'T HELP US RECYCLE.

A key thing for marketers and their agencies working on sustainability is that you have to get your facts straight. It's not easy to do. Life cycle analyses looking at things like embodied energy are always hedged with caveats and assumptions. But you do need to check the numbers.

Last year I worked on a brief for a client who makes mobile phones. One of the ideas in the brief was to get consumers to save energy (or use renewable energy) when using the phone to drive the overall sustainability performance of their hardware. This sounded promising until I looked up figures from the Institute of Electrical and Electronic Engineers:

> A smartphone consumes annually just 4 kilowatt-hours of electricity, less than 30 megajoules during its two years of service, or just 3 percent of its embodied energy cost if the electricity comes from a wind turbine or from a photovoltaic cell. That fraction rises to about 8 percent if the energy comes from burning coal.[85]

If you want to be greener with your phone just don't buy a new one. Keep your old mobile in use longer. Reducing its energy impact in use (like dimming the screen) won't make a big difference. Keeping your phone going for 3+ years will roughly halve its footprint. Keeping it in use for even one extra month will have more impact than all the energy used to charge it.

It would take a public-spirited mobile phone manufacturer to promote this message. But it's a great strategy for a Telco. Working with O_2 in Ireland years ago I pitched the idea of a 'Green 3 Year Phone Contract'. The client calculated that this would roughly double their profit per customer. Not just saving on the handset subsidy, but from the whole cost of marketing when a customer approached renewal and they had to fight to avoid churn. This meant they could afford to make their green phone contract cheaper too.

What about cars? Mike Berners Lee in *The Carbon Footprint of Everything* calculated that around half the emissions associated with a car come from its manufacture:

> If you make a car last to 200 000 miles rather than 100 000, then the emissions for each mile the car does in its lifetime may drop by as much as 50%, as a result of getting more distance out of the initial manufacturing emissions.[86]

That insight fits the car dealership business model to a tee because they make most money not from new car sales but from service and finance.[87] The greener alternative to owning and maintaining a car would be city car clubs, something BMW branched into.

'Nudge' is another topic that was once fashionable. There were some good examples, Like OPower in the US who managed to reduce people's consumption just by telling them how much energy their neighbours were using. OPower got the idea from a Robert Caldini research project. Caldini found that distributing leaflets giving people reasons to save energy or telling them practical ways to save energy had little effect. But a leaflet telling them that many of their neighbours were using fans rather than aircon produced a 6% drop in energy use. OPower showed people in their monthly energy bill how they compared with neighbours. An independent evaluation found that by this means OPower reduced household energy consumption by an average of 2% or 0.62 kWh per day.[88]

One reason 'Nudge' enthusiasts may have loved sustainability was it neatly dodged the main criticism of their method, which is that it is essentially manipulative. I met an internal regulator at Lloyd's banking group who was commissioning a study to ensure *none* of the bank's marketing could be misinterpreted as applying behavioural economics. Because if the government regulator suspected the bank of using underhand tricks like these, they would come down hard. With saving energy it's fair game? Government policy makers were entranced by the prospect of introducing 'nudges' which effortlessly, with little cost, tipped the public into achieving policy objectives. The UK Cabinet Office even set up a 'Nudge Unit' in 2008.

It's not just behaviour change that fell out of favour. The notion of 'consumerising green' has been questioned. A book review in the *New York Times* by the legendary Bill McKibben (environmentalist, author, and founder of 350.org) points out that:

> For 10 or 15 years beginning in the 1990s such consumer-driven environmentalism was a constant refrain, leading to endless disputations about paper towels and disposable diapers versus sponges and cotton nappies. Some fairly small percentage of people read those books, and an even smaller percentage took regular and clear action . . . social scientists estimate that getting 3 or 4 percent of people involved in a movement is often enough to force systemic change, whereas if they acted solely as consumers that same number would have relatively little effect. You can obviously do both, and all of us should try — but fighting for the Green New Deal makes more mathematical sense than trying to take on the planet one commodity at a time.

Extinction Rebellion are one group that are urging us to look hard at behaviour change again. XR wrote an open letter earlier in 2019 to the advertising industry:

'What can I do?' you're thinking.

'I'm just the Founder/CEO/CMO/CCO/CFO/MD/CD of a global advertising agency.'

The answer is: you can do anything you want, and you can shift mass
behaviour in a heartbeat. One of the reasons we've got here is because you've
been selling things to people that they don't need. You are the manipulators
and architects of that consumerist frenzy.

Imagine what would happen if you devoted those skills to something better. No, making a small campaign to give up drinking from plastic straws is not
going to cut it.

Brands can make green lifestyles cool. Oatly is so much more than a non-
dairy milk. It is a lifestyle brand that is trendy and relevant. And marketing
it this way was a conscious decision by the Oatly team. Oatly is the eco
driving of milky coffee – you can still enjoy a cappuccino, but without the
climate impact of dairy farming.

So, there is every reason to keep playing snakes & ladders with behaviour
change. But we do have to deal with a big snake that makes *all* green marketing prone to backfire: the rebound effect.

Rebound is an important topic in sustainability and consumer behaviour
that marketers often fail to grasp. A rebound effect can be understood via the
following scenario. I insulate my loft. Over time this saves me money. However, my finances are managed so that I pretty much spend what I earn. As a
result, I spend the money I notionally saved on something else. My footprint
hence stays roughly the same.

The sobering fact is that every \$1 spent in the economy emits around
0.5 kg of CO_2. Hence if you spend your whole income then you have the
same emissions. And that doesn't really vary all that much if you change the
mix of what you spend it on.

The good news is that carbon intensity (kg/\$) is falling over time. There is
a historical graph at the World Bank website.[89] According to this, the figure
was 0.763 kg in 1990 and fell to 0.325 kg by 2014. In the UK, the figure is
closer to 0.2 kg.

This suggests that the things being done to decarbonise our economy
are working.

The bad news from a climate point of view is that the world economy
measured in GDP terms is also growing. Between 1990 and 2014, the GDP
per capita grew from \$7186 to \$10 156.

And the population is growing. In 1990 it was 5.3 billion. By 2014 it was 7.3 billion.

Multiplying the three numbers gives a much more modest improvement:

1990 = 29 000 000 000 tonnes CO_2
2014 = 24 000 000 000 tonnes CO_2

But it still doesn't add up. Which must be an artefact of GDP and carbon accounting practices.

Because one thing we do know is that global carbon emissions are growing.

1990 = 22 181 807 367 tonnes
2014 = 35 505 827 039 tonnes

If you use these global emissions figures to work back to our true carbon footprint per dollar spent in the economy, you get

1990: 0.58 kg per $1 of GDP
2014: 0.48 kg per $1 of GDP

Hence my number. Roughly 0.5 kg of carbon emitted for every $1 you spend. And – as a 2009 report for the UK government chaired by Professor Tim Jackson went to great lengths to demonstrate – while the economy is decarbonising, it isn't decarbonising nearly fast enough to halt the growth of carbon emissions, let alone reduce them.

It does make a difference what you spend your money on. Some products and services are more carbon intensive than others. But it doesn't make a HUGE difference. There are hidden carbon costs in things that look insubstantial. For instance: Netflix uses 15% of all global internet bandwidth.[90]

The implications of this one number – 0.5 kg/$ – are quite shocking.

For instance, you can either be green or rich. Rich people spend more in the economy and emit more carbon. Even the eco celebrities. According to inequality.org

Inequality has been on the rise across the globe for several decades. The world's richest 1 percent, those with more than $1 million, own 45 percent of the world's wealth.

The world's richest may or may not save their money. But many are also invested in stocks with serious climate impacts. All other things being equal, roughly 1% of humans on the planets are responsible for 45% of carbon emissions, which is a revolutionary thought.

Meanwhile, in green consumerism there is this tricky rebound effect. Allied with the limitless genius of human self-deception that (commentators like Rumi tell us) comes with our ego.

I came to the conclusion decades ago that the only true green consumer act was to put money into savings. A credit card, loan, or mortgage is bringing tomorrow's money (and emissions) forward and spending them today. It is the least sustainable product on any market and directly against the core sustainability ethic of leaving some resources for the future generation's needs. A savings account puts aside money for a rainy day. It creates personal resilience. But also takes some heat out of the economy. And allied with eco savings it also neutralises rebound effects.

Unfortunately for most people in the current economy, saving money is more aspiration than reality. And when you talk to banks you realise that every £1 you do put into a bank savings account goes into their capital reserve, against which they issue credit many times over. So if you save money for sustainability reasons, you need to put it into a long term sustainable bond, invest in green economy assets like windfarms, or go with a sustainable bank like Triodos.

Back to the rebound effect. There are multiple types and each one has significant lessons for sustainability and marketing. The first two are recognised in economic studies of rebound effects. The others here are scenarios I have noticed in consumer research and many will recognise from everyday life:

The direct rebound effect
Something gets cheaper so people use more of it. For instance, after your loft insulation your energy bill falls, so you feel justified in heating the home for longer every day.
The indirect rebound effect
Your home energy improvements save you £100. You have some money left in your account. So, you splash out on a short weekend city break trip.
The halo rebound effect
You buy Fairtrade coffee. And some organic cereal. That feels virtuous – your good deed for the day – so you hardly notice the impact of the rest of your weekly shop.

The eco consumer rebound effect

You feel guilty about the environment but still want to consume. So, you buy a lovely new pair of vegan shoes in this season's style. Rather than sticking with what you had.

The binge rebound effect

As with dieting you maintain discipline some of the time and are careful what you buy. But you can't be sensible all the time or life would be dull. So, you indulge the occasional guilty pleasure. And if it's a far-flung holiday or car, that outweighs a thousand sacrifices.

2.10 Design for Nature and Human Nature

The more time I spend on sustainability, the more I come to appreciate the role of great design.

Design is a way of configuring what's in front of us – whether that's on a screen, in a service, on an advertising poster, or a physical product. Design creates the human habitat. It's our equivalent of the beehive or beavers' dam. Creating our own habitat has big impacts both on the environment and on our way of life, our experiences, and our thoughts.

Design had been captured by overconsumption. Design became an agent of disposability, built in redundancy, excessive packaging, electronics that can't be repaired. None of these were deliberate attempts to pollute or waste. They were side effects of a great idea called modernity. Design showed us materially how far we had progressed. Design whispered to us that our microwave oven was from the same NASA programme that gave us the moon landings. Designers at Penguin brought out the 'disposable' (paperback) book and it felt like progress.

If you break down the culture of consumerism, you start to see some clear design-led narratives:

Keep up with the latest advances.

Mark your distinction with tasteful choices.

Show your status with substantial, expensive looking possessions.

Be more aristocratic, by having less chores and more convenience.

This is just a sample of the many narratives that everyday design carries. But just because we can see through something, like flattery, that doesn't stop it working. These narratives propelled design-forward brands like Apple who gave us computing and communication devices that felt like fashion or luxury, rather than technology. With a price point to match. But always with substance, and a flowing experience. They are well designed.

Design may have carried narratives that encouraged excessive consumption. But I doubt that was the intention of the designers. Most of them simply wanted to express themselves in ways that were gorgeous, functional, and commercial.

Today, urgent, important work is underway to make designers aware of another dimension of design which is its lasting impact on the natural and human world.

Leading designer and circular economy pioneer Sophie Thomas takes groups of designers to landfill and waste processing sites where they sift through the waste stream and try to find something they personally worked on. By choosing better materials, designing for disassembly or reuse, designers can change the impact of everyday objects. One of Sophie's current projects is working with dentists and designers to come up with a sustainable toothbrush.

Design can do more than reduce disposability and waste. Design shapes human life. As Buckminster Fuller used to say: 'If you want to teach people a new way of thinking, don't bother trying to teach them. Instead, give them a tool, the use of which will lead to new ways of thinking.' Design is that tool. Humanity co-evolves with our technologies, designs, artefacts.

Design can change the world.

Let's look at an example. The Brompton has become the signifier of a new sustainable urbanism. Its presence in our cities tells us a story about people who could afford a taxi or their own car but who chose a better mode of transport. It is to the professional green classes what a MacBook Pro is to designers; an emblem of their trade.

Brompton started life in the 1980s as the personal project of Andrew Ritchie, a Cambridge engineering graduate who enjoyed a good challenge. Folding bikes mostly folded in half. At best they were hard to carry and operate. Ritchie was fascinated by the idea of making a better folding and portable bike. He described it as a 'flying carpet you can keep in your pocket'.

Ritchie's prototype was bought by enthusiasts in a (Kickstarter-style) pre-order scheme. Ritchie was lucky in retrospect that the company grew slowly. As many of the original batch he made later failed mechanically. Brompton learned and evolved the design and production process. Today they are now known for the quality of their welding. Some fans even ask for the joints to be lacquered and not hidden behind paint.

Ritchie got Brompton to the point in 2002 where it sold 7000 bikes a year and employed 24 people. Then it went on a growth spurt. Today Brompton has 315 employees and makes 50 000 bikes a year. Sales were up 15% in 2019. And they expect to sell 100 000 bikes a year within five years. Then came their launch of an eBike. They sold 6000 in 2019 but expect eBikes to be half the business within 10 years; 80% of their bikes are exported and Brompton sell in 44 countries worldwide, while still being manufactured by hand in the UK.

That's the Brompton product and business. The Brompton brand is all about the future of urbanism. Brompton support this with a *People for Movement* campaign. With slogans like:

BURN CALORIES, NOT FOSSIL FUELS
SAVE OUR CITIES BEFORE IT'S TOO LATE
UNCLOG ROADS AND ARTERIES

The campaign is pressing for bike friendly infrastructure, for cleaner air quality, more cycling, more physical activity. They point to examples like Copenhagen where research found:

> Cycling results in over a million fewer sick days a year in the capital alone . . . every kilometre cycled in Copenhagen adds 16p to the public purse through savings on transport costs and healthcare. Conversely, every kilometre driven costs the state 65p.[91]

Copenhagen is the epitome of a new urban quality of life – like Berlin, Munich and other cities that feature in the Monocle *Quality of Life* league table. These are low-slung, sparse, green cities, with neighbourhoods full of cafés and local shops, full of culture, community, and spirit. They are cities hipster creative classes want to live in; just as the gleaming metropoles of freeways and skyscrapers – along with garden-lined suburbs – were what people aspired to in the 1950s.

Brompton is based on a design that carries this bigger narrative and mission. They don't see their competition as other bikes, but other ways of moving. Their CEO, Butler Adams, says:

We are in the urban transport industry; the competition for Brompton is the tube or the car. Our customers are urbanites.

This insight drives their marketing strategy. Brompton targets specific cities – selected for the right infrastructure, climate, income level, topography, and culture – rather than whole countries. Their bike isn't for every city. Some are hilly, too car-dominated, or have too many potholes.

A brand like Brompton is more than a company on a mission; it is a community and a movement. Brompton has devotees. Including novelist Will Self who wrote:

> A Brompton folding bicycle is not only a superior means of locomotion, and a perfect antidote to the stresses of the modern world, but also a means of achieving a deeper harmony with place and culture than you've hitherto achieved.[92]

There is a general sense that the public attitudes to climate change are shifting. A new generation demand that brands and employers reflect this. Butler Adams at Brompton says:

> Unless you start giving a shit you are going to go bust. With younger people, if you don't engage with their values then they will walk. Not just in the UK but all over the world.

But then you need to start to build something positive that people want to join.

In my view, design – rather than communications – is the key. Create amazing experiences, understand what people need, what they value, and the rest will happen naturally.

Or as Butler Adams puts it: 'Make a bloody good bike.' The experience is even better on an eBike – this really does live up to the original Brompton vision of having a flying carpet in your pocket. As Butler Adams says:

> The main reason why the e-Bike is so good for the industry is you put someone on it and they flipping love it![93]

You can build a global business on understanding such innately human pleasures and urges.

Brompton taps into our love of cycling, and also the fascination of puzzles and contraptions. LEGO and Minecraft are built on our love of building blocks into towers. The Apple Mouse and iPhone understood that manipulation of tools by hand has fascinated people since the flint age.

Something all people love and are hard wired for is nature. Biologist E.O. Wilson called this biophilia; human beings have an instinct to 'affiliate with other forms of life'.

Biophilia has become a watchword in modern architecture and space design. Google, WeWork, and many others embraced it. Psychologists studying lean offices discovered that the presence of plants or even images of nature significantly increased performance in intelligence, memory, and (document-checking) productivity tests.[94] Numerous studies confirm that natural elements in the workplace, not just greenery but variations in light and temperature, patterns, water features, and natural materials all improve wellbeing and concentration.[95] One study found that people sitting by the window in a call centre were more productive than those in the middle of the room.[96] The philosophy is one of creating spaces that support not just work, but human thriving.

This love and concern for nature can be a powerful driver of system change. The *Blue Planet 2* documentary proved more effective than decades of information about plastic, litter, pollution.

An early example of greenwash was the TV commercials by oil company Chevron about their small scale (but big emotional impact) conservation schemes, looking after butterflies, bears, and sea turtles. What was wrong with this campaign was that the environmental damage done by Chevron made it hypocritical. The very refinery that hosted their butterfly sanctuary was fined for dumping pollutants into nearby Santa Monica Bay. But what was right about the campaign was it appealed strongly to public sentiments. The campaign won an Effie award and featured in a Harvard case study. In its own terms it did actually work. Right message; wrong brand.

Brands with a relevant, credible, and substantial positive connection with nature gain hugely by appealing to this. A brand that stands out in this regard is Patagonia, who might be described as an environmental activist that happens to sell clothing for climbing, skiing, and surfing.

Or as it says in Patagonia's vision: *we're in business to save our home planet.*

Patagonia is famous in marketing circles for a 2012 ad *Don't Buy This Jacket*. Which encouraged people shopping at Thanksgiving to only buy what they needed. This became an icon for those in marketing who wanted to say 'no' to overconsumption.

In 2016, Patagonia donated 100% of its takings on Black Friday to environmental causes. Patagonia backed up this responsible consumption message through their *Common Threads* initiative.[97] Reduce (don't buy what you don't need) was one element. Patagonia asked people to make a pledge. Patagonia's recycling programme, launched in 2005, took back 45 tonnes of old clothes in the following 6 years and turned 34 tonnes into new clothes. Patagonia also launched a repair scheme, promising to get tears and broken zips fixed, and the garment returned within 10 days. They facilitated reselling old Patagonia clothing through eBay. The philosophy – reduce, recycle, repair, reimagine – runs deep into how Patagonia clothes are designed. For instance, Patagonia don't believe in seasons and fashions to encourage people to update their wardrobe with this year's latest colour or look.

One thing Patagonia still has to figure out is their use of synthetic fabric and the microfibres they give off (when washed) that end up in oceans and lakes. Research in 2011 found that despite the 'micro' name, microfibres account for 85% of human-made debris on shorelines. They also pose a risk to human health when ingested by fish.

Patagonia has been researching this issue since 2016. They funded research to help them understand the extent of the problem (in their garments and in less well-made ones). They also looked into the characteristics of fabrics that contribute to fibre release. They have produced education materials for each consumer on how to take best care of garments to minimise microfibre pollution; including washing less often, using a filter (Patagonia is supplying the Guppy Friend bag), and frontloading washing machines. A long-term solution may be waterless washing machines. Patagonia gave funding to Tersus who make washing machines that use pressurised liquid CO_2 (LCO_2). Tersus so far targets commercial washing of workwear and protective clothing. They claim to extend the lifetime of clothes. LCO_2 also cleans better. For clothing contaminated with oil, water washing removes 58%, while LCO_2 removes 98%. The system is closed loop, producing no effluent waste and using no soap. Pretty cool. The next step would be making this technology available to domestic washing. Probably starting with eco launderettes as the system is too bulky and expensive for individual consumers.

Patagonia gives 1% of its profits to environmental causes and innovators. And has done so since it was founded by climber Yvon Chouinard in 1985. By 2019 the total donated was more than $100 million. In 2002, Chouinard started the *1% for the Planet*; an alliance of businesses that pledge to do likewise. In 2019, *1% for the Planet* had more than 1800 business members including ethical brands like Pukka Tea.

As we saw in a previous section, Patagonia also gave its $10 million Trump corporate tax windfall to environmental causes; commenting that in the middle of a global climate crisis, giving corporate America their biggest ever tax cut was 'irresponsible'.

It wasn't the first time Patagonia had clashed with Donald Trump. In 2017, the company joined a lawsuit by five native American tribes and some conservation NGOs, claiming that the president's decision to sign over 85% of the Bears Ears national monument (and 50% of the neighbouring Grand Escalante monument) for mining was illegal. Bears Ears is a holy site for native American tribes who have ancestors buried there; some structures on the site are older than the pyramids. The suit claims that The Antiquities Act of 1906 granted the president the authority to create national monuments, but not to reduce or rescind them. As well as this case, Patagonia is funding multiple conservation NGOs fighting for environmental justice. It also donates to conservation programmes under the themes of land, water, biodiversity, and climate.

In Europe, Patagonia's big recent campaign has been *Blue Heart* – which aims at protecting the last wild rivers in Europe from hydro dams. This involved raising public awareness about the issue and debunking the idea that hydro power is always 'green'. Patagonia made a documentary film to this end. Targeted the financial institutions that invest in a staggering 3000+ hydro power projects in the Balkans. They also got 120 000 signatures on a petition that was presented to the European Bank for Reconstruction and Development.

Recently Patagonia launched a platform called *Patagonia Action Works*. Where people can connect with grassroots local causes and donate money, volunteer, join protests.

Patagonia actively encourages employee activism internally to the extent that they offer all employees training with the Ruckus Society. If graduates of this programme are arrested, Patagonia offer what Ruckus called a 'get out of jail free card': paying bail, legal fees, and time off work. Patagonia commented on this policy saying;

It may sound as if we are training and subsidizing a bunch of tree huggers, hellraisers and brassbound ecologists. We are.[98]

Patagonia's work extends into its supply chain. They are helping communities where partner factories are based be more resilient to climate change; helping them deal with the emotional, physical, and financial consequences. An example was in Sri Lanka where workers at their partner Fairtrade sewing factory could not get to work in 2017 because of flooding. Rather than assume they knew what workers needed, Patagonia started the programme by asking them – and the answers went beyond heatwave conditions in a factory, or difficulty getting to work . . . to emotional stress at home in villages with low crop yields, with children unable to go to school.

Patagonia's supply chain accounts for 97% of its carbon emissions. Hence this is the focus of its efforts to become climate neutral by 2025 (25 years ahead of the Paris Agreement deadline).

Within sewing and fabric factories and the farms that grow their natural fibres, Patagonia's approach is to mitigate, capture, or eliminate emissions. They also are investing in renewable energy for their own facilities. They are already 100% renewable in the USA. They also have the schemes mentioned earlier to reduce, repair, recycle, and to extend the life of garments.

All of which will reduce but not eliminate carbon emissions. To do this they also need to do things that are carbon positive. For this they are investing in carbon capture projects, such as reforestation. And also putting their weight (alongside other forward-thinking natural brands like Dr Bronner's) behind a new Regenerative Organic Certification for agriculture.

Patagonia's activities are impressive and comprehensive. But what sings through in their marketing that listing all these programmes may not capture is a visceral passion for nature, for wild places, for wonderment. Patagonia is born out of love. What E.O. Wilson called biophilia.

Patagonia doesn't advertise much. The exception being getting public attention for things more important than selling jackets. In 2019, Patagonia ran advertising featuring 18 youth activists including Xiuhtezcatl Martinez and Jamie Margolin, with the headline 'Facing Extinction'. At the same time Patagonia closed offices and stores while encouraging people to join the climate strike and to petition Congress from their mobile (by texting CLIMATE to 71333).

It's not the main reason they do it. But activism does drive the business too. When Patagonia launched its *100% for the planet* promotion in 2016 they expected sales of $3 million. But the result exceeded $10 million. (One would hope that the jackets sold were needed.) This shows the public appetite to get involved in brands standing up for nature.

Another example of an organisation run from a total passion for nature (and human nature) is Natura Cosmetics in Brazil. If you want to know what a company might look like in future, visit Natura. That's no accident. One of their executives told me that their ultimate purpose is to show how it is possible for human beings to live and work better together in 25 years' time.

Natura's headquarters look like the setting for a utopian sci fi film. The office campus outside Sao Paulo is set in what Brazilians call 'the woods' (to a visitor from London it looks like lush forest). The factories, lab, and offices have a futuristic, organic modernism that is integrated with nature. In the trees by cafeteria, swooping toucans remind you that you are not in Berkshire. While the round observatory windows in meeting rooms in the conference centre look out on kaleidoscopes of large butterflies in the woods behind (I checked and rather charmingly that's the collective noun).

The architecture is suffused with biophilia design; walkways, natural materials, gorgeous smells, and energy shrines full of large crystals. You would hardly know you were visiting one of the top 10 cosmetics companies in the world. Although when you realise that it is ranked 15th in a list of the 100 most sustainable global companies (and ranked as high as 2nd in previous years) the setting and connection with nature philosophy make more sense.

Natura was founded in 1969 by Antônio Luiz Da Cunha Seabra and Guilherme Peirão Leal. Both are still involved in the business. I had the honour to meet with them during the course of a brand identity project with design agency Pentagram. The philosophy of Natura is a fusion of two kinds of genius. The genius of meaningful products that encourage people to reconnect with themselves, with each other and with nature. And the genius of building a business model that drives social and environmental goods (rather than bads).

Their slogan Bem Esta Bem – well being well – has a circularity that doesn't fully translate into English. It means what I described back to them as 'interbeing'; the insight held by the ingenious people of the Amazon that we are all connected; with nature and with each other. Pentagram poetically re-expressed this as 'the beauty of being as one'.

The Natura philosophy is epitomised by their Ekos range. Sourced with Amazon tribes, to create a business model for preserving biodiversity while bringing new botanicals to market. Or by a range like Sou; soap which is packaged in squishy pouches modelled on water droplets. Enabling Natura to fit 38% more packs on each truck and reduce CO_2 in shipping.

When working on their sub brands Natura developed a fascinating strategic methodology which starts with the question: 'what's the alienation?' Alienation is a condition highlighted by authorities like Karl Marx and the existentialists. It describes modern people as at a 'breaking point' in our alienated relationship with nature, culture, the body. The Natura brand exists to reconnect people with nature and with human nature. To touch and be touched by these.

Luis Seabra says that there is a 'semiotic' in each Natura product. This semiotic creates meaning by acting on some part that has become alienated. It could be, for instance, our relationship with ageing. Other cosmetics will promise to mask or delay this. Natura takes a holistic approach that finds beauty in moments like a grandchild rubbing cream into a grandmother's hand.

Biophilia is a human instinct. We instinctively move towards the natural. This is a huge factor in marketing at the moment, in choice of materials, in experiences, in food ingredients.

Another innate human instinct that can help brands to drive sustainability efforts is generativity.

Generativity is a term invented by American psychologist Eric Eriksson. Eriksson had a model of the stages of life. Like Shakespeare's seven stages of man. At each of Eriksson's eight psychosocial stages a new drama would unfold. Each represents a life crisis that the individual has to work through and survive to keep developing as a healthy personality.

The famous part of Eriksson's model was the *identity crisis* associated with adolescence. Society in his time was obsessed with the new teen culture. What was it with these long-haired youths and their antisocial behaviour? They were a mystery to their parents who had grown up on traditional values like 'duty'. Eriksson's theory explained in psychological terms why teens felt the need to rebel in order to establish their own adult ego identity.

Eriksson's seventh stage of life is the one that interests us here. Generativity. This is encountered in a midlife crisis, somewhere between the ages of 35 and 65. In the previous stage (18–40) Eriksson saw the key task as one of starting a family, forming successful relationships, building your career. With that achieved, you are onto the next question which is 'what is my legacy?'

Eriksson believed the trigger for generativity was feeling your mortality. Then you have a choice. Some choose to cling onto their youth, stock up on anti-ageing cream and hair colouring, have an affair, buy a sports car. Live out a denial that you will decline then die. And that youth is slipping through your fingers. In the process they fail to grow and become a brittle and shallow stereotyped version of themselves. One that diminishes every year.

The alternative is to find something bigger than your ego to invest in. Act in Eriksson's words 'for the good of the species'. Hedge fears of death and demise by contributing things of lasting value that will outlive you. This could be mentoring younger colleagues, starting a business, getting involved with your grandchildren, writing a book, volunteering for a charity . . .

Remember that the whole of sustainability is based on a generative ethic – leaving the world in a decent state for those that come after. The relevance of the idea is doubled today by the climate crisis and a dread feeling of mortality for all human civilisation. Playing a positive role in the face of this crisis is a vital psychological step. The alternative is we stagnate, distract ourselves, indulge in 'golden age' nostalgia and diminish ourselves in the process.

Looking forward creates hope and energy to act.

Random example. What if the next economy was a kelp economy? It's a great source of nutrition, fuel, and also fibre for materials. Seaweed could be the forests of the future and are huge carbon sinks that could also tackle ocean acidification and deoxygenation. Recent reports looked at this and it looks promising. What you can do within sea agriculture that isn't as easy on land is that you can sequester carbon in the deep ocean. One report noted that 'marine calcification is estimated to be the biggest carbon sink on earth over geological timescales by forming layers of calcium carbonate, the basic ingredient of chalk, limestone and marble'.[99]

You get my (ocean) drift. Sounds exciting doesn't it? When you open your mind to a radically different liveable, green economy . . . then positive energy, ideas, innovations start to emerge. This is the gift that comes from the choice to be generative, to invest in the collective legacy.

There has never been a better time in history to build innovative green challenger companies. To pioneer neglected lines of research. Seaweed foods, fuels, and materials. Insect pet food. Community energy. Shoes made of apple skin. Circular economy design. If only a fraction of the effort, imagination, and capital put into WeWork had been put into future proofing societies.

Generativity is seeping into branding. British Telecom's latest TV commercial features a girl (wearing a duffle reminiscent of Greta Thunberg's trademark raincoat) with a script that's all about generativity. It uses the opening words from Dickens' *Tale of Two Cities* to reflect the mood of the times while also putting out a message of optimism.

> It was the best of times, it was the worst of times.
> It was the age of wisdom, it was the age of foolishness.
> It was the epoch of belief. It was the epoch of incredulity.
> It was the season of light. It was the season of darkness.
> It was the spring of hope. It was the winter if despair.
> We had everything before us. We had nothing before us.
> The future is ours to make.
> We're giving 5 million kids the tech skills they need.
> BT. Beyond Limits.

Throughout the commercial there are references that show how Dickens' prose is relevant today: robotics, connected street lighting, fake news, electric car charging, CCTV, and renewable energy. The ad closes with the girl joining her school class where they are learning about tech.

British Telecom have been a stalwart of the business sustainability scene in the UK for as long as I can remember. They funded so many research projects and events in corporate responsibility. And they never made a big deal of this. So, I don't begrudge them the Greta reference, nor feel this is greenwashing. They earned the right to talk about a better future.

But this kind of engagement with generativity – recognising 'the Greta factor' that our own children are now holding us account for what we do next on climate – has to go beyond being a nice corporate ad campaign. It has to be a real process and dialogue.

Marvin and Sandra from *Future Search* hosted a seminal sustainability discussion at IKEA that I attended a decade ago (and wrote about earlier in this book). I was fascinated by their facilitation and spent time in the breaks asking them about it. One story they told me of another project was this: they were engaged to help with an African peace process. For a week before the main meeting they held a conference attended by the sons and daughters of each political leader. At the start of the main event these children came in and made a presentation to their collected parents about their discussions and what they concluded.

It seems to me that if you are a business leader – like the FTSE250 CEO I met recently who told me 'I've got several Gretas living at home' – this kind of approach might be a great idea for the next strategy day you are holding with your directors?

The Irish parliament did this in November 2019. A youth assembly met in the Dail to discuss climate change. As a result, they put 10 recommendations to the government ranging from hemp farming to renewables. Their statement begins with the words:

> We, the youth of Ireland, call on our elected representatives and on adults to listen.

Many reading this will agree that it is high time that we did.

2.11 Build your own Paradigm Shift in 15 Steps

Say you are the leader in a large business. Or the founder of a new venture. Or just a change agent trying to bring your organisation with you. And you buy the need to make a paradigm shift. What processes can you draw upon to make progress in that direction?

What follows is a collection of things that I've seen work. They might not all work in your situation. But some may be worth considering:

1. Restate your Principles

Vision & Values exercises were de rigeur for leadership teams around the 2000s. They would result in a mission statement. At that point it was about having a *Big Hairy Audacious Goal*.

It is often inspiring is to revisit the founding principles of the business. Indra Nooyi, former Pepsi CEO, said that her *Performance with Purpose* programme had its roots in the history of the organization:

The purpose, the character, of a corporation has been woven into the fabric of PepsiCo's DNA from the beginning. The company's founders, Don Kendall and Herman Lay, set out 12 ideas for succeeding in a large corporation, including 'put your emphasis on job fulfilment and a positive working environment, not on making money.'[100]

This kind of bred in the bone principle gives a current CEO leverage. I interviewed Sir Mark Moody-Stuart for a think tank report. I asked him about his time as CEO of Shell during the Brent Spar crisis. Moody-Stuart said that his room for manoeuvre came from a phrase in the Shell statutes about providing 'reasonable returns' to shareholders. His interpretation of 'reasonable returns' allowed him to challenge unreasonable projects with significant environmental and geopolitical risk.

IBM was another organisation that needed to restate and reanimate their principles in recent years. In 1914 – when they made typewriters and other (International) Business Machines – the IBM founder Thomas Watson decided upon three key principles:

respect for the individual,
the best customer service
the pursuit of excellence.

Across the twentieth century, new employees were given this checklist on a laminated card to carry in their wallet. IBM became known as 'Big Blue' – an upright and uptight sort of organisation; corporate and smartly suited. The reality inside was a touch more appealing. IBM had a highly intellectual research culture, home to many of the smartest technologists of their age.

In 2002, a new CEO called Sam Palmisano came on board. I saw them speak at the *Start* conference about IBM's *Smart Planet* vision. It was a compelling big picture vision originally launched by a similar speech Palmisano gave at the United Nations. *Smart Planet* was the culmination of an internal revolution. This started with Palmisano getting IBM to revisit its core principles. The context was the dotcom boom and subsequent crash. Leaving organisations like IBM scratching their heads and wondering: what now?

Palmisano realised that with more than 300 000 employees in over 170 countries, top down organisation wasn't going to be the core operating model in future. He needed a distributed organisation of teams and individuals taking the initiative. The way IBM initiated this was to host a simultaneous massive virtual conference using their IBM Jam platform. Online discussions ran for 72 hours and 50 000 employees contributed. These comments were content analysed and distilled into key themes. New values were proposed as a result of the Jam:

> Dedication to every client's success
> Innovation that matters – for our company and the world
> Trust and personal responsibility in all relationships.

These were further brought to life in a statement of what it means to be an IBMer:

> . . . forward thinkers. We believe that the application of intelligence, reason and science can improve business, society and the human condition.
> . . . love grand challenges, as well as everyday improvements. Whatever the problem or the context, every IBMer seeks ways to tackle it creatively – to be an innovator.
> . . . strive to be first – in technology, in business, in responsible policy.
> . . . take informed risks and champion new (sometimes unpopular) ideas.

2. Make it the Reality

You have restated your principles. What now?

Many organisations put the values up on the wall, then carry on doing what they did before.

IBM's effort to make the values a living reality included an initiative called the '$100 million bet on trust'. Managers on the ground had a $5000 budget to do the extraordinary, without having to go through the usual approvals. If a client had an issue, they could hire people on the spot to fix it. The scheme was a success and was extended to 22 000 managers (hence the $100m).

One big lesson of the Values Jam was how proud IBMers were of their historical contribution. IBM marketer David Yaun commented that:

> We'd never considered how strongly people feel about IBM's role in shaping the modern world and their pride in the fact that our technology helped man get to the moon and helped to create the first social security system and is now being applied to fighting cancer and AIDS and mapping the human genome. Although we had an inkling that there would be something around innovation and being the technical leaders, the societal aspect was eye-opening for us.

This was the genesis of the *Smart Planet* idea. Seeing that what you do matters in the bigger scheme of things. It was a beautiful way of aligning what's Net Good for the world with their strategy, via the pride of people who work there.

3. Meet the World

People in business can wear blinkers. They are removed from the reality of what they make, the lives that they serve. They live in a narrowed, tidy, formal reality of meeting rooms, desks in rows, smart clothing. Some frontline and service workers might experience the messy world beyond this. But most work is abstracted from the real meaning and impact of what you do.

It is this ivory tower abstraction that leads to many of the 'bads' in sustainability. It is the unseeing pressure for 'results at all costs' that can leads to worker suicides, slave labour, emissions test cheating, and unsafe products.

The implication is this. Don't read reports. Go and meet the world.

If you want to be more digital, spend a week in Silicon Valley.

If you want to understand logistics, put yourself as a human package inside your own transport and warehousing system.

If you want to understand child labour, go to India and meet people affected by it.

I have known leaders of corporations who have done each of these things. And the vivid human direct experience has made all the difference in spurring innovation.

It's not just about intellectual understanding. It's about humanly getting it. It's about seeing solutions and having a feel for how they work. It's about the motivation to innovate in the first place. Warby Parker got into spectacles because one of the founders lost a pair travelling and couldn't afford to replace them. These first-person stories make it feel like a problem worth fixing. They also make it easier to communicate the business idea and transmit the culture.

When Dave Lewis, CEO of Tesco, started their turnaround in 2014 the first thing he did was take the leadership team away to shop and cook together in a holiday cottage in Norfolk.

4. Hold a Jam

IBM's original Jams back in the 1990s were sessions where engineers threw ideas around. The word meant jamming like a jazz band – improvising ideas. They used videophone to facilitate the flow of ideas and interaction (meeting face to face without having to travel).

Whether you meet online, in virtual spaces, in a local hall . . . giving a diverse and qualified group of people some sharply honed challenges is sure to result in fresh ideas.

You can also host a hackathon, getting engineers and developers to build something in a day.

I remember brainstorming with an engineer from Unilever at a Forum for the Future innovation session. What we came up with was a gym where your clothes were washed and some of the energy came from the gym equipment. The key insight was that they already had the technology to wash clothes with zero waste in water and soap (like LCO_2). It's just the machines cost $1 million. I said: we need to go back to the launderette then. And he said: we tried that, but it was low status and too much effort for most people. So, I said: what if it was part of your gym? Gyms have high status and you go there anyway . . .

There could be a hundred other solutions. The key thing was bringing together diverse people with different thought styles. It's why internet incubators put together teams of business strategists, designers, and developers. Like the electrons, neutrons, and protons that make an atom.

5. Where Can We Have an Impact?

It's a deceptively simple question. But not a simple one to answer.

You can go for an off the shelf answer. Take the Sustainable Development Goals. Pick three. Or indeed measure yourself against all of them. These are certainly great points of inspiration about what the world needs. But can lead to generic or incremental ideas.

The usual way of answering a strategy question like this is to analyse. Past performance. Sustainability data. Competitor moves. Developments in parallel industries.

But numbers won't get you to a paradigm shift where you flip from Not Bad to Net Good. For that you need imagination, jamming, a flow of ideas, hypotheses, investigative sprints.

I met yesterday with a food ingredients company. Within the food industry, the obvious impacts are from agriculture and the human health impacts like obesity. But their core is processing agricultural products to extract value. They could apply this to new plant-based materials rather than food. Or to new crops like seaweed. Both could see explosive growth in the green economy. Those are the kinds of impacts that won't occur to you through reductive analysis.

It can be that it is hard to answer without investigation. Doing some R&D. Meeting small companies and attending fringe events. That's because the opportunity itself may be emergent. An unforeseen opportunity that comes from a new technology or approach. Viagra was originally developed as a heart pill. But then Pfizer started to get reports back from field trials saying male heart patients were reporting unexpected side effects!

6. What Business are We In?

Simple question. But it can open the door to innovation if pursued with imagination.

Are we in the energy business or the warm home business?

If it's the latter, then well sealed houses could be your model, or district heating, or air circulation (a room has its warmest air by the ceiling). Or get into making warmer clothes.

It's much easier to recast your business model if you start with the human needs you serve.

But sometimes the pivot comes from what you physically do. The founder of Blockbuster Video was previously in waste management and knew a thing or two about shifting boxes, unblocking bottlenecks, high volumes, and efficient logistics.

The trick is finding a restatement of what business you are in that is true to the present but has ample room for growth and purpose. Working with executive search firm Heidrick & Struggles we came up with the phrase: 'we're in the business of character'. For the Lloyd's of London insurance market, the phrase was 'underwriting human progress'.

One simple test is: does it make employees proud of what they do and inspired to do more?

7. Science-based Targets

At the top of the world's to do list is halving carbon emissions by 2030 and reducing net emissions by 2050 to zero.

We have made negative progress in this direction so far (carbon emissions are still growing).

Many companies joined the Science-based Targets movement and committed to radical action on climate.

Whatever your plans to be Net Good – you might be out to tackle obesity, job skills, or mental health – you will need to be on this carbon journey in order to be Not Bad.

There could be a new kind of M&A strategy which builds a portfolio, some parts of which are massively carbon reductive in order to balance out others with an unavoidable footprint.

One percent of the world's emissions come from online video streaming. And streaming video (in $ terms) is growing at 20% a year. Netflix and Amazon Prime both use Amazon Web Servers. Imagine if Amazon, the biggest spending R&D organisation, made clean energy and CO_2 reduction a core business? It could take a huge chunk out of their energy bill. Hence why companies like Google already made huge investments in clean energy and cleantech R&D.

8. Up the Future Ambition ×10

The best kind of target is the one so ambitious you don't yet know how you will reach it.

This gives the moon-shot factor. It forces you to create the means of achieving the goal along the way. Even if you don't achieve your goal, you will probably go much further than if you started with sensible objectives.

LEGO are dropping the (made from oil) plastic brick by 2030.

LEGO already introduced some trees and similar made from a sugarcane based alternative material. But this is not strong enough to make LEGO bricks. They don't know yet what they will make bricks from in future. They just know that it will be sustainably sourced, and it won't come from oil. And they have committed $1 billion and 100 people to the task. LEGO have also committed to 100% renewable energy and a carbon neutral supply chain by 2030.

9. Hack the Present System

LEGO makes 75 billion bricks a year. This has been growing with the global success of its franchise, movies, games, and partnerships. They only made 20 billion bricks a year when I worked with them in the mid 2000s. Even back then they estimated that they had already manufactured 400 billion bricks. By 2019 my estimate is they have sold 1000 billion.

That is 133 bricks for every person on the planet. There are roughly 1.3 billion children aged 5–14. Each could have 770 bricks – a pretty decent collection.

There's just one catch. How to get old LEGO to new users? It's not the sort of thing (I hope) most people put in the bin. LEGO says their research shows that '97% of LEGO owners keep or share their bricks, passing them on to friends or family'.[101]

LEGO have started moving to a circular economy of LEGO through their *Replay* scheme. This collects the bricks from families who want to pass them on, repacks and distributes them via Give Back Box to places like Teach For America. LEGO are a pro social company. I'd say their biggest positive impact is inspiring the next generation of engineers and makers. But it's great to see them managing their footprint too (and I wish them luck with the new materials).

10. Skunkworks

It's amazing what you can make these days in an incubator.

Internet incubator YCombinator started only 15 years ago. But in that time has launched over 2000 companies including Stripe, AirBnB, Reddit, Twitch, and Dropbox; 100 of their graduating companies are valued at more than $150 million and 19 of them at more than $1 billion. Every year there are fresh examples and some of them are way 'out there'. One of this year's graduating companies (Kern Systems) uses DNA to store data. Apparently, it's a cost effective, low energy way to store the big data sets that modern information systems are drowning in.

In a big company you have huge resources but can tend to stifle things that start from scratch.

In this case, a separate radical skunkwork incubator can be just the ticket.

Google is often named the most innovative company in the world. And even within their organisation they separate off moon-shot projects into a division called X. The remit of this group is to invent and launch wildly new technologies that aim to make the world a radically better place. Some of the existing graduating programmes include molten salt renewable energy storage, wind energy from kites, and a deep learning AI system called Google Brain that have already more than paid for the whole of X. The lab is 'semi-secret' about what it is working on, but I couldn't help noticing they are seeking interns with a background in quantum computing.

11. The Can-Do Plan

It's one thing to claim it can be done.

It's another to show how it can be done.

One approach that has proved effective is using modelling to work out – with current technologies if possible – how to make it from here to there.

The moon-shot plan of my (future energy grid building) client Wärtsilä was the idea that it is now possible for each local energy market in the world to transition to 100% renewables. The path to 100% was different in different regions; more wind in the UK, more solar in Saudi . . . Wärtsilä worked with a think tank to develop a model. And took this to energy utilities. It's clarifying for their clients to be able to make long term investment plans based on this modelling and a clear idea of what, when, and how much it will cost.

In a previous era, Greenpeace used the Department of Energy & Climate Change's own published modelling tool to show how we could achieve UK climate commitments and also meet all our energy needs without any nuclear power. This caused a lot of debate and it wouldn't have been possible if DECC hadn't made their My2050 tool available.

12. It Takes an Ecosystem to Save an Ecosystem

My guess is that LEGO will solve its challenge not through its own R&D efforts, but through some innovation that lives on a science park. There is a promising new material I saw in Finland that makes something as hard as plastic out of wood cellulose, for instance. The material named Woodly is designed to be recyclable, so that as well as coming from a renewable source (FSC certified forests) it can be part of a circular economy. Should any Woodly end up being incinerated, it generates 70% less CO_2 than burning traditional plastics.

Most companies are used to building relationships with the digital start-up ecosystem. Companies like Walmart, Target, Unilever, and Diageo have corporate venture funds and incubators. There is a growing global cohort of eco and social disruptive innovators and these could become a next wave of corporate venturing.

Many sustainable disruptors are held back by lack of funding and market access. Water technology enjoyed a rush of interest. In 2013, there were 113 deals totalling $400 million. That's a decent chunk, but a fraction of what goes into tech investing. It is only 4% of the amount VC fund SoftBank invested in WeWork, for instance. And then the water tech market slumped. By 2016 there were only 37 investment deals with a total invested of $148 million, according to the Cleantech Group. Most funding comes from water utilities and their suppliers like GE and Suez. ImagineH2O, a water-tech focused accelerator, had 181 applications from promising new water tech start-ups in 2018 – double the amount in 2017. And they expected 250 in 2019.

I saw an amazing water tech start-up when I was working with Natura. A team in Start-up Chile developed a cheap and easy to use way to provide unlimited clean water. And they had proved it worked in the José de Cerrillos community. Their solution was to put a simple low energy device into a pipeline so that the water was purified. Unlike conventional water purifiers, this gizmo uses a patented plasma technology developed by a NASA engineer.

Plasma is the fourth state of matter (solid liquid gas plasma). In simple terms, it is a gas so hot that the atoms split into electrons and ions that can move separately. A brief moment in a plasma state ensures that anything living in the water is no longer living. The innovation was working how to do this in a plumber's pipe at a low cost in money and energy. The technology was developed by a radical organisation called AIC who are attempting to link advanced technology innovation with the poorest of communities. This was easily the most exciting start-up I saw that year. But languishing in a water tech sector that is not attracting investment and whose support is too slow and selective. It needs a big push. Why not from drinks brands who have identified water stress as one of their key impact issues? Such as PepsiCo.

13. Getting Granular

Unilever was one of the first modern global corporations to set itself a moon-shot target to halve its ecological footprint relative to its size (what they actually expected was they would double in size while keeping the footprint the same). It was a big enough commitment to call for radical change and innovation rather than just incremental change.

To make this a reality, Unilever held Brand Imprint workshops with each brand team, along with internal specialists (such as sustainability, supply chain, and packaging) and some invited external experts (including yours truly). The goal of the two-day workshops was to review where they were, get inspiration from the experts, and then agree on three simple and bold new actions which could help Unilever achieve its overall Sustainable Living Goals.

14. Open Innovation

How to conduct meetings that drive radical innovation and escape old paradigm thinking? One answer to that question is to look at how software developers pulled it off. What hackers, open source software, home brew hardware tapped into was actually working like amateur enthusiasts. As Linus Torvalds (founder of Linux) put it, they did it 'just for fun'.

There was a huge surge in innovation after the dotcom crash. This was when web 2.0 developed – the fusing of community and computing – one example being the social network.

The bigger shift to come out of web 2.0 was social production. Groups of people self-organising outside the old corporate model. Like Linux, or Wikipedia. We found that ten thousand hobbyists could build almost anything, especially in software. Later this model extended to politics (Obama as the first crowdsourced president) and Kickstarter.

You can tap into this trend directly by starting an open innovation platform. LEGO has one called LEGO ideas. Anybody can submit an idea for a new LEGO set. They have to build a model and take some photos and write a description. The community then upvotes their favourites. Past winners include Women of NASA, Sesame Street, and International Space Station. The winning sets have a chance to go into production and earn 1% royalties.

The same model can be applied to social and environmental impact ideas. Check out OpenIDEO. Founded in 2010 by the leading product design agency IDEO, Open IDEO 'enables people worldwide to come together and build solutions for today's toughest societal problems. Online and around the globe.' If you are a company or an NGO with a big challenge you can join the scheme as a sponsor. Non-profit sponsors have included Ellen MacArthur foundation and USAID. Corporate partners have included Starbucks, Ford, Nike, and Unilever.

15. DIY Paradigm Shifts

Many of us hold and attend workshops on a weekly basis.

The plus points are that these workshops take people away from the day to day and put them in a space where they are not distracted, with a mindset to innovate.

The less than positive reality is that attendees go to workshops every week, just like you do. And quickly fall into workshop-based stereotyped thinking and constraints. They know how to brainstorm, collect ideas, report back. And can sleepwalk through your session while feeling great about how engaged they were, how well they listened and built on ideas, captured notes, reported back, and were a nice team player.

A group of us held some sustainability workshops as part of the London Design Festival. My favourite presentation came from a young comedian and artist called Miriam Elia, who stood up in a conference room at the Design Council that was full of canvas shoe-wearing millennial hippies holding handwritten flipcharts and said:

> . . . our group really struggled with this task emotionally.
> It's like . . . you know . . . like when a baby is screaming, and you don't know whether to beat its head against the wall or throw it out of the window?

It was literally the first surprising thing anybody had said all day. While I know it offended a few people, I felt it was the shot of adrenalin our discussions had needed. Plus, it was funny. Even more so because some didn't seem to fully realise that she was joking.

There's no way around the fact that your workshop will be full of sleepwalkers who are acting the 'the way I think and behave in workshops'.

But at least you can plan around it – here are a few tips and tricks I have pulled together over the years:

Invite their inner child. I often get people to do a warm-up exercise using LEGO. I decide what the actual exercise is based on the subject – in one workshop we built a new supply chain with LEGO, in another we built a model of a cultural value you hold dear. But the real point is to get them playing like a child and building with their hands.

Bring some gate-crashers to the party. The casting will depend on the task. But for instance, when we held a get together at IKEA to talk about eCommerce, we invited some successful dotcom entrepreneurs in their 20s to come and join the discussions and chivvy them along.

Get people to mark themselves against high ambitions. Score your ideas out of 10 after every session against things like 'Breakthrough' and 'Never Seen Before'. People are lazy (I know I am) and will spend three days contributing their 'old chestnut' ideas unless you jolt them out of this by getting them to score their ideas in this way.

Serendipity. Give people a random element to use as a nucleus for further ideas. I was running a workshop on future water solutions. And all the ideas looked similar. Desalination plants. River treatment. New filtering and piping systems. So, I gave groups random pictures torn from a magazine. One group was given a beer bottle and they started to think about 'bottlenecks' in the system. Another was given a picture of a human body and started to think 'maybe the answer is to give people a pill?'

Rupture. Change the way you judge how it's going. Don't look for smiley engaged people and a slap on the back from the client in the coffee break. Look for building frustration, conflict, tension, breakdown, mutiny. Because those are steps on the way to breakthrough when *finally*, somebody actually says something new.

Change scenes. Go for a walk together and tell people that on their way they will find the answer. Plan sessions so they break for sleep, dinner rather than packing it all into a day. Tell people to bring one great idea that comes from a dream the next day. Taking the group into nature is a key part of this. I am sure we might not have come up with the 'like a forest' sustainability vision for IKEA if we hadn't held our workshop in a forest.

Empathise. Don't just sit there shooting ideas off. Go deep into the experience of the people you are trying to serve. Follow their journey. If possible, invite them, visit them, call them up and ask them stuff. And put yourself in the heart of the system as a subject – Einstein figured out relativity by imagining being a photon travelling the universe.

Ultimately all you need is a free-flowing conversation with some people who know enough to make radical ideas workable, plus some crazy enough people able to suggest radical enough ideas in the first place.

And you need to commit to playing, doing it 'just for fun' and not being so adult about it.

Problems are serious, but breakthrough creativity seldom is.

Notes

1. https://www.theguardian.com/environment/2019/jan/25/our-house-is-on-fire-greta-thunberg16-urges-leaders-to-act-on-climate
2. https://www.theguardian.com/world/2019/oct/26/young-people-predisposed-shake-up-established-order-protest
3. https://www.khanacademy.org/humanities/us-history/postwarera/postwar-era/a/the-baby-boom
4. https://www.ipsos.com/en-us/news-polls/Gates-goalkeepers-youth-optimism
5. https://www.edelman.com/sites/g/files/aatuss191/files/2019-02/2019_Edelman_Trust_Barometer_Global_Report.pdf
6. https://blogs.scientificamerican.com/cross-check/revolt-against-the-rich/
7. https://www.ers.usda.gov/topics/food-nutrition-assistance/food-security-in-the-us.aspx#.UelqMdLVBQg
8. https://thehill.com/hilltv/what-americas-thinking/428747-new-poll-americans-overwhelmingly-support-taxing-the-wealth-of
9. https://www.scientificamerican.com/article/the-american-economy-is-rigged/
10. https://www.thetimes.co.uk/article/china-quick-to-soak-up-blue-planet-3nh8h9zfl
11. https://uk.reuters.com/article/uk-environment-un-pollution/nearly-200-nations-promise-to-stop-ocean-plastic-waste-idUKKBN1E02FY
12. https://es.reuters.com/article/idUSKBN1E02F7
13. https://www.bbc.co.uk/news/business-46835573
14. https://www.bbc.co.uk/news/uk-43224797
15. https://www.nationalgeographic.com/news/2017/07/plastic-produced-recycling-waste-ocean-trash-debris-environment/
16. https://www.ft.com/content/0bf645dc-d8f1-11e7-9504-59efdb70e12f
17. https://www.bbc.co.uk/news/business-43724314

18. https://www.letsrecycle.com/news/latest-news/terracycle-unveils-loop-shopping-platform/
19. https://www.circularonline.co.uk/news/blockchain-technology-to-revolutionise-the-trade-of-recyclables/
20. https://www.sciencedaily.com/releases/2019/04/190415144004.htm
21. https://www.bpf.co.uk/press/oil_consumption.aspx
22. https://www.vegansociety.com/news/media/statistics
23. https://www.waitrose.com/content/dam/waitrose/Inspiration/Waitrose%20&%20Partners%20Food%20and%20Drink%20Report%20 2018.pdf
24. https://skepticalscience.com/animal-agriculture-meat-global-warming.htm
25. http://planetearthherald.com/eating-meat-is-a-major-cause-of-global-warming/
26. https://www.fern.org/news-resources/eu-consumption-of-beef-and-deforestation-91/
27. https://skepticalscience.com/animal-agriculture-meat-global-warming.htm
28. http://www.fao.org/fileadmin/templates/esa/Global_persepctives/world_ag_2030_50_2012_rev.pdf
29. https://www.plantandfood.co.nz/file/protein-china-perspective.pdf
30. http://www.ox.ac.uk/news/2018-06-01-new-estimates-environmental-cost-food
31. https://www.bbc.co.uk/news/uk-england-49440639
32. https://fashionunited.uk/news/retail/the-rise-of-vegan-fashion-in-stats/2019021841635
33. https://www.bmj.com/content/365/bmj.l1613
34. https://www.momsacrossamerica.com/gmo_impossible_burger_positive_for_carcinogenic_glyphosate
35. https://www.ncbi.nlm.nih.gov/pubmed/10749030
36. https://medium.com/thrive-global/good-things-take-time-words-of-wisdom-with-bjorn-oste-ceo-of-good-idea-ab60912339a6
37. https://thechallengerproject.com/blog/2016/oatly
38. https://www.plantbasednews.org/culture/its-like-milk-but-made-for-humans-oatly-campaign-uk

39. https://www.chinadaily.com.cn/a/201910/28/WS5db64ccca310c-f3e35573eaf.html

40. https://www.gglaw.us/giannuzzi-brand-of-the-month-oatly/

41. https://scholar.harvard.edu/files/mankiw/files/know_what_youre_pro-testing.pdf

42. Alexis de Tocqueville [1856] (2011). *The Old Regime and the Revolution*, Paris: Levy, p. 157

43. https://www.blackrock.com/hk/en/insights/larry-fink-ceo-letter

44. https://www.dw.com/en/blackrock-the-secret-world-power/a-18653761

45. https://www.businessroundtable.org/business-roundtable-redefines-the-purpose-of-a-corporation-to-promote-an-economy-that-serves-all-americans

46. https://www.businessroundtable.org/business-roundtable-redefines-the-purpose-of-a-corporation-to-promote-an-economy-that-serves-all-americans

47. https://www.forbes.com/sites/christianweller/2019/05/30/the-2017-tax-cuts-didnt-work-the-data-prove-it/#5af5a28658c1

48. Hills, T.T., Proto, E., Sgroi, D. et al. (2019). Historical analysis of national subjective wellbeing using millions of digitized books. *Nat Hum Behav*: doi:10.1038/s41562-019-0750-z.

49. https://globalwellnessinstitute.org/press-room/press-releases/global-wellness-institute-releases-report-and-survey-on-the-future-of-wellness-at-work/

50. https://www.wri.org/blog/2019/08/new-business-roundtable-statement-are-200-ceos-stuck-yesterdays-corporate

51. https://www.unilever.com/news/news-and-features/Feature-article/2016/businesses-must-embrace-the-disruptive-power-of-young-people.html

52. https://www.theglobeandmail.com/report-on-business/careers/man-agement/how-unilever-won-over-shareholders-with-its-long-term-approach/article36538572/

53. https://www.sharedvalue.org/about-shared-value

54. https://www.ft.com/content/d8b6d9fa-4eb8-11e8-ac41-759eee1efb74

55. http://news.mit.edu/2013/footwear-carbon-footprint-0522

56. https://www.wired.com/story/veja-running-shoe/

57. https://www.mirror.co.uk/news/uk-news/revealed-actual-number-shoes-british-9660645

58. https://www.mckinsey.com/industries/healthcare-systems-and-services/our-insights/how-the-world-could-better-fight-obesity
59. https://www.bustle.com/p/outdoor-voices-cotton-campaign-features-a-model-who-uses-a-wheelchair-the-representation-is-so-vital-18233782
60. https://www.sharedvalue.org/sites/default/files/2017%20Summit/Shared%20Value%20-%20An%20Inflection%20Point%20in%20the%20Making.pdf
61. https://www.sharedvalue.org/sites/default/files/2017%20Summit/Shared%20Value%20-%20An%20Inflection%20Point%20in%20the%20Making.pdf
62. https://www.statista.com/chart/16903/microsoft-stock-price-under-satya-nadella/
63. https://www.microsoft.com/africa/4afrika/about-us.aspx
64. https://www.strategy-business.com/article/11518?gko=9b3b4
65. https://www.euractiv.com/section/energy/news/bp-shareholders-demand-climate-action-but-reject-calls-for-hard-targets/
66. https://www.forbes.com/sites/danschawbel/2017/11/21/indra-nooyi-achieving-both-financial-growth-and-purpose-at-pepsico/#1d0236cbeaa6
67. https://www.warbyparker.com/assets/img/sustainability/report-2018.pdf
68. https://www.bbc.co.uk/news/world-europe-44545860
69. https://www.edie.net/news/7/Sustainable-Living-Brands-delivered-record-75--of-Unilever-s-2018-turnover-growth/
70. https://www.thedrum.com/news/2019/06/19/unilever-chief-alan-jope-keith-weed-s-successor-working-with-networks-and-the-need
71. https://www.thedrum.com/news/2019/06/19/unilever-chief-alan-jope-keith-weed-s-successor-working-with-networks-and-the-need
72. https://adage.com/article/cmo-strategy/nike-ad-age-s-marketer-year-2018/315795
73. https://immigrationforum.org/article/immigrants-as-economic-contributors-immigrant-entrepreneurs/
74. https://www.warc.com/newsandopinion/news/how_airbnb_mixes_politics_and_brand_values/40647

75. https://www.varkeyfoundation.org/media/4487/global-young-people-report-single-pages-new.pdf

76. https://newsroom.statestreet.com/press-release/corporate/state-street-global-advisors-reports-fearless-girl-impact-first-anniversary-

77. https://www.marketingweek.com/heineken-on-its-new-marketing-strategy-its-an-evolution-not-a-revolution/

78. https://www.tescoplc.com/news/2018/tesco-and-wwf-join-forces-to-make-food-more-sustainable/

79. https://news.pampers.com/fact-sheet/about-1-pack-1-vaccine-unicef-pampers-partnering-save-lives-mothers-and-babies

80. https://www.karmacola.co.uk/our-story

81. https://www.tandfonline.com/doi/full/10.1080/14693062.2018.1551186

82. https://pdfs.semanticscholar.org/7745/c3ef0c8501be31ea6859144dc-c3ee97d8ccb.pdf

83. B. Drysdale, J. Wu, and N. Jenkins (2015). Flexible demand in the GB domestic electricity sector in 2030. *Appl Energy*, 139: 281–290.

84. https://www.telegraph.co.uk/finance/personalfinance/household-bills/10157963/Overfilling-the-kettle-wastes-68m-a-year.html

85. https://spectrum.ieee.org/energy/environment/your-phone-costs-energyeven-before-you-turn-it-on

86. https://www.theguardian.com/environment/green-living-blog/2010/sep/23/carbon-footprint-new-car

87. https://www.forbes.com/sites/jimhenry/2012/02/29/the-surprising-ways-car-dealers-make-the-most-money-off-of-you/#4e35b52d1e6f

88. https://www.povertyactionlab.org/evaluation/opower-evaluating-impact-home-energy-reports-energy-conservation-united-states

89. https://data.worldbank.org/indicator/en.atm.co2e.pp.gd

90. https://fortune.com/2018/10/02/netflix-consumes-15-percent-of-global-internet-bandwidth/

91. https://www.brompton.com/news/posts/2019/cities-for-movement

92. https://www.independent.co.uk/news/uk/this-britain/the-wheel-thing-will-self-on-the-brompton-bike-926741.html

93. https://cyclingindustry.news/were-about-to-see-a-mega-transformation-of-the-bicycle-says-brompton-boss/

94. https://www.researchgate.net/publication/264395358_The_Relative_Benefits_of_Green_Versus_Lean_Office_Space_Three_Field_Experiments
95. https://www.terrapinbrightgreen.com/reports/the-economics-of-biophilia/
96. https://aceee.org/files/proceedings/2004/data/papers/SS04_Panel7_Paper09.pdf
97. https://www.patagonia.com/blog/2011/09/introducing-the-common-threads-initiative/
98. https://ruckus.org/patagonias-get-out-of-jail-free-card/
99. https://www.independent.co.uk/news/science/can-seashells-save-the-world-813915.html
100. https://www.directorsandboards.com/articles/singlecharacter-corporation-profit-and-purpose
101. https://www.lego.com/en-gb/campaigns/replay

SECTION III

Aim, Frame, and Game

How to Aim, Frame, and Game

How can you incorporate sustainability and purpose into everyday marketing practice?

I've summarised my toolkit here – how I develop marketing and brand strategies from objective setting through to creative execution. I've used these in contexts ranging from independent eco entrepreneurs to giant global corporations. You do need to flex the approach in different contexts. But the same core tools seem to work pretty well.

Principles and processes are best explained through examples, so there are plenty of those to chew over in what follows. You also might have a different thought style and approach and still find these examples helpful.

I hope this is helpful and if you have questions, do send me a message on LinkedIn.

3.1 AIM – Defining the Task

Every marketing challenge, from designing a new product or service, to deciding a pricing and ranging strategy, has an aim. When marketing and business is pushing for Net Good, it also has a purpose – some way of improving life and supporting ecosystems.

It's important when developing plans, ideas, campaigns to set an aim. If working in the directions defined by this book this is likely to be a blend of commercial purpose and social purpose. This is often an 80:20 mix. For instance, if the product is super ethical the aim might simply be how to grow. If the product is quite mainstream the aim might be to drive some social good with your marketing – adopt a social purpose like the Unilever brands.

It is best not to approach this aim in a rational, dry, reductive way. Defining the problem that you are setting out to solve in an innovative way can make all the difference.

In my old agency St Luke's, we reduced the creative brief to two headings – Why? and How? Usually the strategies were driven by the 'Why?' – the identification of an unusual problem. For instance, instead of promoting IKEA, we set out to modernise British tastes and values. I worked on a project last year with one of the founders of the Stanford D-School and he also told me that problem-finding was also their key step – the pivot point of user-centred design.

Quite often you will start with a fairly obvious, functional task. We need to target this audience and achieve such and such for the business – in broad terms 'how to grow'. Some block, sticking point, or gap might be holding that growth back. For instance, the problem could be that your product is bought too infrequently to work well in ecommerce.

A friend has an eco shoe company (Po-Zu). It is hard to build momentum, word of mouth, repeat business in an infrequent market like shoes. This makes it expensive to market your shoes as you are fighting all the time for fresh awareness and acquisition.

Po-Zu's main marketing in the past has been about partnerships. They make the footwear used in Star Wars movies and get orders from fans who want the genuine Rey boots as part of their costume. It's a viable strategy (that also worked well for LEGO), but movies and fashion partners can't necessarily solve the frequency issue.

The aim I suggested when we talked was: why not sell your insoles as a standalone product?

Po-Zu has an amazing comfy insole that uses coconut fibre based on bio-mimicry design. This makes for a healthy, supportive insole that moulds itself to your foot. I can testify that it makes for the most unfatiguing shoes I've worn when (in workshops and events) I spend all day on my feet. The insole is a product people might buy more regularly for multiple existing pairs of shoes. It can be posted through a letterbox. It's not a big consumer decision. It could even breathe fresh life into old shoes and increase their longevity. By finding this regular place in people's shoe-rack, Po-Zu would then have a cost-effective ecommerce platform to offer their shoes. They'd be a contender.

I don't know if that's a great idea. But it's a clear example of 'think of an unusual aim'.

As with most marketing, the process of setting an aim is iterative. Often you will define an aim, have some ideas and then one of these creative ideas will give you a sharper definition of the problem, which will lead to more focused ideas.

The definition of an aim will also likely include some thinking about the target segment.

It could be an audience insight led strategy. For instance, one of my past agencies did the advertising for the government to promote safe sex using condoms. The target segment they identified was courting couples. The aim being to overcome the reticence they had about raising the subject of condoms. And not have unprotected sex because they were simply too shy to raise this. The advertising solution was to make hilariously frank cinema commercials featuring old aged people talking about condoms and sex. One was a gentleman with a reusable condom left over from the Second World War era that he had nicknamed 'Geronimo'. Another featured a woman working on the production line of a condom factory. The ads were designed to break the ice and get young couples talking. And the key to the media strategy was recognising the need to reach couples while they were dating.

There can be multiple stakeholders. Sustainability people usually have a long list. A useful exercise can be to draw a target diagram with concentric circles and debate who to put in the centre. For one brief I worked on, the key audience was the environmental head of city councils. But we decided that the best way to get them on board was engaging the public. That could sound expensive – targeting 10 million people rather than just one. But what if you could catch the imagination of the media, public, and politicians with one smart stunt?

The client in question (Vaisala) makes air quality monitors. The latest generation have internet of things sensors. And the new approach is to dot these all over the city rather than just have a few expensive devices integrated into weather stations. More sensors, better data; you can localise your reading of air quality to know where and how to intervene – with actions ranging from traffic calming, to street cleaning, to visiting some polluting factories.

One idea that caught our eye was Plume Labs creating little backpacks containing the sensor chip plus a GPS tracker to put onto messenger pigeons. The birds then recorded air quality as they flew over the city on defined routes. The readings were transmitted to the *Pigeon Air Patrol* Twitter account. It was a demonstration project aimed at raising awareness of poor air quality in London. But it catapulted the Plume Labs sensors to a public fame they never could have achieved with public sector trade media and events. It wasn't expensive to execute. It just took imagination. We used that example to evidence our strategy.

It's best to be quite functional in the wording of your aim. Put the imagination into the model of how it might work (that comes later) not semantics. It's better to be clear and distinct. To an experienced strategist there is a taut, minimalist beauty to an unusual problem definition. But it doesn't have to be grounded in alliteration or a pun. Much better if it can be shown as a simple diagram. Even if it is just an arrow showing from/to.

When working on strategy definition, it's often helpful to zoom in or zoom out.

Zooming out can mean stretching the boundary of a problem. I ran a workshop once for design students who were working on a competition brief to get people to drink less bottled mineral water and drink tap water instead. The students had lots of initial ideas. There were cool drinking bottles. Some with exotic filters. There were fun water taps in interesting places. There were refill schemes for restaurants. In other words, there was nothing new.

I started the workshop by holding up two drink bottles. One Coca-Cola, the other Evian. Which is more sustainable, I asked?

It turns out to be an interesting question. Dutch Scientist Arjen Hoekstra invented a measure called the water footprint that measures how much water is used in total to make what we consume. By this measure it takes around 700 litres of water to make a t-shirt. Mainly because of the water used in cotton agriculture. A quarter pound hamburger has a water footprint of 260 litres, due to things like the water used to grow cattle feed crops. Hoekstra introduced the concept of water footprint because by UN predictions around half the world's population could face water shortages by 2030. Coke had faced criticisms for depleting the water supply in countries like India. And they responded to these criticisms by saying that they were committed to be 'water neutral' by 2020. Coke CEO Doug Isdell announced this in 2007:

> the Coca-Cola Company pledges to replace every drop of water we use in our beverages and their production to achieve balance in communities and in nature with the water we use.

Coca-Cola adopted Hoekstra's water neutrality methodology and calculated that it took 70 litres of water to make one litre of Coca Cola: 56 litres in sugar beet agriculture; nearly all of the rest making the plastic PET bottle. With a small amount (close to the volume of the actual drink) being used in manufacturing. How could Coca-Cola balance the water used in making their beverages? The company used impact investment in water development (sanitation and supply), water purification, and water metering and distribution systems. Coca Cola became a player in water tech. Coca-Cola were subsequently able to announce they gave back

> 191.9 billion liters of water to nature and communities in 2015 through community water projects, equalling the equivalent of 115 percent of the water used in Coca-Cola's beverages last year.

Note that this is measured as 115% of the volume of their products. Not the 70 litres it takes to produce one litre including agriculture. So, while it is laudable achievement, it is not strictly water neutral. They still got plenty of credit for their efforts. Carter Roberts, World Wildlife Fund president, said: 'This is an important milestone in Coca-Cola's continued leadership on water stewardship and sets a standard for other water users to build from.'[1]

Back to the brief. Bottled water is rightly a target of environmental campaigners (in countries where the tap water is good to drink). But when you look into the water footprint of drinks, you realise anything with a crop in it adds much more water stress than just water. Coca-Cola is an easy target. But the same calculation can be applied to tea. The Carbon Trust estimated that a typical cup of milky tea uses 52 litres of water (30 litres for growing the tea, 20 for the milk, 12 litres for two spoons of sugar).[2]

If you look at the sustainable water brief now, you realise that a more radical aim would be to get people to switch one soft drink or tea per day to a mineral water. This would save 50–70 litres which is equal to the UK average mineral water footprint *per year*. It's also good for people's health. You could also start looking at the other parts of people's footprint. If Coke could subsidise water efficient showers, US water footprint calculators show that this would easily cancel out the entire impact of drinking several litres of soda a day.

What this example shows is:

the importance of deeper research into sustainability;
the importance of data and analytics;
being flexible in problem defining and the boundaries.

What has Coca-Cola itself done against the brief I mentioned at the start of this chapter?

They have made and popularised smaller drinks – the mini can.

These formats are showing double digit growth; so significant in fact that they were mentioned in Coke's latest financial results as helping to boost the company's overall revenues.

Mini cans are a win for climate, obesity, and water conservation.

They also work for consumers. You want a soda. You don't necessarily need a big soda. Just a something to pep you up.

We won't save the world with smaller pack sizes, but it's a surprisingly big step in the right direction. Because it has the potential to achieve real scale.

Look deep into the research; then take a Swiss army knife approach to the Aim.

I would have been super-impressed if one of the design students in the tap vs bottle project had come forward with idea of making mineral water bottles 10% smaller.

Every brand needs to look again at their business through the eyes of a climate and environmental crisis. The standards we set even a year ago may just not be high enough now. Not every brand has the scale to save much of the world. But every one of us is now accountable to try our best to contribute. And make a proportionate contribution.

A lot of brands are looking to adopt a cause. How to avoid 'wokewash'?

The best way to avoid that is one simple question. What do you truly measure yourself against? In the current climate you need to be so ambitious with your environmental goals that it would be a telling sign if you don't have a real impact KPI (beyond those you use in PR saying how nice you've been). I mean a KPI like Coke's water neutrality.

Take Persil's *Dirt is Good*. I think you can make a reasonable case that the brand contributed positively to more than just its own sales. They hired Sir Ken Robinson (educationalist and giver of one of the most viewed TED talks ever) as a brand spokesperson. They created an Outdoor Classroom Day and partnered with 3500 schools, reaching 480 000 children in 52 countries.

I like the question that an amazing Lebanese slow food activist called Kamal Mouzawak asked when I interviewed him. We were talking about sustainability. This, Kamal said, was the word used by big companies that tear up the world, then plant a few trees in order for people to think of them more fondly. Kamal's question was this:

WHAT IS YOUR CONTRIBUTION TO LIFE?

It's the day of judgement question.

You could ask that question of a meeting, a campaign brief, a website, or product. It doesn't matter what the contribution is, whether it is even noticed. The question is purely about the net impact.

Making a contribution to life could mean making the sustainable option cheaper than the nasty option. That was the conclusion the Friendly Soap company came to. They make artisanal soap for other brands that is sold for up to £18. But when they sell their own vegan, ethical, gorgeously scented soap it's £2.25. Why? Because Rob and Geoff the founders believe that it's important that most people can afford the sustainable option. So, they charge a similar price to what someone would pay in a supermarket for an industrial soap bar or shower gel.

It's not that every single thing that you do will make a positive contribution, some things will be depleting. But if, like Google, you have moon-shot projects which alter the course of human history, we might live with you making your money from digital ads.

Corporate purpose exercises need to be approached in this same strategic way.

The aim isn't 'to have a purpose' because it's a management fad. Sataya Nadella's 'empowering individuals and organisations' at Microsoft was intended to unify a disparate organisation (from Xbox to Windows to Azure to Office to Skype . . .) and direct the culture to be more open, led by learning and growth. It made sense for the business as well as being good for the rest of us.

I can't emphasise enough how valuable it is to keep coming back to the Aim.

3.2 Frame – Cultural and Cognitive Positioning

The concept of a brand, its personality, its USP (unique selling proposition) stems from the Madmen era. Based on influences like psychoanalysis and industry stalwarts like Leo Burnett and David Ogilvy, this was a theory suited to selling stuff using characterful TV adverts. Even back then there were people that thought more broadly about brands. Like Bill Bernbach whose agency branded the VW a 'Lemon' and used Mobil's advertising dollars to teach road safety.

Framing is a broader idea than branding. Whereas the brand is a commercial/cultural construct that we attempt to build and manage, the frame is part of the human mind. Deciding a frame for your brand suits the broader canvas of modern marketing where the output could be content, a community, a partnership, or cause. It also sits well with having a purpose.

The idea of a frame originated in anthropology. George Bateson was walking in the zoo and saw chimps playing. They were teasing each other in ways that could have led to violence. But they all seemed to know they were 'only playing'. Bateson called this a frame. A shared understanding giving meaning to isolated acts or utterances. It's totally different when you utter the words 'I do' in a church, or in answer to the question 'who wants ice cream?'

Cognitive linguist George Lakoff adopted this idea and suggested that it is fundamental:

> Reason is actually 98% unconscious. Frames are the unconscious neural circuits that define how we think and talk. They are conceptual structures made up of metaphors, narratives and emotions, and they are physically part of the brain. We cannot avoid framing. Words activate frames. That's why words are so important. A single word can activate not only the defining frame, but also the system its defining frame is in.

You could say that framing is the new branding. Our concept of brands has broadened – it no longer is just a façade of personality attached to a product. It can be about the social context, having a purpose; the frame of 'United Colors' for Benetton or 'Real Beauty' for Dove.

To give an example: TESLA as a classical brand is based on the persona of Nicolai Tesla – wrapped up in the glamorous design and performance of sports cars like Ferrari.

But from a framing point of view, TESLA is here to pioneer. It makes grid sized batteries. Its sister company SpaceX does space exploration. TESLA exists to pioneer the sustainable energy transition. It is the car of choice for Silicon Valley pioneers who share the mindset – it expresses their entrepreneurial spirit, eco values, and also appeals by being more software than hardware, a constantly tuning and updating smart vehicle. Pioneering is a frame. It is a mode of life, not just a pose or a desirable personality. TESLA makes sense when you see Elon Musk in front of an image of the Earth at a press conference to announce something incredible.

It's a subtle difference. But frames can trace out a destiny for your brand. Whereas the old theory of branding will likely wrap you in yesterday's news like a fish and chip dinner.

The importance of words that trigger frames is dawning on brands today. George Lakoff advised the Obama08 campaign and they were one of the first to adopt the lexical marketing so apt for an era of hashtags – at the heart of the campaign were just two words:

HOPE
CHANGE

Framing has always been here. Brands always trigger frames. We just didn't notice it because the brands in each market played within such narrow common confines. Brands seldom realised that you could differentiate yourself through a total rethink of your context.

Undifferentiated framing is common in sustainability-themed corporate marketing. When pitching to work with Wärtsilä Energy, we did a review of how others in cleantech were communicating. We found a number of clichéd visual themes. And we then showed how *every single one of them* was also used in Wärtsilä's own website:

The city of lights
Earth redesigned
Data abstraction and virtual models
Sunflowers, fields, wind turbines
Future blueprints.

The frame is one of sci fi future vision. None of those cleantech ideas communicates pioneering. They are *literally* communicating that the industry is doing nothing. If the industry was doing something, they would show pictures of projects they had built. Not fantasy graphics.

The fact was that Wärtsilä's competitors took full page ads in industry magazines to share their 'future vision' but few had built any actual projects. The two biggest names, GE and Siemens, had – Wärtsilä told us – only one live project of any size between them. Whereas Wärtsilä Energy had dozens of energy transition projects underway across the world.

Wärtsilä is an industrial company mainly known for making engines or turbines – their parent company makes ships, and they started out in energy with infrastructure for ports. In a rapidly changing energy market, they were well placed to be 'the new kid on the block'. After all, before the mobile revolution Nokia was known for making rubber boots.

Wärtsilä's approach was to act as the *energy systems integrator*: combining energy storage (batteries and similar), energy management (complex IT overlaid on the grid), energy plant (quick firing gas boilers as a transition technology enabling more renewables in the mix), and of course building renewable projects (Wärtsilä had acquired a solar division). The 'internet of energy' is key to all of these. Large amounts of energy are lost because of inefficiencies and waste. Clever software and configuring the right mix of generation, plus waste strategies like combined heat and power and district heating all can play a role.

The most useful part of the early framing discussions is working out roughly where the brand and company wants to be positioned. For this exercise with Wärtsilä we mapped out a grid with two axes: projects vs people, leader vs challenger.

And then we started the strategy journey together by looking at four frames:

WÄRTSILÄ PRESENTS (projects, leader)

show your real projects, be the storyteller of energy transition
CITIZENERGY (people, leader)
drive the agenda by bring communities together for climate emergency action
NEXT GEN (people, challenger)
the Gretas of the world spearhead your campaign – design solutions with them
MESH (projects, challenger)
rename 'the grid' – the new version is intelligent, responsive, and internet-like

There were some proposed words that trigger frames in the mix:

WE (Citizenergy) short for Wärtsilä Energy – considerably easier for a global audience
MESH stood for MIXED ENERGY & STORAGE HARMONISED

We had a lively workshop with Wärtsilä hosted by Superson, the Helsinki agency I worked with on this. The team liked WÄRTSILÄ PRESENTS. They had already taken a step in the storytelling direction by producing a book about one US energy company's transition. They also loved the MESH positioning. (But not the name which they worried could sound like MESS.) Overall, they agreed with the analysis that they had to stand apart from the industry – in the same way TESLA had broken ranks with the car industry with a pioneering frame.

The key early on in these framing projects is to break up the ground and explore as widely as possible. There are a multitude of different frames these can hook into. Most have advantages and disadvantages. If you don't explore a diverse set of frames, you may not find the best one.

Another Superson project was with Vaisala. We did a project with the air quality division. The frame we defined was Breathable Cities. A marked contrast from the negative frame projected by their website and everyone else (a typical web page would have a picture of a Chinese schoolchild wearing a smog mask). Then we got a brief from their industry division. The initial brief was for the biogas measuring equipment. But when we took the CMO through our framing map, she decided it could be applied across the whole division.

Vaisala makes innovative measuring technology. For instance, they are the leader in weather stations. This brief was about the monitoring equipment Vaisala make for biogas plants.

Biogas makes fuel out of decomposing organic waste: agricultural waste, food scraps, manure. The process called anaerobic digestion is a kind of fermentation (using microbes) to produce methane gas. This would happen naturally anyway if the waste were not processed, leading to methane emissions with high global warming potential. Capturing the gas 'closes the loop'; capturing value and reducing emissions. The other output of biogas production is organic fertilisers – better than the chemical sort. Biogas is a prime example of the circular economy where something that would have been waste is turned into a valuable resource.

The problem with biogas is the process is inefficient and the resulting gas can be impure and this can corrode vehicles. This is where state of the art monitoring helps – raising the quality and using data to drive process improvement. It's a huge leap, basically taking biogas and making it a key part of the future energy and waste management mix. When we reviewed competitor marketing, it was boring and technical; just like any industrial equipment sales brochure.

We wanted to find a way to communicate the key benefits and establish Vaisala as the place to go to if you own a biogas plant and can see an exciting future.

What we did for the first meeting (I'm sharing it here to show there are many ways to skin a cat when it comes to framing) was show eight separate frames; two per quarter of a grid we drew with two axes. One axis was SENSOR (talk about the product) vs BIOGAS (talk about the end use and benefits). The other was PERFORMANCE vs (higher) PURPOSE.

The thing missing from this written account is the visuals. I always use pictures in these framing exercises because they help to amplify and make clearer the differences. But hopefully you can picture those in your mind's eyes:

1. Higher Standards (biogas × performance)
   1A. High Grade Bio
        We create a new standard, like Super-Unleaded in petrol, that commands a price premium (you need state of the art monitoring to check your biogas hits this standard).
   1B. Hate Waste, Hate Wasting

Publish transparent data about client biogas plant efficiency. Made possible by sensors. If you make biogas out of waste, you should be proud of being less wasteful.

2. Cutting Edge Sensors (sensor × performance)

   2A. Molecular Sensing

   Process monitoring in biogas is different than most industries. It's about tracking a nonlinear living process. That's why we redesigned sensing for biogas from the molecule up.

   2B. Finland Grade

   The country with the cleanest air, happiest people and most advanced eco standards has just raised the bar in biogas sensors. How? Finnish engineering design.

3. For a Better World (Biogas × Purpose)

   3A. Where it Matters

   Biofuels innovation in communities that really need it – for instance development & disaster relief (the image was a news story about biogas innovation in Yemen).

   3B. Humble Heroes

   The bacterium and the biogas engineer. These unsung heroes are applying a precise and controlled blend of life science – the alchemy behind tomorrow's fuel.

4. Game Changers (Sensors × Progress)

   4A. The Measurers

   When methods of detection are refined, whole new fields of progress open up. Scientific breakthroughs often start with measurement: the telescope, the x-ray . . .

   4B. If It Works on the Surface of Mars

   Vaisala made sensors on NASA's Mars Curiosity Robot. Able to withstand hellish extremes and deliver precise results, 55 million miles from the nearest maintenance engineer.

The most 'on brand' frames according to the Vaisala were the 'Better World' ones.

But the team felt that all had some merits, and each could potentially find a role somewhere in the marketing for their industrial division.

The frames closest to how Vaisala went forward with biogas specifically were Molecular Sensing and Hate Wasting.

Once you have your aim and frame (and remember this is an iterative cycle) you are ready to come up with concrete creative marketing strategies.

3.3 Game – The Greener Marketing Grid

I've been arguing for 20+ years that marketing needs to see itself as a participative game played with consumers, rather than communications done to or aimed at consumers.

Old marketing thinks of itself as controlling, influencing, persuading, and herding people. Brands are analysed by smart ambitious brand teams into diagrams with detailed lists of values, propositions, supporting evidence, and so on. They are then communicated through ruthlessly consistent and disciplined messaging and design. Is it any wonder people don't like most brands? When all they do is shout at you and clutter up your media with their messaging?

This old marketing culture did co-opt the idea of having a brand purpose. But never really questioned the ethics behind what brands do. The products are all too often processed crap or carelessly inhuman services, engineered to cost as little as possible and doing untold damage in their supply chain. The advertising systems around these were designed to compensate and to create the illusion of humanity. Over the decades the façade wore thin.

In the 1990s it seemed like brands were hitting a brick wall. Levi's was a test case. For over a decade the top creative advertiser in the world (measured by awards). And during that time its value as a business declined steeply. This was nothing to do with marketing. Levi's just were not fashionable. They were seen by a new generation as 'the jeans your uncle wears'.

Levi's have gone on to become a more interesting marketer since those days. The migration of marketing from 'saying stuff that makes you look cool' to 'doing stuff that actually is cool' has been the saving of them. Their turnaround CEO Chip Bergh tells the story of how he visited a customer in Bangalore who showed him her jeans. One was a pair of Levi's she had kept since college. Her phrase you wear jeans, but you 'live in Levi's' became their new tagline. Levi's fixed their fundamentals like ecommerce, innovated fabric and design, did collaborations. They had a decent growth spurt in 2018. And in 2019 returned to being a public company.

Chip Bergh became famous in sustainability circles when he told a conference 'don't wash your jeans' and the phrase went viral. He was alluding to research in sustainability showing most of the water footprint (despite the cotton agriculture) is in customers' washing machines.

Levi's is also moving to respond to the climate crisis and the wave of public concern. They have joined the Science-Based Targets Initiative (SBTI) which commits them to setting targets in line with the Paris Agreement. Levi's targets for 2025 (against a 2016 baseline) include a 90% reduction in greenhouse gases and 100% renewable energy for their own facilities and a 40% reduction in Greenhouse gases across their whole supply chain. They signed the UN Fashion Charter for Climate Action. And Levi's joined 75 other major businesses in calling on the US Congress to pass significant climate legislation, including a meaningful level of carbon tax.

Levi's have the scale to make a real impact and reach mainstream consumers. They have the issues associated with cotton to deal with. They also have a durable product that gets better with age. One that you can keep hygienic by putting it in the freezer (kills 99% of bacteria) rather than the washing machine.

Nudie Jeans offers free repairs for life, whenever or however you bought your jeans. Their network of repair shops takes damaged Nudie Jeans in for repair, or if beyond repair takes them in for the fabric to be reused in their recycling programme. If you aren't in a city where there is a repair shop, they also have repair partners and a touring mobile repair station.

Nudie were ahead of the curve in offering this service, launching it in 2010. In 2018 they repaired 55 000 pairs of jeans. It's just one of the programmes that form part of Nudie's vision to become the most sustainable denim company. In 2018, 98% of their garments were made from sustainable materials including organic cotton and recycled fabrics. And a constant stream of initiative like a Re-Use range and replacing leather patches with patches made from paper. They've looked at every aspect of their business including production and living wages.

Nudie is one hundredth of the size of Levi's (€50 million vs $5 billion). But the standards that they set, including all organic cotton since 2012, are the standards bigger brands like Levi's will be judged by. They are the Craft Beer to Levi's Budweiser and the key danger is ceding authenticity. If any brand could challenge Levi's on the 'lived in' positioning, Nudie could.

What Levi's could do with its scale and creative firepower is make jeans the definitive thing to wear if you worry about the environment. Yes, I know they are made of cotton. But so are most clothes. As Livia Firth says, 'The biggest message is every time you buy something, always think, "will I wear it a minimum of 30 times?"'[3] I have jeans still going that are 10 or 20 years old. They are just so incredibly durable *and* the more they age the better they look.

So, what I would do (just to illustrate) if I were Levi's is the following:

AIM: establish Levi's jeans are the most sustainable thing to wear
FRAME: Levi's are for Life.

You keep a pair of jeans a long time. And they become a companion. And like a journal. That rip from a festival fence aged 23. The patch your daughter sewed when you were 37 . . . The jeans are truly lived in. And you keep them alive through repair, remodelling, freeze cleaning . . .

GAME: . . .

Now the creative fun starts. Here are a couple of starting point ideas:

- 100-year jeans. Design denim jeans to last a century. They might be tough and durable. Or might be designed with modular parts that are easy to replace.
- Born on. Give each pair a unique born on date. Encourage people to track these, share stories, attach photos, give the life of their jeans and lived in their jeans a timeline.
- Influence. Donate $3000 to an environmental cause every time an influencer posts a pic of themselves in a pair of Levi's that they have worn every day for a month (to popularise the 'wear each garment 30 times' maxim from Livia Firth).
- Born Again. Partner with Re/Done and scale this across the global Levi's user base.

One inkling of how far Levi's could go into the circular economy is provided by Re/Done. This fashion start-up from LA takes pre-loved Levi's jeans apart at the seams and remakes the fabric into new jeans, making a fashionable, hand-made, hand-cut, and unique pair of new jeans. One that is full of characterful imperfections like frayed pockets, torn knees, and faded colours.

Now imagine this was available in every city and it created jobs (gig economy seamstresses).

Fashion brands need to think radical. Not least because activists are calling the industry out. They might not have the impact of oil, meat, or banks. But they are a super visible target. And if you have an eco-puritan mindset then fashion shows in the midst of a climate emergency looks decadent. Extinction Rebellion called for London Fashion Week to be closed out of respect for the crisis and held a funeral signalling a 'symbolic death for the status quo'. Sound unrealistic? Bear in mind that the Swedish Fashion Week *did* close in 2019 due to climate concerns.

XR followed up by inviting the public to join a 52-week (one year) boycott of fashion, by pledging not to buy any new clothes or textiles, instead learning to make do with what they already have. I'm not sure yet how widespread this will prove but it does send a very clear signal to fashion, consumer brands, and marketing that they are in the last chance saloon.

If nothing else, this illustrates that the bar has been raised. There is a climate crisis. Extinction Rebellion have raised the alarm. More than 50% of people in the UK think of this as a climate emergency – which was unthinkable five years ago. Companies that respond to the climate crisis can still thrive, but there are significant challenges ahead for those that don't.

The ultimate challenge is to reinvent your business model. Start to think (like Nudie do) of *jeans as a service*, rather than a product made to be discarded.

How do brands, marketers, communicators, and companies respond?

First be Not Bad. Many of marketing's basic practices are not fit for a climate emergency. Your two for one offers. Your January 'everything must go' sale. Your hard to recycle plastic packaging. Pick some examples where there are substitutes. Physical direct marketing campaign in unrecyclable envelopes? Consider email newsletters or loyalty apps.

Beyond that, look at what behaviour your business model rewards. Cheap products may cost the Earth. How about a deposit for reusable packaging? Setting up sharing schemes or exchanges where consumers can resell your goods at their end of life.

Ask bigger questions like: what is your role in unsustainable consumption? It's easy to target fast fashion (and Extinction Rebellion have done just this). But there are also campaigns looking at less recognised topics like digital sobriety. The Shift Project points out that online video

> generates 60% of world data flows and thus over 300 million tons of CO2 per year. This is far from being 'dematerialized'. It represents 20% of the greenhouse gas emissions of all digital devices (use and production included) and 1% of global emissions.

Shift details the carbon emissions (in millions of tonnes of CO_2) of the top four internet video uses: video on demand (104), pornography (82), YouTube etc. (65), social video (56). It looks like it could be time to revisit the video lending library. Love Film discs by posts worked great and many people still do have disc players in the form of console gaming machines.

In no way can we soften the message and offer the comforting illusion that we can go on as we were with a few tweaks. It's not all about marketing. We've seen businesses step up – even Walmart and Tesco – with strong commitments to ambitious targets. Our role as marketers in many cases will be to make all of this work as fully as it can, bringing people with us.

Brands have been responding in all sorts of ways to the climate crisis in 2019. And there is so much exciting happening right now it seemed worth writing up.

What I have done is take the old 'green marketing grid' from my last book (written at a time when launching a hybrid car was state of the art) and repopulated it with examples from 2019 – a year of marketing responses to the climate crisis.

Partly to reinforce a point that while the aims are new, the 'game' of marketing hasn't changed.

	post green standards	post green collaborations	post green business models
business	*Science-Based Targets*	*Architects Declare Alliances*	*Prada Sustainability Linked Loans*
brand	*The* Guardian	*Covering Climate Now*	*Hurr sharing economy fashion*
products & services	*Vivobarefoot Earth Positive Shoes*	*Regenerative Organic*	*Insect Grub*

Post Green Standards for Business: Science-Based Targets

To be on the right side of climate history, business should as a minimum be aiming to reduce their greenhouse gas emissions in line with the Paris Agreement.

One option to achieve this is join the Science-Based Targets Initiative. And base your targets on what is necessary rather than what feels afford-able and achievable. We've seen across the book that numerous businesses joined this movement from Levi's to Unilever. This ensures that you take a consistent, long-term approach (that reassures media, NGOs, and publics) while also putting you ahead of the game when meaningful carbon pric-ing kicks in.

You could always go further and aim for Net Zero emissions or even bet-ter for climate positive targets. Patagonia are committed to being climate neutral by 2025. Max Hamburgers claim to be climate positive already. Something they achieve through three actions: measuring all their emissions (including those emissions from their farms and the customers journey to the restaurant), reducing emissions by every means possible including encour-aging customers to try one of their range of vegan options, and planting trees. They are quite transparent about this, having their programme inde-pendently audited. And it doesn't look like greenwash because they've been on about climate friendly food choices for over 10 years.

There is a strong argument for aiming higher like this. In brand terms, if you want to be seen as a leader on this issue, it doesn't do to be just 'average'. And logically since so many are not achieving the basic standards, the lead-ers need to do more than their fair share if they are serious about a collective effort to achieve the Paris Agreement goals.

Post Green Standards for Brands: The *Guardian*

The greenest thing to do with your brand is to influence people. That doesn't mean asking them to do little things to make a difference. It means making a big noise about the climate emergency and the drastic changes we need to make to avoid fatally high global warming.

Media brands have a double responsibility. They keep the public informed and also play a big role in shaping the cultural attitudes and lifestyles. And some parts of the media have been admirably forward on climate change. Some, like the *Guardian*, have a long track record of outspoken reporting on climate. Others are surprising additions to the fold – doubly valuable as they are preaching to those who might not be converted. The *Economist* carried a whole climate issue. And the *FT* made a video about climate change with the Royal Court theatre.

The *Guardian*'s new brand campaign is framed around strong, mobilising statements (similar to those in Obama08) that

CHANGE IS POSSIBLE
HOPE IS POWER.

The aim is to restate the *Guardian*'s core purpose, build solidarity with its readership, and boost the growing numbers voluntarily contributing to support the *Guardian* in its mission. One million readers have already done so. Making this one of the most extraordinary examples of mass public crowdfunding since Obama08.

You don't need to be a media to declare. A poll conducted by Kin & Co found that half of the British public would like their preferred brands to declare a 'climate emergency' while more than two thirds of UK consumers think climate change is an 'urgent issue' for brands.[4]

Post Green Standards for Products and Services: Vivobarefoot

Ethical shoe brand Vivobarefoot is one of the new generation of brands that thinks beyond sustainability to having a regenerative role. From their website:

> Vivobarefoot is a business fixated on reconnecting people and nature. Sustainability is having the health of ecosystems and people embedded in its DNA. Here, it's not just about doing less harm, but about actually enabling life to flourish on Earth.

This vision leads to two main aims. First is for their materials to be 100% sustainable by 2021; biosynthetic (made from plants not oils), natural, or recycled. What helps is a product philosophy about making shoes that are as close as possible to going barefoot. Ensuring that they are light on the materials in the first place, focused on foot health and comfort and hippy living.

This also makes them distinctive. Second aim is to use their influence. They estimate that over a million people have engaged with the brand's sustainability vision. And a radical vision it is too. Emma Foster Geering, head of sustainability at Vivobearfoot, describes it like this:

> Look, the time to go greener is gone. If your business doesn't stand for regenerating the planet right now, you are obsolete![5]

Vivobarefoot was founded by Galahad Clark, a pioneering member of London's sustainability community for as long as I can remember (with Terra Plana eco shoes and using upcycled materials with Worn Again). Galahad is a descendant of the Clarks shoe dynasty, yet he calls conventional shoes 'foot coffins'. He is on a mission to create the most sustainable footwear in the world. Vivobarefoot have been actively involved in climate activism. This is from their Facebook page:

> At Vivobarefoot we support Extinction Rebellion and we will be joining their global campaign starting October 7th.
> There is no doubt we are facing a climate emergency and we want to be part of the change that needs to happen for our collective future.
> We recognize that 'being sustainable' CANNOT just be about doing less harm. For us sustainability means we must only set goals to restore and regenerate the planet.
> The barefoot wisdom we ascribe to has now become a movement of sustainability vigilantes: a global community of health and well-being activists, indigenous tribes rich in ancient wisdom and active urbanites who still find a way to play and raise families in nature. With this community we grow, thriving on our united ethics of peace, feet and environmentalism.
> Part of this is supporting Extinction Rebellion.
> Find out more at //rebellion.earth and by following @vivobarefoot and @vivobarefoot.kids on Instagram to find out about our Ambassadors speaking at Extinction Rebellion events and the planned barefoot walk through London.

Vivobarefoot took some flak for this in social media. Foster-Geering commented:

> We believe in nature and restoring the planet. Therefore we're with them (XR). If a portion of our consumer base don't want to be with us that's a loss we're going to have to take.

Post Green Collaborations for Companies – Alliances

Alliances are a staple of purpose led business. For decades, coalitions got together to advance sustainability in ways that individual organisations could do on their own.

Some have gathered around their common interest in particular commodities – for instance, sustainable sourcing coalitions for seafood, for palm oil, and for rubber.

Others have gathered around a particular agenda; for instance, the Natural Capital Coalition is dedicated to appreciating the ecosystems services that underpin the healthy workings of business. If that sounds 'far out', this is hosted by the Institute of Chartered Accountants and has 300 member organisations. They also (as systems thinkers par excellence) give a handy definition of what a coalition is and why it is needed:

> Coalition organizations share a common belief that we can do more together than we can alone and an understanding that it is only by bringing the many different parts of the system together (in) a purpose-led conversation that we can we affect real change.

The climate emergency and the public responses to this have crystallised a new set of alliances.

One was convened in the architecture and construction engineering sector. I will let their declaration speak for what they are up to:

> The twin crises of climate breakdown and biodiversity loss are the most serious issue of our time. Buildings and construction play a major part, accounting for nearly 40% of energy-related carbon dioxide (CO_2) emissions whilst also having a significant impact on our natural habitats. For everyone working in the construction industry, meeting the needs of our society without breaching the earth's ecological boundaries will demand a paradigm shift in our behaviour. Together with our clients, we will need to commission and design buildings, cities and infrastructures as indivisible components of a larger, constantly regenerating and self-sustaining system. The research and technology exist for us to begin that transformation now, but what has been lacking is collective will. Recognising this, we are committing to strengthen our working practices to create architecture and urbanism that has a more positive impact on the world around us.

The declaration had 788 signatures at the time of writing and the names underneath are a rollcall of the leading firms in engineering (e.g. Arup) and architecture (e.g. Foster + Partners).

Post Green Collaborations for Brands – Coordinated Campaigns

Brands instinctively want to hog the limelight. But often can achieve more by joining forces.

I used to hold 'brand date' sessions where brand teams could share what they were working on find projects where they could collaborate. One such session was with the *Guardian* and innocent drinks. One of the outputs was that the *Guardian* came and hosted an area of the *innocent village fête* festival, where people built a model forest out of recycled newspapers.

There are numerous brand alliances for climate change springing up in various industries. We've already mentioned the UN Fashion Coalition for Climate Action. Another was an alliance of media titles under the banner of Covering Climate Now: *a global journalism initiative committed to bringing more and better coverage to the defining story of our time.*

The initiative was co-founded by *The Nation* and *Columbia Journalism Review* and managed to bring 323 media titles on board, reaching a global audience of billions. The *Guardian* was a natural fit with this. But other more surprising titles joined, like *Admap*, who provided the advertising industry with a week of inspiring brand stories and climate related marketing coverage.

The result of the whole programme was climate coverage reaching its 'highest level globally in nearly a decade' according to the Media and Climate Change Observatory programme at the University of Colorado.[6]

Post Green Collaborations at a Product Level – Regenerative Organic

How to develop a model of farming (if you are a food brand or make things from agricultural produce) that is regenerative?

If you are a small brand you could source from permaculture and deep ecology farmers committed to what often turn out to be traditional practices. One of these is no-till farming. (Tillage is when a plough turns over soil and has only been used for several hundred years.) According to Regeneration International 'Studies have shown that organic no-till practices, when combined with cover cropping and organic management, help increase soil organic carbon by up to 9 percent after two years and 21 percent after six years.'

The role of healthy soil in mitigating climate change has been a hot topic in recent years. The UN made 2015 'International Year of Soils'. A report by the UNFAO set out the benefits:

> When managed sustainably, soils can play an important role in climate change mitigation by storing carbon (carbon sequestration) and decreasing greenhouse gas emissions in the atmosphere. Conversely, if soils are managed poorly or cultivated through unsustainable agricultural practices, soil carbon can be released into the atmosphere in the form of carbon dioxide ($CO2$), which can contribute to climate change.

By the time of the Paris Agreement, the French government launched a campaign called 4 per 1000. This was based on scientific studies showing that increasing the organic carbon capture by soils by 0.4% globally would offset the entire CO_2 emissions increase in 2015.

If you are a larger brand, you can do more than just source crops grown in a regenerative way. You can put your budget and fame to work promoting this style of farming. Patagonia, Dr Bronner's, and Thrive Markets along with a whole host of organic food brands and retailers have joined the new Regenerative Organic Certification. The standard has been defined and the scheme is at the pilot stage currently.

MegaFood are a pioneering brand that link soil health to vitamin quality – the only farm to table vitamin company with a direct relationship with its farmers. MegaFood is committed to regenerative farming. Sarah Newmark at MegaFood says: 'you can't nourish people without nourishing our soil'.[7] MegaFood have joined another soils for climate alliance, along with Danone, Ben & Jerry's, and Green America. This idea involves making a global standard where farms can show measurable progress towards soil health. Their Soil Carbon Initiative, as I understand it, will use soil tests to verify how much carbon is sequestered and hence progress on soil health. The project is at an early stage so there are not too many details yet, but we do know they recruited 150 partners, including major food companies.

Chefs these days are powerful and influential brands too. Numerous initiatives have seen chefs come out and raise awareness for the importance of healthy soil in the food system. *Chefs for Soil* brought out Chefs Table superstar chefs like Dominique Crenn.

It's time to get the generation who grew up on hipster farm to fork food, farmers markets, urban gardening, and so on behind the regenerative soil revolution. And behind organic in general. Bringing sharply positioned brands to popularise this will help no end. Ultimately, if consumers value it and are willing to pay more for this, it will move a lot faster than if we wait for governments who are missing their carbon targets to subsidise the development.

Post Green Business Models Adopted by Companies

Business needs to do some smart thinking to make space for Not Bad and Net Good in their business. And you know what? That's not such a stretch. Business accommodated the huge burden and bonanza that is digital already. Companies like Amazon spend billions on digital R&D to ensure they can play a leading role in future. And as a result, barely break even. Only the Amazon Web Servers part of their business empire actually makes any profits, the rest – Prime same day delivery, Alexa, Amazon Fresh, Kindle . . . – keep turning in a loss.

There is a religion of 'we must be digital at any costs' and companies pursue this while working hard across the rest of the business to somehow balance the books.

We need to do the same Indian rope trick for Not Bad and Net Good. One report I quoted earlier found the world is about to spend $90 trillion on infrastructure of all kinds – buildings, energy, transport, distribution, retail, technology . . . – and with little additional net cost these investments could be decarbonising and make a huge leap towards Paris Agreement goals.

Prada is one of the latest companies to take out a Sustainability Linked Loan. According to the company's press release, it was the first in the luxury industry to take this kind of loan. Although they had been increasingly common for infrastructure and industrial companies.

This new facility, named *Sustainability Term Loan,* is a EUR 50m five-years term loan which interest rate can be reduced following the achievement of targets related to: number of stores assigned of a LEED Gold or Platinum Certification; amount of training hours for the employees and the use of Prada Re-Nylon (regenerated nylon) for the production of goods.

Sustainability Linked Loans are a subset of the burgeoning area of Green Finance. The difference between a Green Loan and a Sustainability Linked Loan (like Prada's) is that with the former you have to spend the money on defined Green investment projects; for the latter you can use the money for any corporate purpose, but the terms of the loan (the interest rates due) are linked to significant sustainability improvements that are measured objectively.

Post Green Business Models Adopted by Brands

We have seen a new wave of direct to consumer online brands that integrate a service model (like subscription) with lean online operations and heaps of creativity. One such start-up launched in a year when the climate crisis hit the front page was Hurr. This is the AirBnB of fashion. A carefully vetted club share their wardrobes online for others to rent.

The founders say this is a natural step for a generation who prefer living light and having access, rather than being weighed down by hoarding and owning. Think City Car Clubs and other 'living light' millennial services. Hurr stress that it's not just for party dresses but also for changing up your wardrobe for holidays and workwear. Also perfect for those taking Extinction Rebellion up on not buying any new clothing and fabrics for the next 12 months.

Hurr partner with eco-friendly dry-cleaning service Blanc. They also provide insurance cover. And use trust ratings to build confidence and reward considerateness.

There's something quite lovely about how Hurr combines purpose with the glamour of fashion and ends up being just common sense. As founder Victoria Prew says:

> With Hurr we're striving to bring sustainability to fashion, one of the world's most polluting industries. Our members are a collective of forward-thinking women that believe renting makes both economic and environmental sense.[8]

Post Green Business Models Applied to Products

In the perfect storm of climate change, population growth, water stress it seems likely our diets are going to change a lot. We've already looked at vegan and flexitarian diets. Another idea that always sparks controversy is that we should switch to eating insects.

Around 20% of the human population already does eat insects according to a report by the UN FAO. There's a London start-up called Horizon Edible Insects that is farming mealworm and crickets fed on food waste. According to founder Tiziana Di Costanzo the insects have an earthy to nutty flavour. Insects such as these contain up to three times as much protein as meat or eggs, while also being low in fat. Worm burgers are already on sale in supermarkets in Belgium and Germany. Some try to hide 'insectiness' but others wear their origins proudly – like Eat Grub (as sold in Sainsbury) or US start-up Bitty Foods.

Farmed insects use about 2% as much land and 4% as much water to farm as meat. Dutch insect farm Protix claims they can grow a tonne of insects per month on just 10 square metres. Their excretions make great fertiliser and they require very little by way of energy or input.

There is a clearly a divide between countries where insects have been eaten traditionally and are prized – such as Japanese hornet larvae, or South African termites – and the West where insects are regarded with some revulsion. It's a funny hang up when many will happily eat very similar marine creatures like prawns and don't mind honey?

This would be a fascinating marketing challenge to work on.

Perhaps there could be a new fad diet based on protein and nutrients from insects?

There are other ways to go with insect farming. One is insect pet food. Which makes sense because pet animals don't seem to care or know the difference – and pets are estimated to eat up to 20% of all meat products consumed globally. Which is a lot.[9]

If we can't take on hard challenges like this as creative marketers, what good are we to anyone?

A YouGov poll found that 37% of respondents thought we'd be eating insects in the next 10 years. The ingenuity of marketing could make all the difference.

One piece of research found that people more readily adopt insects (a chocolate truffle with meal worm) when they are told they are delicious, pleasurable, and on trend – compared to being told they should eat them because of health and climate change. The researchers called this 'sushification', pointing out that most Western consumers saw raw fish as disgusting only 20 years ago.[10]

There's also just good old-fashioned creativity to be applied.

Find the fun, the cool, the playfulness.

Swedish agency Forsman & Bodenfors produced a gorgeous set of 'Play food from the future' featuring a 'Bug Mac' among other sustainable options like 'Tasty Waste' and a non-meat meatball made from algae. Nothing could be more fun if you are four?

If you want to make a family day out of it and learn all about insect farming, then do check out Bug Kitchen in Wales. According to its award-winning chef Andy Holcraft:

> Kids love the edible insects – they don't have that fear factor.

That lack of fear, openness to change, and the climate activism driving the school climate strikes could point to a bigger lesson for brands: let's go back to marketing to kids? Kids are after all the change agents in every household.

Notes

1. https://www.coca-cola.eu/news/first-fortune-500-to-replenish-all-the-water-it-uses-globally/
2. https://www.carbontrust.com/news/2015/07/how-much-water-does-it-take-to-make-a-cup-of-tea/
3. https://www.standard.co.uk/fashion/news/livia-firth-attacks-throwaway-fashion-as-she-suggests-women-only-buy-clothes-theyll-wear-30-times-a2952856.html
4. https://www.prolificlondon.co.uk/marketing-tech-news/other-media-news/2019/05/half-uk-consumers-want-brands-declare-climate-emergency
5. https://www.thedrum.com/profile/the-humblebrag/news/how-can-brands-take-a-stand-on-the-climate-emergency
6. https://www.cjr.org/covering_climate_now/climate-journalism-collaboration.php

7. https://www.greenamerica.org/story/megafood
8. https://www.standard.co.uk/fashion/hurr-collective-wardrobe-swap-dress-rental-a4085371.html
9. https://www.bbc.co.uk/news/science-environment-49450935
10. https://www.theguardian.com/commentisfree/2018/oct/15/edible-insect-save-planet-global-warming-tasty-trendy

What Now? (Concluding Thoughts)

The years ahead could be exciting.

A key thread running through this book has been the stories of individuals, brands, and companies who have decided to step up to the challenge. They might have started out wanting to run a carpet company or make vegan brownies. But they have decided to make the climate crisis, or some other vital cause, the main aim of their business.

I'm excited to keep working with brands who make a difference. I'm right in the middle of a project with ethical and organic pioneers Evolve Beauty and can't wait to get stuck back in.

I've got a brand of my own in the offing called Chikola. It is made with reforestation cacao and aims to be the Red Bull of sustainability. If we get it off the ground, it will be a very good year.

I also convened a group called URGE. A collective of like-minded people from the creative industries who want to help leaders and organisations make radical paradigm shifting climate responses. We've already started meeting companies and have exciting plans.

Getting this book launched will take a bit of effort too. And from the experience of previous books, that could get me into some really worthwhile conversations with amazing people.

But I don't want to conclude this book with my plans – but rather with yours, dear reader.

So, here is a space to write three new things you commit to do as a result of reading this book.

1.

2.

3.

And you can sign below these here:

Thanks for coming on the journey, let's do what we humanly can and be better people for it.

May the Life Force be with You

Index